D0382718

# Sweet Designs

*Bake It*
*Craft It*
*Style It*

**HYPERION**
NEW YORK

Developed in conjunction with The Stonesong Press.

Photography by Johnny Miller
*Except* photograph by Aran Goyoaga: p. i; photographs by Gemma
Comas: pp. 3, 106–107 (middle), 146–160, 161 (bottom), 290–291,
293, 294 (left), 297–298, 300–302, 305–307, 309; and photographs
by Amy Atlas: pp. viii–ix, 6–7, and 346–347.

Interior Design: BTDNYC

LIBRARY OF CONGRESS CATALOGING-IN-PUBLICATION DATA
Atlas, Amy.
      Sweet designs : bake it, craft it, style it / Amy Atlas. – 1st ed.
          p. cm.
    ISBN 978-1-4013-2440-7
1. Desserts. 2. Confectionery. 3. Cookbooks. 4. Decoration and
              ornament. 5. Handicraft. I. Title.
      TX773.A89 2012
      641.86'539—dc23
                      2011034003

ISBN: 9781401324407

Hyperion books are available for special promotions and premiums.
For details contact the HarperCollins Special Markets Department
in the New York office at 212-207-7528, fax 212-207-7222, or email
spsales@harpercollins.com.

FIRST EDITION

10  9  8  7  6  5  4  3  2  1

SUSTAINABLE
FORESTRY
INITIATIVE
Certified Fiber Sourcing
www.sfiprogram.org

*For my beloved late dad*

who taught me to reach for the stars and
ignited a fire in me that will never stop burning.
As we always said, I love you "immensely."

*For my sweet Zach, Josh, and Rick*

who complete me.

*And for my supportive and
wonderful readers*

who inspire my work every day.

# Contents

MALTED
MILK BALLS

# Introduction

The
Sweet
Life

*"Life is uncertain. Eat dessert first."*

—ERNESTINE ULMER,
Early Twentieth-Century Writer

I'll raise a slice of frosted chocolate cake to that. But seriously, I find this oft-quoted (and misquoted!) advice to be as relevant to my life on the whole as it is to mealtime. For as long as I can remember, I have loved sweets. My brother Jonathan can attest to that. He used to find me lurking in front of the fridge, fork in hand, eating straight from the Entenmann's box. At midnight. His favorite word was "busted," which he said to me often. The truth is, back then, I'd forgo a good meal for America's favorite course any day of the week. (I still would, although I can't admit that to my kids!) My dad and I were the sugar fanatics in the family, while my mom and brother went for anything savory. Dad and I enjoyed our best moments late at night around the kitchen table, talking while eating whatever treat happened to be on hand. Many times, Jonathan joined us. Indeed, in the days before he passed away, my ailing father asked for just one more of those memorable nights, which sent my brother and me racing to the nearby deli for every confection we could carry home (including my dad's favorite, halvah, and mine, Reese's peanut butter cups). We sat together, eating our trove with abandon, our last and perhaps sweetest moment with him.

Mom loved that my father and I had such a strong bond, no matter what it was that brought us together. She's a great cook and she's known for her killer Thanksgiving spread, but my romance with baking is un-

doubtedly and inextricably linked to my beloved grandmother, whose rocky road cake is to me what Proust's madeleine was to him. The very thought of that Willy Wonka–esque concoction of chocolate chips, marshmallows, and caramel buttercream takes me right back to her sunny kitchen, where she would whip up the caramel while the cake baked, and I would watch her every move in anticipation of licking the bowl.

It was my grandmother who gave me my first baking lessons. When I became old enough to use the oven on my own, I anointed myself the family baker—of birthday cakes, sweet breads, and my famous candy-packed gigantic chocolate chip cookies. In college, even the small-

est occasion gave me a reason to whip up sweets for my sorority sisters. The baking frenzy didn't stop when I graduated, either. When I started working, I became known for the cookie baskets I put together for my colleagues. Right after I married my husband, Rick, we entertained like crazy. At the time, I was practicing law at my father's firm by day and spending hours in the kitchen by night. My parties invariably culminated with an elaborate dessert spread, which I concocted from a mix of sweets I had made myself, gourmet confections, and treats I picked up at the grocery store. Not only did I take pride in these spreads, but I was a stickler for presenting them with style. I got so much satisfaction from working the right side of my brain after spending my days "up to there" with the left! Even more fortunate than getting to practice law with my father was the fact that throughout my life, he supported me in all of my endeavors, including taking time off to raise my boys.

It wasn't until I had my sons, Zach and Josh, that I realized I needed to turn my affection for creating confectionery tableaux into more than a hobby. When Josh was born, I scoured the Internet for all sweets related to the "We're Bananas Over You!" monkey theme I had chosen for a party I was throwing—and that's when the lightbulb went off. I knew of no one who was combining confection, crafts, and creative direction. I began keeping a database of candy and crafts by color, pattern, and flavor. I kept copious notes on candy sources, specialty items, and expert confectioners.

After creating dozens of tables for family and friends out of sheer joy (and being duly rewarded with their swooning over them), my father's credo hit me: Life *is* too short. I needed to spend my days doing what I loved. Fast-forward five years (and what a speedy five years it's been!) and my hobby-turned-passion is now a full-fledged and thriving business. Metaphorically speaking, I eat dessert first every day.

The truth is, others have been offering up tables of sweets for centuries. The custom of the dessert pyramid originated in Europe in the early eighteenth century, where it graced tables in castles and palaces from the German states to the French court at Versailles. I'm with Elizabeth Raffald, the Miss Manners of the period, who, in her book *The Experienced English Housekeeper*, wrote, "As many dishes as you have in one course, so many baskets or plates your dessert must have and it must be set out in the same manner." Now *there's* someone I can relate to! In 1850s America, the British colonists were building centerpieces of stacked cake stands and loading them up with sweets—like I've done on pages 187 and 311. In fact, large households would employ their very own confectioner, whose sole task it was to prepare sweets and sugar sculptures for the dessert course.

But we live in the twenty-first century, and betting on the unlikelihood of your having a personal confectioner, I've designed fourteen original, fully dressed dessert tables with that in mind. Based on themes most often requested by my clients and how I'm inspired—a favorite color palette, a pattern, a fashion designer's look, a flavor, a destination, a passion, or a holiday—I deconstruct each table to show you how to do it yourself.

Each chapter is divided into **two** sections:

- **BAKE IT**
  Provides recipes and decorating instructions for all of the home-baked desserts on the table.

- **CRAFT IT**
  Includes step-by-step instructions for making all of the decoration elements—paper garlands, upholstered backdrops, table runners, candy bags, and cups, to name a few. Many of the instructions make use of templates, which allow you to adapt my techniques to create your own unique decorations, and which you can download from my website at http://blog.amyatlas.com.

Within these two sections, there are several types of boxed text that contain important tips and information:

- **SHOP IT** provides a list of the goodies on the table that are easily picked up from the grocery store, candy shop, and gourmet food store—and tips you off to my specialty sources for the rest.

- **DISPLAY IT** points out all of the items I use on the table, ceiling, and wall—platters, pedestals, floral arrangements, buckets, baskets, and crates—to achieve the overall effect.

- **STYLE IT** reveals my special styling tips to improve the look of your table and make it jaw-dropping.

- **SWITCH IT** offers ideas for shifting the vibe of the table to suit your crowd. For example, In Forever Chanel, page 47, you can "Grow It Up" with a Lemon-drop Cocktail for adults, or "Grow It Down" with simple lemonade garnished with lemon slices for the kids. Instead of using a yellow and white color palette, "Color It" with sea green and white. I'm not one to back anyone into a creative corner, so feel free to experiment!

- **EASY DOES IT** recommends shortcuts when you can't bake or craft from scratch while still achieving the same polished look.

- **SWAP IT OUT** encourages you to replace roses with daisies, cookies with cupcakes, white chocolate with dark chocolate, or cream cheese frosting with a simple glaze. Don't be afraid to do the unexpected!

# How to Use This Book

I'm a wife, mother of two, and founder of my own company. I know what it's like to be long on obligations, short on time, and stretched in too many directions. But that's the subject for another book! Because we all experience demands on our time differently, I encourage you to approach each table in this book in a way that suits your particular needs. **You can:**

1. **Deconstruct any of the dessert tables**
   and use just one or two of my ideas anytime, anywhere (for instance, put together my signature candy boxes for family movie night, or make my mini apple pies for a host gift). Think of this book as a dessert cookbook and a craft book in one, and mix and match the sweets and projects as you please, the same way you do individual pieces in your wardrobe.

2. **Swap in new colors, DIY crafting projects, or sweets,**
   depending on the vibe you want to create and your available time. For example, swap out pink for yellow in Forever Chanel, page 47, for a baby shower; use a giant chalkboard for Apple of My Eye, page 211, to turn it into a bake sale; and use Jell-O pudding instead of my homemade strawberry mousse in Perfectly Preppy, page 243, if time is short.

3. **Duplicate the tables just as you see them pictured**
   and still let them multitask. My Perfectly Preppy table, page 233, is perfect for a wedding anniversary, Father's Day, a graduation celebration, a his-and-hers wedding shower, or a job promotion celebration.

My hope is that this book gives you the same kind of encouragement and guidance my father, my mother, my husband, his family, our sons, and my friends have given me throughout my life. I hope it's a blueprint that will inspire you to draw on your own right-brained reserves, a handbook that will make your own lightbulbs go off, and a visual feast that brings you sweet pleasure.

*Amy Atlas*

*New York City*

# Sweet Basics

They're essential, fundamental, elemental. Yes, I'm talking about brownies, crispy rice treats, vanilla buttercream, custom candy bar wrappers, pretty pedestals, and candy cups. For a sweets stylist, these are just a few of the recipes and crafts that are tapped again and again to complete a table. If you master the items in this chapter alone, you can put together a sweets table with the flair of a pro. In the chapters that follow this one, you will find references back to these recipes and crafts, accompanied by decorating and crafting instructions specific to the table. I encourage you to read through the entries in this chapter before moving on to the tables; as with a successful wardrobe, you should feel comfortable in the basics before piling on the accessories!

*Bake It*

# Tool Time

I use little in the way of fancy kitchen equipment to make the Bake Its. Apart from a few cookie cutters that you may want to order (or you can use the templates I've provided; see page 335 for instructions), it's likely you'll have most of the items I call for. In recipes in which I use a standing mixer, it's perfectly fine to use a handheld version; the best are the kind that have both standard and whisk-style beaters. The standing mixer simply allows me to walk away and prepare something else if the mixing to be done goes on for a few minutes! You'll notice I use pastry bags and tips *a lot*; Wilton tips are my favorite and can easily be purchased online (see Find It, page 348).

To create the tables in the following pages, you will need:

CLOCKWISE FROM TOP:

1. 2 9-inch round cake pans
2. 2 8-inch round cake pans
3. 2 standard sheet pans or baking sheets
4. rubber spatula
5. mixing bowls
6. hand whisk
7. strainer or sieve
8. rolling pin
9. offset spatula
10. wooden spoon
11. candy thermometer
12. standing mixer or handheld beaters
13. 2 standard cupcake tins
14. 1 9- × 9-inch baking pan
15. 1 8- × 8-inch baking pan (not pictured)
16. 1 9- × 13-inch baking pan (not pictured)
17. bench scraper
18. measuring spoons
19. pastry tips
20. pastry bag or resealable plastic bags with coupler
21. pastry brush (not pictured)
22. lemon zester
23. small bowl (for holding candies or egg whites)
24. food processor (not shown)

# Basic Recipes and Techniques

For the most part, the ingredients in the Bake It sections can be easily found at your local supermarket. Occasionally, a specialty ingredient will show up—isomalt for making the Oscar statuettes on page 260 stand up, fondant for covering the cakes on pages 90, 130, and 236, for example—for which I point you to the places I buy the ingredients in Find It, page 348. I have tried to stay away from food coloring and gelatin, but you will occasionally see them pop up in recipes. Chocolate figures largely (because what would a sweets book be without it?), and I do have a preference when it comes to that. There's a lot of melting and rolling and dipping going on in these pages, and the brands I prefer to do that with include Ghirardelli, Valrhona, and Callebaut.

# Vanilla Butter Cake

**Makes 3 cups batter, enough for one 9-inch cake (½ of a 4-inch-high tier) or 12 cupcakes.**

- 1  stick (½ cup) unsalted butter at room temperature, plus more for pans
- 1  cup sugar
- 2  large eggs
- 2  teaspoons vanilla extract
- 2  cups all-purpose flour, plus more for pans
- 2  teaspoons baking powder
- ½  teaspoon salt
- ¾  cup whole milk

*Please see recipe on page 130.*

1. Adjust oven rack to middle position and preheat the oven to 350°F. Line a standard cupcake pan with cupcake liners, or spray a 9-inch square baking pan with nonstick cooking spray and line the bottom with parchment paper.

2. In the bowl of an electric mixer fitted with a paddle attachment, beat the butter and sugar until light and fluffy. Scrape down the sides of the bowl and continue to beat, adding 1 egg at a time along with the vanilla until thoroughly combined. Scrape down the sides of the bowl with a rubber spatula. Sift the flour, baking powder, and salt together in a small bowl. With the mixer on a low speed, add the flour mixture in two parts, alternating with the milk. Beat for 1 to 2 minutes, until the cake batter is smooth.

3. If you are making cupcakes, divide batter equally among the cupcake liners and bake until just set and a toothpick inserted in the center comes out clean, 17 to 20 minutes. Let cool in pan for 5 minutes, then transfer to a wire rack to cool completely.

4. If you are making a 9-inch tier, pour the batter in the baking pan and bake until just set and a toothpick comes out clean, 18 to 20 minutes. Let cool in pan for 5 minutes, then transfer to a wire rack to cool completely.

*Storage:* The layers or cupcakes can be frozen for up to two weeks before frosting and serving. When frosted, the frosted cake or cupcakes can be kept in an airtight container in the refrigerator for up to three days.

# Sugar Cookies

**Makes about 20 square 2-inch or 30 round 2-inch cookies.**

½ cup (1 stick) unsalted butter, softened
1 cup granulated sugar
½ teaspoon salt
1 large egg
1 teaspoon vanilla extract
2 cups all-purpose flour

*Please see recipe on page 133.*

1. In the bowl of a standing mixer fitted with a paddle attachment, combine the butter, sugar, and salt on medium-high speed until just combined. Add the egg and beat until combined, scraping down the sides of the bowl as necessary. Add the vanilla and beat until combined. Reduce speed to medium-low and add the flour. Beat until just combined.

2. Place the dough onto a piece of plastic wrap and press firmly into a 1-inch-thick circle. Wrap tightly and chill until firm, for at least 1 hour.

3. Roll out the dough on a lightly floured surface to ¼-inch thick. Cut out the cookies with a cookie cutter or, if using a template, use a knife to cut them out. Transfer the cookies to a baking sheet, spacing them 1 inch apart. Chill in the refrigerator for at least another 30 minutes before baking.

4. Meanwhile, place oven rack in middle position and preheat oven to 350°F. Line two baking sheets with parchment paper.

5. Bake until light golden, 6 to 12 minutes, depending on the size and shape of the cookie, rotating pan from front to back halfway through baking. Let cookies cool on pan for 5 minutes, then transfer cookies to a wire rack to cool completely.

# Crispy Rice Cereal Treats

**Makes approximately 24 2¼-inch squares.**

- 4 tablespoons (½ stick) unsalted butter
- 10 ounces marshmallows
- 1½ teaspoons vanilla extract
- 6 cups crispy rice cereal

1. Spray a 9- × 13-inch pan with nonstick cooking spray. In a large saucepan or stockpot, heat butter over medium heat until melted. Add the marshmallows and stir until they are melted. Add the vanilla and stir until combined.

2. Remove the pan from the heat and add the cereal to it, stirring until evenly coated. Immediately pour mixture into prepared pan and smooth top. Let cool until set, about 1 hour.

3. Run a knife around the inside rim of the pan to loosen the rice crispy treat. Flip the pan over onto a clean work surface to release it. Cut out as directed.

*Please see recipe on page 314.*

# Fudge-y Brownies

Makes 12 brownies.

These moist, dense brownies offer clean, sharp edges when stamped out with shaped cutters. After brownies are cool, cover tightly with plastic wrap and let them sit overnight before cutting them into shapes.

- 1¼ cups all-purpose flour
- ¼ cup Dutch cocoa
- ¾ cup (1½ sticks) unsalted butter, softened
- 8 ounces unsweetened chocolate, finely chopped
- 4 large eggs
- 2 cups granulated sugar
- ½ teaspoon salt
- 4 teaspoons vanilla extract

1. Adjust oven rack to middle position and preheat the oven to 325°F. Line a 9- × 13-inch baking pan with parchment paper, letting paper drape slightly over the short edges. Spray parchment with nonstick pan spray. Sift flour and cocoa into a bowl; set aside.

2. In a medium saucepan, melt butter and chocolate over low heat, stirring frequently; set aside to cool. Whisk eggs, granulated sugar, salt, and vanilla in a large bowl until combined and smooth. Whisk in chocolate mixture until combined. Whisk in flour mixture until just combined.

3. Spoon batter into prepared pan and smooth top. Bake until just set and a cake tester inserted in the middle comes out clean, 25 to 30 minutes. Transfer pan to a wire rack to cool completely. Cover with plastic wrap and let them sit overnight. Cut out as directed.

# Quick Vanilla Buttercream

**Makes about 4 cups.**

- 1½ cups (3 sticks) unsalted butter, softened
- 4 cups confectioners' sugar
- ⅛ teaspoon salt
- 1 teaspoon vanilla
- 2 teaspoons milk

1. In the bowl of a standing mixer fitted with a whisk attachment, combine the butter, confectioners' sugar, salt, vanilla, and milk and whisk on medium-low speed until smooth.

2. Increase speed to medium-high and beat until light and fluffy, about 4 minutes. To store, place a sheet of plastic wrap over the buttercream so that it is touching it, cover tightly with a lid, and freeze up to 1 month. Thaw in the refrigerator and rewhip before using.

# Cream Cheese Frosting

**Makes 3½ cups, enough to cover 12 to 24 cupcakes, depending on the application.**

- ½ cup (1 stick) unsalted butter, softened
- 8 ounces cream cheese, softened
- 2 cups confectioners' sugar

In the bowl of a standing mixer fitted with the paddle attachment, combine the butter and cream cheese and beat on high speed until smooth, about 2 minutes. Reduce the speed to medium-low, gradually add the sugar, and beat until smooth and fluffy, 1 to 2 minutes.

*Please see recipe on page 112.*

# Simple Glaze

# Royal Icing

**Makes 1 cup.**

> 2 cups confectioners' sugar plus more to thicken if necessary

Pass the confectioners' sugar through a sieve into a medium bowl. Add 4 tablespoons of water and stir until the icing is smooth and coats the back of a spoon. If the icing seems too thin, gradually pass a bit more of the sugar through a sieve into it and stir until smooth. If it is too thick, add water *by the drop* and stir until smooth.

**Makes about 2½ cups.**

If you choose to use meringue powder, follow the instructions on the package to make the equivalent of 2 egg whites. If preparing this ahead, cover the icing with plastic wrap so that it is touching the icing surface to prevent it from developing a hard skin.

*Note:* Uncooked egg whites should not be consumed by very young children, pregnant women, or people with compromised immune systems.

> 3 cups confectioners' sugar
> 2 large egg whites or meringue powder (prepared according to directions to make egg whites)
> 1 teaspoon vanilla

1. In the bowl of a standing mixer fitted with the whisk attachment, whip sugar and egg whites on medium-low speed until combined.

2. Increase speed to medium and add vanilla. Add water, one tablespoon at a time, up to 3 tablespoons, until desired consistency is reached. Increase speed to medium-high and whip until thick enough to pipe but not so thick that it will be difficult to squeeze through a tip. The icing will keep, covered tightly and refrigerated, up to three days. Stir vigorously before using.

*Please see recipe on page 117.*

# How to Melt Chocolate

Either way you melt it, molten chocolate is ideal for coating pretzels, topping brownies, and incorporating into frostings.

### In the Microwave

Place 2/3 of the chocolate in a medium microwave-safe bowl and heat on medium power until the chocolate is melted, stirring every 30 seconds. Remove from the microwave and stir in remaining chocolate until it is completely melted.

### On the Stovetop

Place 2/3 of the chocolate in a heatproof bowl. Set it over a saucepan filled with 1 inch of water on low heat. Do not let the water touch the bottom of the bowl. Cook, stirring, until the chocolate is completely melted. Remove the pan from the heat and stir in remaining chocolate until completely melted.

# Outlining and Flooding Cookies with Royal Icing

If using one color (as in Honey, I Love You Cookies, page 169), tint the Royal Icing with the specified color. If using two colors (as in Dots and Lines Sugar Cookies, page 156), divide the icing equally between two bowls. To determine if the consistency of the icing is right to outline the cookies, do the knife test: Drag a butter knife across the surface of the icing, making a streak. The streak should smooth over in 8 to 10 seconds. If it takes longer than this, your icing is too thick. Thin with another egg white or, if using meringue powder, thin with water, 1 drop at a time.

1. Fill a pastry bag or resealable plastic bag fitted with a small round tip (Wilton Round Tip #3) with ½ of the icing. Pipe around the rims of the cookies, alternating the colors if using two, and allow to dry for at least 1 hour.

2. Return whatever icing remains in the bag back into the bowl(s) and test the icing for a syrup-like consistency to fill in, or flood, the cookies. To achieve this, thin with additional egg whites, or water if using meringue powder. Using a pastry bag or resealable bag fitted with a round tip (Wilton Round Tip #2), fill in the cookies with the icing(s). Alternatively, drizzle some of the icing with a spoon and smooth with a toothpick or other tool specified in recipe. Allow the cookies to dry for several hours or overnight, until dry and firm to the touch, before decorating with intricate detail.

# Decorating a Cake with Fondant

Rolled fondant creates a clean canvas for beautiful design and brings a refined look to a cake. Honestly, I was initially concerned about how to incorporate into this book the stunning cakes that I often get from my vendors, but with the help of some of the best cake decorating talents in the industry, I've boiled down the basics so you can create some beauties in your home kitchen. It's a lot easier to work with than you think!

*A few helpful hints:* Fondant hates humidity and loves flexibility, which can be achieved by kneading it, turning it forty-five degrees after each roll, and dusting the work surface and rolling pin with confectioners' sugar.

My recipes for the larger cakes in this book include both real and fake tiers because sometimes I want a show-stopping centerpiece but I don't need to feed a hundred people. Fondant works on both fake tiers (which are usually made of Styrofoam) and real ones. Keep in mind that one tier equals two nine-inch cake rounds.

WHAT YOU'LL NEED:

Cake such as Vanilla Butter Cake, page 11

Quick Vanilla Buttercream, page 14

Rolled fondant, see Find It, page 348

Corn syrup (if using a fake tier)

Confectioners' sugar

Food coloring gel, if desired

TOOLS

Serrated knife

Cardboard cake base equal to the dimensions of your cake

Offset spatula

Pastry brush (if using a fake tier)

Rolling pin

Smoothing tool

Small, sharp kitchen knife

## Leveling and Filling

1. Baked cakes usually are on the top; to create a perfectly level surface, you need to trim away the top so that it is flat. A serrated knife works like a handsaw—the best results come when you use it that way to remove the portion of the cake that slopes

from the center. It won't rip the cake the way a straight kitchen knife does. Trim away the top of the cake with the serrated knife, using a sawing motion and working slowly across the surface until the knife comes out the other side. Brush away any crumbs that remain on the top of the cake.

2. To make one tier, place one cake on the cardboard base. Cover with about 1 cup of buttercream and stack the second cake on top of it so that the edges are flush.

## Crumb Coating

Using an offset spatula, apply a thin layer of the buttercream to the top and sides of the cake to lock in any crumbs. Refrigerate the cake until the buttercream is firm to the touch, at least 3 hours.

*Note:* If you are covering a fake or dummy cake tier (see my Forever Size Four Cake, page 58), omit the buttercream and brush a thin layer of corn syrup over the fake tier.

## Rolling Out the Fondant

1. On a clean surface lightly dusted with confectioners' sugar, knead the fondant, working quickly, until it is smooth. To keep it from sticking, lift and move the fondant around as you work. To color the fondant, dip a toothpick into the food coloring gel and dab it onto the fondant. Knead the fondant until the coloring is thoroughly incorporated.

2. Using a rolling pin, roll the fondant into a circle about double the width of the cake and ¼-inch thick. Move the fondant around as you roll it out, dusting with the confectioners' sugar to prevent it from sticking to the work surface or rolling pin.

## Applying Fondant to the Cake

1. Carefully roll the fondant onto the rolling pin, position the pin over the cake or Styrofoam, and unroll the fondant over the surface.

2. Smooth the top and sides of the cake with your hands or a smoothing tool. Trim the edges with a sharp knife. Repeat with additional layers, if using. Decorate according to individual cake instructions.

## Assembling a Tiered Cake

TOOLS

Dowels

Cake board

1. Follow the instructions for Decorating a Cake with Fondant, page 18. Apply a few tablespoons of frosting to the cake pedestal and underside of the cake board fitted to the bottom tier. This is used to "fix" the cake or cake board to the cake pedestal.

2. If using tiers of baked cake, you will need to support each layer with dowels. If you are using just one baked cake and faux cakes for the other tiers, there's no need to use dowels. When stacking tiers, carefully spread some icing onto the underside of the next cake tier and center it over the cake beneath it. Repeat if using another tier or tiers.

### DOWELS

Dowels provide support for cakes and stop tiers from "sinking" into each other. Use at least 4 cake dowels per tier.

1. Using a dowel, gently mark 4 points on the top of the bottom tier of the cake, within at least 1 inch of the rim of the tier you will be placing above.

2. Carefully push the dowels all the way through the cake at the marks. Mark the dowels just above the surface of the cake with a pen. Remove the dowels and trim at the pen mark, making sure they are even in length. Replace them in the holes. Spread the frosting on the underside of the next tier and carefully center it over the dowels. Repeat with remaining tiers.

# Tool Time

Scissors, double stick tape, Glue Dots, a bone folder—these seem to be my go-to tools, the few I use over and over again to put together almost everything in this book. There are additional items, all of which are easy to amass in a single trip to, say, Michaels or your favorite craft store. If you stock the following tools and materials, you will be able to make almost everything in this book.

OPPOSITE PAGE, CLOCKWISE, FROM TOP

1. wood glue
2. chalk
3. scalloped craft punch
4. felt
5. hot glue gun
6. ribbon
7. double stick tape
8. ruler
9. Glue Dots
10. glue and paint brushes
11. edible markers
12. decorative paper (rice paper/mulberry paper)
13. masking tape
14. X-Acto knife
15. dressmaker pins and corsage pins (not shown)
16. scissors
17. floral wire
18. Mod Podge
19. glitter
20. hole punch
21. bone folder
22. needlenose pliers
23. circular craft punch (with scrapbook paper)
24. fishing wire
25. gridded ruler, such as Omnigrid
26. Command hooks (not shown)
27. thumbtacks (not shown)
28. jump rings (not shown)

There's nothing like a length of ribbon to dress up even the most prosaic jar, bag, pedestal, or box. I love every kind of ribbon there is—double face satin, grosgrain, baker's twine, rickrack, velvet. The options are endless.

# Custom Tablecloth

I rarely, if ever, use a premade tablecloth on my table; there are too many amazing fabrics out there to choose from! If your table is placed in the middle of the room (called a floating table) rather than against a wall, you'll need to stitch two lengths of fabric together. Fabric is generally available in 36-inch, 45-inch, 54-inch, 60-inch, and sometimes 72-inch lengths.

MATERIALS

Length of desired fabric

TOOLS

Dressmaker pins

Sewing machine

A standard table is 30 inches high, 30 inches deep, and 96 inches long.

Calculate the finished dimension of your tablecloth by using the following formula:

1. Table set against a wall = (height + depth + 4 inches) × (2 × height + length of table)
2. Floating table = (2 × height + depth of table) × (2 × height + length of table)

To determine how much fabric you need, use the following examples:

1. For a standard table set against the wall:

(30 inches + 30 inches + 4 inches) × (2 × 30 inches + 96 inches) = 64 inches wide × 156 inches long

* If you are using fabric that is at least 72 inches wide, no stitching is necessary. Simply divide the length of the tablecloth by 36 inches (a yard). 156 inches ÷ 36 inches = 4⅓ yards.

* If you are using fabric that is less than 72 inches wide, you need to stitch two lengths of the fabric together and double the amount of fabric, or 2 × 4⅓ yards = 8⅔ yards.

2. For a standard table floating in the middle of the room:

(2 × 30 inches + 30 inches) × (2 × 30 inches + 96 inches) + 1 inch for seam allowance = 90 inches × 157 inches

* No standard fabric is 90 inches wide, so you need to stitch two lengths of fabric together to achieve that width. So, double the amount of fabric you need, which is

157 inches ÷ 36 inches (1 yard) = approx. 4½ yards × 2 = approx. 9 yards

*Note: If using patterned fabric, measure the length of the repeat and add this amount to the amount of fabric calculated above.*

To make the tablecloth, fold the fabric in half crosswise and press. Cut along the fold. With right sides together, pin the two pieces of fabric together along one long side. If using a patterned fabric, make sure the patterns on both pieces of fabric are running in the same direction and are aligned. Stitch a ½-inch seam along the pinned edge. Press seam open. Trim excess so that width of tablecloth measures 64 inches for a table set against a wall and 90 inches for a floating table, with the seam running down the middle of the table.

# *Pretty Pedestal*

If you've wrapped a gift box, then you can make every single pedestal in this book. The details are below, but it may be just as easy for you to wrap the pedestal as you would a gift.

MATERIALS

Length of fabric

Gift box, Styrofoam, cake dummy, floral foam, or other base

Dressmaker pins

1. Cut a length of fabric as you would if wrapping a gift.

2. On a clean work surface, lay the fabric wrong side up. Center the base on it. Bring one edge of the fabric to the center of the box and secure it with dressmaker pins. Bring the opposite edge of the fabric to the center of the box. Secure it with dressmaker pins.

3. Repeat step 2 with each of the remaining sides, making sure that the edges are pushed in as far as they will go to create crisp corners and that the fabric is sharply creased at its folds. Secure with dressmaker pins and embellish as directed.

Dark Chocolate

Milk Chocolate

White Chocolate

TIED THE KNOT
Betsy & Ryan 8/28/10

TIED THE KNOT
Betsy & Ryan 8/28/10

# Custom Candy Bar Wrappers

MATERIALS

Foil-covered 5½- × 2¼-inch candy bar or
purchased foil wrapper for candy bar
(see Find It, page 348)

Decorative paper

Double stick tape or Glue Dots

TOOLS

Bone folder

Ruler

1. If you purchase a foil wrapper, wrap one foil around the candy bar.

2. Measure and cut a piece of decorative paper to size so it wraps around the candy bar. You may or may not want some silver foil to peek through at the ends.

3. Place the paper wrong side up on a work surface with the long side facing you. Center the chocolate bar on it, wrong side up, and tightly fold the top and bottom of the paper onto it, creasing the edges. Remove the paper. Use a bone folder to make sharp folds at the creases.

4. Wrap the decorative paper around the chocolate bar, right side out, and secure neatly on the back side with double stick tape or Glue Dots.

# Candy Cups

Around my company, these are referred to interchangeably as candy cups and popcorn cups because they are the shape of the classic, old-school movie popcorn containers. Use the templates specified in individual chapters for custom candy cups.

MATERIALS

White printer paper or light card stock

TOOLS

X-Acto knife or sharp scissors
ruler
Bone folder
Double stick tape

1. Refer to the Template Index, pages 335–345, to find the specific template, then go to http://blog .amyatlas.com to download, and print the template onto the paper. Cut out with an X-Acto knife or sharp scissors.

2. Score along all lines, using a ruler and bone folder to guide you, so that the folds are crisp.

3. Fold along the score lines and secure the side edges with double stick tape.

4. Secure the three short bottom edges to each other with double stick tape.

5. Secure the remaining long edge to the others with double stick tape.

# Decorative Candy Bags

# Drink Stirrers and Flags

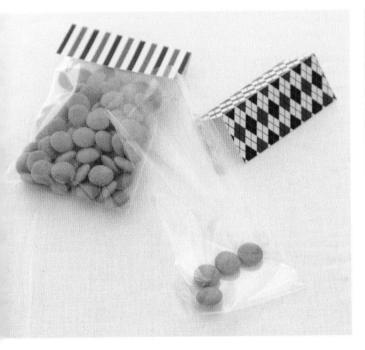

MATERIALS

Cello bags, 3-inch-wide × 5½-inch-tall
(see Find It, page 348)
Decorative scrapbook or construction paper cut
into 3-inch-wide × 2½-inch-tall pieces, folded
in half with a bone folder
Double stick tape or Glue Dots

TOOLS

Bone folder

Fill the bag half-full with candy. Fold the top of the bag onto itself by ¼ inch. Place the folded paper over it and secure with double stick tape or Glue Dots. There should be a I¼-inch flap of decorative paper on each side of the candy bag.

An embellished stirrer makes any drink—milk, cider, juice, champagne—festive and can be easily made with coffee stirrers, lollipop sticks, skewers— you name it. See the next page for lots of ideas for stirrers. For flags, I've provided templates that you can access on my blog, http://blog.amyatlas.com (see page 335 for instructions), which you can print onto card stock. Or you can make your own with decorative paper.

Print the flag template onto card stock or trace the template onto decorative paper and cut out. Fold the paper in half crosswise to make the flag. Place the stirrer in the crease of the fold and secure with Glue Dots.

## Style It

If it can stand up to liquid (or in some cases, if you can lay it across the rim of the glass, as in a ladyfinger) and it's appealing, it can be a drink stirrer. Think outside of the box: who doesn't have childhood memories of sipping a drink through a licorice straw? For an adult party, even a crochet needle can be charming if the theme (say a crochet/knitting party) allows for it. I've used all kinds of items—from the craft closet, kitchen, stationery store, cookie aisle, and party shops—for embellishing drinks. Or top standard drink stirrers with decorative flags. Don't limit yourself!

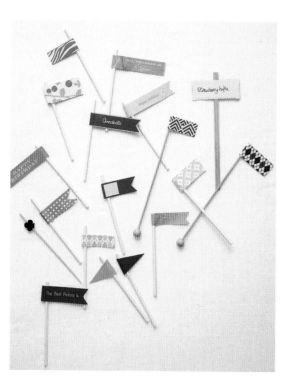

**Mix and Match
Drink Stirrers**

FROM LEFT TO RIGHT

ROW 1
- *Pirouette*
- *Chocolate Covered Pretzel Rod*
- *Fabric + Lollipop Stick*
- *Card stock + Lollipop Stick*
- *Golf Toothpicks*
  *(Pick-On-Us)*
- *Honey Stick + Honeycomb Flag*
- *Cherry on Wooden Skewer*
- *Ladyfinger*
- *Marshmallow on Lollipop Stick*
- *Oreo Mini Cakester on Lollipop Stick*
- *Hammond's Candy Stick*

ROW 2
- *Licorice Stick*
- *Paper + Ribbon on Craft Stick*
- *Lollipop*
- *Fruit Roll-Up*
- *Fondue Skewer*
- *Ribbon on Popsicle Stick*
- *Crochet Needle*
- *Plastic Spoon + Ribbon*
- *Knitting Needle*

ROW 3
- *Straw + Crepe paper + Froot Loops*
  *(Peas in a Pod)*
- *Rock Candy Swizzle Stick*
- *Raffia + Wooden Skewer*
- *Patterned Straw*
- *Cucumber*
- *Hammond's Candy Stick*
- *Cardstock Cutouts + Wooden Skewer*
- *Vanilla Bean*
- *Cinnamon Stick*

# Candy and Dessert Tags

The variety of candy tags you can make is only limited by the range of paper products there are in the world. Think burlap, honeycomb, scrapbook paper, or fabric scraps. Tags can be anything that relates to the table's theme and color palette.

CANDY

LIME POPSICLES

Picnic Lunch!

Red Velvet Cupcakes

MARASCHINO CHERRIES

MAPLE WALNUT

Brownies

My Favorite Teacher

S'MORE CUPCAKES

JELLY BEANS

Petit Fours

PRINCESS Candies

honey beehive cake

MOON PIES

Ribbon

Printer paper or card stock

If using the tag templates in the book, refer to the Template Index on pages 335–345, go to http://blog.amyatlas.com, download, and print the template onto the specified paper. Cut out. You can simply write your copy on the tags. Alternatively, you can create your own design using inspiration from the opposite page. Punch a hole in the tag if using a ribbon or another type of tie. Slide ribbon through as directed.

Alternatively, lean the tag against the platter, tuck it into the candy tray liner, or affix it to the jar with Glue Dots, as instructed.

**SHOP IT**

# Getting the Sugar High:

*A Walk Down the Candy Aisle and Around the Grocery Store*

Candy and treats are king (or queen) on these sweets tables, and both run the gamut. Good old-fashioned general store style candy—licorice wheels, Necco Wafers, pillow mints, malt balls, ribbon candy, and saltwater taffy—are among my favorites. Current candy emporium-style sweets—think Dylan's Candy Bar—are here in full force, too: Jujubes, Gummy Sours, Fruit Roll-Ups, M&M's, colorful Good & Plenty's, sourballs, gourmet jellybeans. Couture candy—calissons, spangled truffles, dragées, penny candy, marshmallows—is also part of the mix. For these last and any other hard-to-find treats, I provide a purveyor in Find It, page 348.

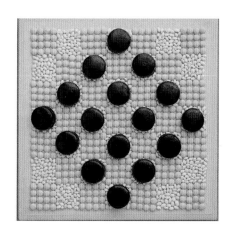

What really gets me going, though, is styling up a few beloved packaged desserts on my tables. MoonPies, Entenmann's pound cake, Oreo Cakesters, boxed cake mix, Little Debbie cakes, Manner wafer cookies, donut holes—they're all fabulous when you combine them with a few home-baked treats and some noteworthy candy.

Candy and confections' raison d'être is to satisfy a sweet craving, of course. But as a sweets stylist, I am constantly looking at both not for what they *are*, but for what they *can be*. Once you begin to look at sweets through a design lens, you start to see them for their shapes, patterns, textures, and colors. I encourage you all to look at items in your grocery aisle with a different eye. Look at shapes and colors of sweets to see how they can be translated in different ways. A licorice wheel looks a lot like a film reel, doesn't it? Necco Wafers are essentially colorful dots. Flaked coconut mimics freshly fallen snow unlike any other edible treat. A pile of

coffee-colored malt balls, artfully stacked, recalls honeycomb. When I see a mini powdered donut, I see a life preserver. An Oreo Cakester looks like a checkerboard piece.

If a store-bought goody isn't as obvious to translate into a design as those above, then there's no reason not to manipulate some store-bought favorites to suit your theme: I cut MoonPies into small rectangles, then arranged them on a platter in a zigzag pattern on the Mad for Zigzag table, page 109. Macaroons become bumblebee bodies with the addition of chocolate stripes and almond wings. I turn to the grocery store if time is tight (which it always seems to be!), and so can you. Boxed cake mix and premade sugar cookie dough are fine to use if you're in a pinch. And those yummy chocolate pirouette cookies? They're not only great drink decorations, but they make excellent tray liners. Stroopwafels, too. Let your imagination soar.

FROM LEFT TO RIGHT

**ROW 1**
- *Gummy Hearts*
- *Licorice Wheel*
- *Corn Husk Candy Corn*
- *Chocolate Milkies*
- *M&M's*
- *Lime Gummy*
- *Mellowcreme Pumpkin*

**ROW 2**
- *Chocolate Straw*
- *Marbled Malt Ball*
- *Sour Patch Apple*
- *Pretzel Malt Ball*
- *Ribbon Candy*
- *Yellow Sugar Candy Beads*
- *Hammond's Pillow Mints*

**ROW 3**
- *Yellow Sprinkles*
- *Flower Marshmallows*
- *Jordan Almonds*
- *Jelly Beans*
- *Necco Wafer*
- *Glitter Truffle*
- *Sanding Sugar*

**ROW 4**
- *Nonpareils*
- *Candy Dots*
- *Chocolate Lentils*
- *Chocolate Wafers*
- *Rock Candy Crystals*
- *Candy Coated Sunny Seeds*
- *Taffy*

**ROW 5**
- *Jujubes*
- *Licorice Bites*
- *Gummies*
- *Sixlets*
- *Skittles*
- *Black Licorice Diamonds*
- *Good & Plenty*

# Candy Couture

 *Gummy Hearts:* A candy after Marc Jacobs's, well, heart: If he can plaster hearts all over a handbag and incorporate them into the heel of a shoe, you can go crazy with them on your sweets table.

 *Licorice Wheel:* It's a film reel, it's a spider-web, it's a tray liner; think of it as an accessory you can't live without.

 *Candy Corn in Husk:* Holiday wear only.

*M&M's:* A candy wardrobe workhorse, perfect for trimming a cupcake, lining a serving tray, or filling a candy bag.

 *Lime Gummies:* A statement piece, not for the inhibited!

 *Mellowcreme Pumpkins:* They're like those sample-sale purchases—you can't always get them, except once a year. Everyone offers these on Halloween and that's the point. Something isn't quite right about a table without them.

*Chocolate Straws:* The pencil skirt of the holiday candy cupboard.

 *Marbled Malt Balls:* The ultimate bauble, as versatile as a string of giant pearls, in which case, more is more.

 *Sour Patch Apples:* Like sequins and lamé, a little bit goes a long way!

 *Pretzel Celebration:* They're what Donna Karan is to DKNY, Calvin Klein is to CK, and Michael Kors is to Kors—the couture candy pretzel.

 *Ribbon Candy:* Retro, in a good way. Think of it as your prized vintage find.

 *Yellow Sugar Candy Beads:* The costume jewelry of the candy jar. They come in every color under the sun and are simply fun.

 *Hammond's Pillow Mints:* Remind me of the perfect summer wardrobe, pretty, light as a feather, and unfussy.

 *Yellow Sprinkles:* Use with a light hand to add a little shimmer.

 *Flower Marshmallows:* The Peter Pan collar of candy.

 *Jordan Almonds:* Some call them dragées, but no matter, these symbols of fertility (particularly at traditional Italian weddings) are the little black dresses of the dessert table. They always, always, always look good—all on their own.

 *Jelly Beans:* Like flip-flops, they come in every color under the sun and convey a casual vibe.

 *Necco Wafers:* Old-school candy with modern design applications (see page 140).

 *Glitter Truffles:* The cocktail ring every sweets stylist must bring out when the occasion calls for a dash of panache.

 *Sanding Sugar:* Lipstick, in another life. Cover basic buttercream in it, and you've given a dessert just the right amount of polish.

 *Nonpareils:* If Coco Chanel designed candy, these would be in the collection. Eminently wearable, these chic little disks can give a cupcake a certain je ne sais quois.

 *Candy Dots:* The press-on nails or false eye-lashes of candy; peel and apply—to marsh-mallows to make dice (see page 193) or to give a frosted dessert a polka-dot coat.

*Chocolate Lentils:* Size 4 Chocolate Milkies.

 *Chocolate Wafers:* Like scarves, they're nothing until you do something with them. Once they're melted, these disks can coat pretzels and swathe brownies, for example.

 *Rock Candy Crystals:* The diamonds in the dessert stylist's jewel box. Use them, pavé style, to line trays, or more sparingly on frosted confections.

 *Sunny Seeds:* The seed pearls of sweets, best used in clusters.

 *Taffy:* Like blue jeans, it's been around forever and never fails to deliver comfort, especially with that stretch!

 *Jujubes:* The semiprecious jewelry in the candy cupboard, these jewel-tone chews bring a pop of color to the table.

 *Licorice Bites:* They come in Bakelite colors and recall vintage jewelry in heft and appeal.

 *Gummies:* Some are ghoulish, others girlish, and still others Goth. Alexander McQueen would have swooned.

 *Sixlets:* Size 0 Chocolate Milkies.

 *Skittles:* If they were clothing, they'd be summer wardrobe staples; these chewy candies let a little sunshine in.

 *Black Licorice Diamonds:* Another Chanel-esque piece that needs little more than the sleek surface of a frosted cupcake.

*Good & Plenty:* A classic that will never, ever go out of style.

# CANDY MATH:

## How Much Do You Need?

When you buy as much candy as I do, it becomes easy to eyeball just how much will fill a certain container. While 6 ounces of candy per guest is enough, you always want a bounteous spread. See my ideas in Go for Abundance, page 42.

I use the following guidelines to fill a half-gallon vessel to almost full:

Licorice Pastels ..............................4 pounds

Pillow Mints ...................................2½ pounds

Taffy ...................................1½ pounds

Malt Balls ...................................2½ pounds

M&M's...........................................3 pounds

Jordan Almonds....................................3 pounds

## DISPLAY IT

Displaying tantalizing treats beautifully is as important as making sure they taste and look good. Presentation makes the first impression, and it's right up there with a firm handshake and a stylish outfit when it comes to creating a successful tableau. There are a few essential moves I make on every table that you should make, too; if you get them down, you can put together any table with ease—and panache.

## Look Around for Inspiration

It's everywhere. A pattern on a rug, a simple floral arrangement, the shape of a lamp, the cut of a dress, the indescribable color of a Weimaraner, the composition of a chef's special preparation on a plate, the trim on your grandmother's lace handkerchief—once you begin to do this, you won't be able to stop! And then you'll start piecing together a table that, while it may not directly incorporate the thing that inspired it, owes its gestalt to it.

## Go High, Go Low

There's nothing more unflattering than a table full of plates and platters of the same height. The eye doesn't know what to look at first, no depth or dimension is created, there is no composition, and in a word, it's just boring. When you look at the still life paintings of the great masters—think Chardin, Morandi, and Matisse—what makes them so dynamic (beyond the obvious) is the variation in form.

Throughout the following chapters, you will read the word *vertical* again and again. On every table, there's a distinctly vertical element or elements, whether it's a tiered cake, a pair of pie stands, a pair of candy boards (see page 147 or 187), a tower of cupcakes, a floral arrangement, or a series of graduated pedestals. The vertical element can be the baked sweet itself or the serving pieces you put it on. You'll also note that the vertical element is not always centered. An asymmetrical arrangement can have as much verve as a symmetrical one; it all depends on the other elements you are using. I always tackle the vertical element first, then determine how to plate and tray the remaining items on the sweets menu. Graduate the height of the serving pieces, from footed compotes and cake stands to rimmed platters and plates, and arrange them on the table from the highest pieces in the back to the lowest in the front. Any other way and it's awkward and impractical to get to the low-lying offerings.

# Embrace the Backdrop

In the same way that a stage production needs a backdrop to create an environment and frame the stage, so does a sweets table. First, look to see if you have an existing wall that will complement your sweets spread. Maybe the wallpaper in your dining room suits, or if you're celebrating in a restaurant, perhaps there's a beautiful boiserie wall. In fact, I occasionally begin with the backdrop of a particular venue and design my table to incorporate it. If the right backdrop doesn't exist, I make my own. But not to worry . . . it doesn't have to be elaborate—for one table I used lengths of fluffy mohair hung from a rod; for another, diaphanous curtain panels did the job beautifully, and in yet another, I affixed pieces of card stock to the wall to make a bold zig-zag design. How easy is that? The key is to create a backdrop that's related to the table. For example, I used Mylar fringed panels in red, silver, and gold to up the glitz factor on my Movie Night table, page 257, an homage to film and the Oscars. I fell in love with a bolt of colorful peacock fabric that reminded me of resort wear, so I made two panels from it to frame up the fabulous cake in Take Me Away, page 87. Not all backdrops have to cover a wall or windows; for example, a festive cluster of paper lantern lights hung from the ceiling in the New Year's Eve Buffet, page 311, and a group of overlapping folding fans backgrounded Spooktacular Halloween, page 291. The sky is the limit here, so let your creative juices flow.

# Go for Abundance

Which would you rather have, three malt balls in a small bowl or an urn full of them? But seriously, a bounteous spread is a successful spread. Even budget-friendly pillow mints or marshmallows look as elegant as truffles when piled high into a pyramid in a beautiful compote (see Pastel Pretty, page 127). That doesn't mean you have to load up on enough malt balls to fill an urn, however, to achieve a look of plenty. When I need to bulk up for beauty, I fill the container with crumpled wax, parchment, or craft paper (see Apple of My Eye, page 211, and Perfectly Preppy, page 233). This is a clever way to convey a generous spirit without overloading on the sweets.

# Work the Whites

It's not the first thing that strikes you when you look at one of my tables, but on closer inspection, you'll notice that I use a lot of white. It's essential for creating a resting place for the eyes, and it gives a table breathing space. Using white pieces brings clarity and crispness to a table; there's a fine line between a spread that's bountiful and one that's just plain cluttered. This is especially true when you are working with a bold palette and pattern (see Mad for Zigzag, page 109). One way to incorporate white is through using basic white serving platters and trays. Not only are they timeless, but they allow the desserts to stand out. As you will see, they are my go-to serving pieces. If you buy them in pairs—square, round, and rectangular platters; footed compotes, cake stands, and bowls in various sizes—you'll never be lacking for smart presentation pieces. The same goes for table linens. I love to use interesting colors to cover the table, but often I'll spread a white runner on top of the tablecloth to ground the tableau.

## Make It Original

My tables have a very distinct vibe. Most of them are marked by the use of striking and unexpected color palettes. For example, in Apple of My Eye, page 211, I used red, of course, but the predominant color is yellow-green, a shade that takes the palette from cliché to cool with the merest shift on the color wheel. The same goes for Vineyard Afternoon, page 279, in which I combine berry and chartreuse to stunning effect. The point is to bring your own sensibility to your tables, to create a signature look. Maybe it's the inclusion of a dramatic flower arrangement, the use of particular fabrics, or the way in which you arrange desserts on a platter—you'll know if your choices feel right to you; it's similar to the feeling you have when you try on a pair of shoes or a dress that seems to have been made for you.

## Pick a Focus: Design or Flavor

Both are important, but when a client wants to focus on one over the other, I employ a strategy that allows me to make sure both are given equal attention. I first map out the table's design, then choose its color palettes and patterns, followed by the menu. Say, for example, you want to use blue. There aren't too many appetizing blue foods out there, so use blue in the decor to obscure the fact that none of the food falls into the palette. On the other hand, if flavor is the focus yet none of it falls within the chosen color palette, simply hide the dessert. Use mini candy cups for bulky chocolate-covered strawberries, wrap glasses in decorative paper to disguise out-of-palette drinks, bake cupcakes in colorful wrappers, and use bakeware that goes with the color scheme.

## Shop Your Closet

In the following pages, I use my husband's neckties to make one table runner and deploy my own fringed scarf to create another. A favorite tunic can provide the inspiration for an entire table, as can a preferred color palette. Shop your closet, as my friends and I like to remind one another, and you can't go wrong!

# Use Sense and Sensibility!

With every decision you make for your table, ask yourself if it suits the sensibility of the theme. For example, I love the idea of pulling out the fancy china and using it, but it just doesn't work on a table such as Apple of My Eye, page 211, or Vineyard Afternoon, page 279. In the same way, a beautiful tweed is ideal for Forever Chanel, page 47, but it would look too fancy on Darling Dots, page 147. This applies to the sweets themselves, the table linens, tableware, backdrop, ribbon, tags, stirrers, and favors.

# Use Tray Liners Liberally

Do this little experiment: Place a batch of cookies on a bare ceramic platter, then try it again with a decorative paper liner. It's an easy, simple detail that goes a long way toward giving a table a finished, professional look. Paper, however, is just the tip of the ice pop when it comes to dressing up trays. The options are seemingly endless; just be sure the liners are safe for food (if they're not actually edible!) and that they can safely handle holding whatever you put on them. If they can't, then make sure the sweet is in its own container (cupcake wrapper, ramekin, pie dish) and then place that on the liner. Fabric, ribbon (woven into a checkerboard!), flattened cupcake wrappers, graham crackers, tiny candies, rock candy crystals—there are as many liner options as you can visualize.

## Mix and Match Tray Liners

CLOCKWISE FROM TOP LEFT

- *Straws*
- *Patterned Fabric*
- *Pirouette*
- *Grosgrain Ribbon (woven)*
- *German Tissue Paper (with 3-inch scalloped-edge punch-outs)*
- *Waxed Honeycomb with Graham Crackers*
- *Patterned Card Stock*
- *Rock Candy Crystals*
- *Cupcake Wrappers*
- *Nonpareils*

# Forever Chanel

## 1

*Fashion is not something that exists in dresses only. Fashion is in the sky, in the street, fashion has to do with ideas, the way we live, what is happening.*

—COCO CHANEL

**W**ords to live by, right? I pinned this quote smack in the middle of the bulletin board in my office so that every time I look up, I'm reminded that inspiration is everywhere. When I find myself stuck in a creative vacuum (and believe me, I get stuck!), I go right back to the gal who broke all the rules when she put men's trousers, pea jackets, raincoats, and sweaters on women's bodies.

Coco Chanel's raison d'être was to create elegance through simplicity and refinement, and that's what I went for in this table, a shout-out to the legendary designer of the classic tweed suit. I've always been partial to her pastels and, of course, would have loved to own one—what woman wouldn't? But the truth is I can't deny that my first impulse was to translate such masterpieces into a pastiche of desserts.

So, by sticking with a limited palette and an equally restricted set of design conceits—tweed, pearls, and tailored bows—I put together a chic table that's ideal for a spring gathering—Mother's Day, Easter, or lunch with the ladies. I took my cues directly from those tweeds; the fabric store—where I have many aha! moments—is brimming with inexpensive materials that beautifully mimic tweed. The table itself required a simple draping of an extra-large piece, and the cylindrical glass vases and the cake pedestal needed only an easy wrap. Once I dressed them up, the next step was that oh-so-Coco finishing touch, a tailored bow.

When I see yellow and white, my thoughts turn to the flavors I love—banana, lemon, and pineapple. Here they are all folded into sweets that not only taste incredibly yummy, but make references to Chanel's iconic style. Bites of pound cake read like diamonds and pearls. Windowpane Check Squares are a nod to Mademoiselle's weakness for men's suiting and echo the tweed pattern on the table. Banana Whoopie Pies, with their bold stripe of mascarpone, recall the designer's uncanny ability to elevate the common to couture. The pièce de résistance, however, is a three-tiered faux cake. It's a prop (and shush, a styling secret) that comes in very handy when a table really needs a vertical element but the menu is full. There's plenty for guests to indulge in, including the goodies inside sunny yellow hatboxes. I filled them with lemon and coconut jelly beans, but the options are only as limited as your imagination. And isn't that the only way Coco would have had it?

INSPIRATION: Fashion

PALETTE: Yellow and white

PERFECT FOR: Mother's Day, Easter, ladies' luncheon, bridal shower

Bake It

# Tangy Lemon Bars

I've served these gorgeous squares with and without the powdered sugar, as the perfect ending to any dinner that calls for a zesty dessert. They may look fragile but they hold up well when transporting.

*Makes 16 bars.*

FOR THE COOKIE CRUST:

- ¾  cup all-purpose flour
- ¼  cup confectioners' sugar plus extra for dusting
- ⅛  teaspoon salt
- 6  tablespoons cold unsalted butter, cut into ¼-inch pieces

FOR THE LEMON FILLING:

- 1½  cups granulated sugar
- ¼  cup flour
- 2  teaspoons cornstarch
- ½  cup fresh lemon juice
- 4  large eggs

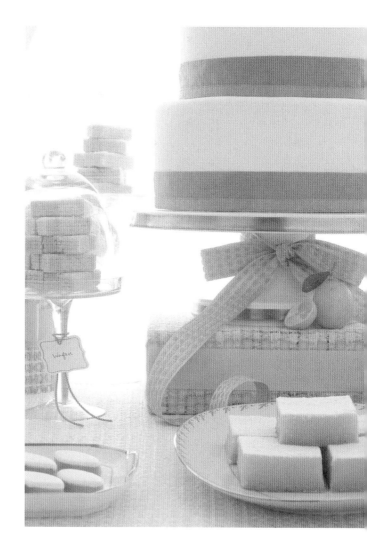

1. Adjust oven rack to middle position and pre-heat oven to 350°F. Prepare an 8- × 8-inch baking pan with nonstick cooking spray. Place a piece of heavy-duty aluminum foil in the bottom of the pan, allowing excess foil to hang over the sides. Spray the foil with non-stick cooking spray.

2. In the bowl of a standing mixer fitted with the paddle attachment, combine the flour, sugar, salt, and butter and mix on medium-low speed until the mixture resembles coarse wet sand. Don't overmix or let mixture come together into a dough.

3. Firmly press the dough into the bottom of the pan, using the bottom of a measuring cup to firmly press the mixture down. Chill dough in the freezer for 15 minutes.

4. Bake until light golden brown, 20 to 25 minutes. Remove the crust from the oven and set aside. Reduce oven temperature to 300°F.

5. Meanwhile, make the filling. In a large bowl, whisk together the sugar, flour, and cornstarch until combined. Add the lemon juice and eggs and whisk until combined. Strain the mixture into a bowl.

6. Pour the filling over the baked crust and bake 30 minutes more, or until the filling does not jiggle when tapped. Cool on a wire rack for 15 minutes, then refrigerate at least 2 hours to set.

7. Cut the lemon bars into 16 equal squares. Use a small offset spatula to remove them from the pan. Tap a bit of confectioners' sugar through a sieve over the top of the bars. Arrange 5 or so on an oval platter and set on the table. Replenish as necessary. The lemon bars will keep, tightly covered, in the refrigerator up to 1 week.

## Style It

To get razor-sharp cuts through the curd and crust, use a very sharp knife dipped in warm water. Rewet it every few cuts to maintain those ultra-precise edges.

# Banana Whoopie Pies

I swoon over these cute little chubsters! Whoopie pies are a universally loved and classic treat that add just the kind of offhand flair to a sophisticated table that I bet Coco would have loved. Ladies, if she could hang a fisherman's striped shirt in her atelier, you can put whoopie pies on an elegant table.

**Makes about 12 3½-inch Whoopie Pies.**

  2   cups all-purpose flour
  ¾   teaspoon baking powder
  ½   teaspoon baking soda
  ½   teaspoon salt
  ¼   teaspoon ground cinnamon
  8   tablespoons (1 stick) unsalted butter, softened
  ½   cup granulated sugar
  ½   cup packed light brown sugar
  1   large egg
  2   ripe bananas, mashed (about 1 cup)
  ¼   cup sour cream
  1½  teaspoons vanilla extract

FOR THE FILLING:
  2   cups mascarpone at room temperature
  4   tablespoons sugar

1. Adjust oven racks to lower-middle and upper-middle positions and preheat oven to 350°F. Line 2 baking sheets with parchment paper.

2. Sift together the flour, baking powder, baking soda, salt, and cinnamon into a medium bowl; set aside.

3. In the bowl of a standing mixer fitted with the paddle attachment, beat butter with sugars on medium-high speed until light and fluffy, about 3 minutes. Stop mixer, scrape down the bowl and beater, and beat in egg on medium speed until combined.

Beat in banana, sour cream, and vanilla until combined. Reduce the speed to medium-low and add flour mixture in batches until completely combined, scraping down the sides of the bowl as necessary.

4. Transfer the batter to a pastry bag or a resealable plastic bag fitted with a Wilton Round Tip #2A pastry tip. Pipe six 2½-inch round mounds onto each pan, spacing them 3 inches apart. Bake until light golden, 12 to 15 minutes, rotating pans from top to bottom and from front to back halfway through.

5. Remove pans from oven and slide the parchment sheet of cookies onto a wire rack to cool completely. Line baking sheets with fresh paper and repeat process with remaining batter.

6. Meanwhile, make the filling. Combine the mascarpone and sugar in a small bowl and mix with a rubber spatula until the sugar is thoroughly incorporated.

7. Once the cookies are cool, spread 2 tablespoons of the filling onto the flat side of ½ of the cookies. Top with the remaining cookies and arrange on a platter in a single layer. The whoopie pies can remain at room temperature up to 3 hours. To store, cover with plastic wrap and refrigerate.

Whoopie Pies

***easy does it*** *Substitute banana-flavored MoonPies or easy-to-find golden Oreo Cakesters and arrange as you would the fresh-baked version.*

# Windowpane Check Squares

The story goes that Chanel was invited to a fancy party while staying on the estate of her lover, had nothing to wear, and so went through his closet. She was so taken with the luxurious fabrics she found that she immediately transformed one of his shirts into what became one of her iconic designs. I wouldn't doubt if she fell for windowpane check, a popular pattern at the time, and the design that inspired these tweed-like shortbread cookies.

*Makes 16 bars.*

1 cup (2 sticks) plus 2 tablespoons unsalted butter, softened

½ cup granulated sugar

⅛ teaspoon salt

1½ teaspoons vanilla

2½ cups all-purpose flour

1 cup good quality pineapple topping

1. Adjust an oven rack to the middle position. Spray a 9- × 9-inch baking pan with non-stick cooking spray. Place an extra-large piece of heavy-duty aluminum foil in the bottom of the pan, letting the excess foil hang over the sides. Spray the foil with non-stick cooking spray.

2. In the bowl of a standing mixer fitted with the paddle attachment, beat the butter, sugar, and salt on medium speed until light and fluffy, about 3 minutes. Add the vanilla and beat until combined. Reduce the speed to medium-low and gradually add the flour until combined.

3. Place dough on a clean work surface and divide into three equal parts. Wrap and refrigerate one part. Firmly press the remaining two parts into the bottom of the pan. Place pan in freezer for 15 minutes.

4. Meanwhile, preheat the oven to 350°F. Bake dough in pan until crust is set and light golden, about 25 minutes. Remove the pan from the oven and let cool 5 minutes. Spread pineapple topping evenly over top. Increase oven temperature to 375°F.

5. Remove the remaining dough from the re-frigerator and divide into 16 equal pieces. On a lightly floured work surface, roll each piece into an 8-inch rope. Working horizon-tally, place 8 ropes, spaced 1 inch apart, across the top of the filling, beginning and ending with a rope hugging the side of the pan.

6. Repeat with the remaining 8 ropes, working vertically to create a lattice top. Bake until top is golden brown, 20 to 25 minutes. Let cool on wire rack.

7. Run a knife along the sides of the pan that are not covered with foil. Holding onto excess foil tabs, carefully lift the tart out of the pan and place on work surface. Using a very sharp kitchen knife, carefully cut into 16 equal squares.

## Style It

To get a clean cut through the lattice crust, chill the windows in the pan before cutting them with an extra-sharp kitchen knife. Most stylists set a standard school ruler across the rim of the pan to guide them to nice, straight cuts.

Malt Balls

Pound
Cake

# Diamonds and Pearls

I love these tiny pound cakes drizzled with simple glaze for so many reasons: they're the perfect size for satisfying a sweet craving (a chronic one for a candy lover like me), and they're super-elegant and ridiculously simple to make. I use petit four cutters for diamonds, ovals, and squares here, but the possibilities are limited only to the shapes of cutters you have. I like to think Coco would have approved.

**Makes 24 1-inch petits fours.**

2 loaves store-bought pound cake

Simple Glaze, page 15

Yellow pearlized sprinkles or sugar pearls

## Style It

Go classic and traditional, if you like. There's no better time to pull your wedding china or Grandma's china out of the closet; the more simple the design, the better. Gold-rimmed plates and platters work beautifully with domed glass stands, footed compotes, a pitcher and drinking glasses. I think Coco would have concurred.

1. Prepare a baking sheet with parchment and set a wire rack over it. Set aside. Make the Simple Glaze in a medium bowl. It should be thick enough to coat the back of a spoon. If it is too thin, gradually add more confectioners' sugar. If it is too thick, add water by the drop. Set aside.

2. Using a serrated knife, trim the crust from the pound cakes on all sides. Slice the pound cakes into 1-inch-thick slices, using an exaggerated sawing motion to get a smooth cut. Cut out 1 × 1-inch shapes as desired and transfer to the rack.

3. Using a teaspoon, drizzle the glaze over each petit four, then patch the exposed parts on the sides with more. Using an offset tweezer, place a single pearlized sprinkle in the center of each petit four. Let set in a cool, dry place for at least 1 hour. Arrange on a platter in a single layer and set on the table. The petits fours will keep, stored in an airtight container, up to 2 days.

# Forever Size Four Cake

In food, as in fashion, some things are an illusion. I took a page from the dozens of wedding planners I've worked with and set a super-tall—yet phony—tiered cake covered with rolled fondant on this table, using it as my vertical element and focal point. Most wedding caterers bake the top tier so that the bride and groom can cut into it, then the whole thing is rushed into the kitchen, where sheet cakes are sliced and served to guests. What a sly little catering secret, right? I didn't bother with a fresh-baked top layer for this cake since the occasion didn't call for one, but if there are a bride and groom in the equation, arrange to have the top tier baked and decorated (or you could bake the Vanilla Butter Cake on page 11 and make a square cake). The beauty of this trick cake is that it will keep in a sealed container for up to 2 years or more. No lie. And you can swap out the ribbon to suit the color scheme and/or design of your table.

**Makes one 3-tiered fondant-covered cake.**

MATERIALS

 1   10 × 4-inch round cake dummy
 1   8 × 4-inch round cake dummy
 1   6 × 4-inch round cake dummy
 5¾  pounds white rolled fondant

   Here is the amount of fondant for each tier:
   10 × 4-inch round cake dummy:
   2½ pounds fondant
   8 × 4-inch round cake dummy:
   1¾ pounds fondant
   6 × 4-inch round cake dummy:
   1½ pounds fondant

 1½  yards 2-inch-wide satin ribbon
 2   yards ½-inch-wide satin ribbon
 3   decorative straight pins
     (pearl-tipped version is nice)
 5   Meyer lemons with leaves for garnish

TOOLS

   Rolling pin

1. To dress the cake, see Decorating a Cake with Fondant, page 18. Of course, you won't need to begin with leveling, filling, and applying a crumb coat of frosting, since a dummy produces no crumbs.

2. Once you've covered the three tiers, stack them in descending order onto one another. (See Assembling a Tiered Cake, page 20.) Run a length of 2-inch-wide ribbon around the bottom of the largest tier, cutting the ribbon so that the ends meet seamlessly. Secure with a decorative straight pin. Repeat on the second tier. Use the ½-inch-wide ribbon on the top tier, proceeding in the same manner to wrap and secure it. Add ½-inch ribbon over the 2-inch ribbon for the two bottom tiers.

3. Cut 2 lemons in half. Arrange 2 whole lemons and 3 halves, with their leaves, on the top of the cake. Place the remaining lemon half and a whole lemon on the pedestal.

# Tailored Tweed Tablecloth

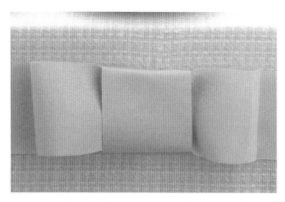

I chose a soft yellow and white tweed for this table because the colors are versatile, for a Mother's Day brunch, ladies' lunch, or afternoon tea. I'm all about the shortcut, and here's a perfect opportunity to skip the time-consuming task of hemming a tablecloth. Raw edges have been a signature design detail of Chanel suits in recent decades.

If your table is set against the wall, there's no need to run the ribbon around the entire circumference. If it is floating in the middle of the room, though, go for wrapping the entire thing to get a totally finished look. Take your time affixing the ribbon to the tablecloth; keeping it perfectly straight is the key to a couture look.

MATERIALS

Length of tweed fabric

Length of yellow
    grosgrain ribbon,
    4 inches wide

Glue Dots

TOOLS

School chalk

Dressmaker pins

1. See Custom Tablecloth, page 24, to make the tablecloth.

2. Use the following formulas to determine how much ribbon you need:

Band for table set against a wall = long side + short side + short side + 6 inches

Band for floating table = (2 × long side) + (2 × short side) + 3 inches

Bow = (2 × length of bow desired) + 1 inch

Bow band = 10 inches long

3. Using white school chalk, measure and mark the fabric 2 inches below the top edge of the table at 3-inch intervals. Next, measure and mark the middle of the table to indicate where you'll place the bow. Fold the length of ribbon in half to find its midpoint. Using dressmaker pins, affix the midpoint of the ribbon to the center front of the tablecloth, aligning the top edge with the chalk marks just enough to cover them. Continue pinning the ribbon to the cloth until it is securely in place. Stand back and eyeball it, making adjustments as necessary to make it perfectly horizontal. Use Glue Dots to affix the ribbon at the bottom and top edges to the cloth, removing the dressmaker pins as you move around the table.

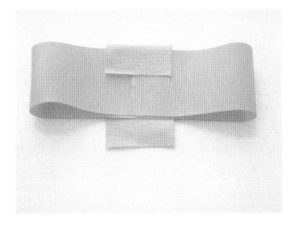

4. To make the bow, fold a piece of ribbon into a loop with the edges overlapping by 1 inch and secure along the short side with Glue Dots. Place a Glue Dot on the inside center of the loop where the edges overlap and pinch it together to make two loops. Wrap the bow band around the center and secure the loose ends at the back with Glue Dots. Affix the bow to the table band at its center with several dressmaker pins so that it is tightly secured.

# Couture Vase Cover

I used 6-inch-high glass cylinders with 5-inch and 3-inch diameters on this table, but I've written the instructions so that you can adapt the cover to whatever container you decide to use. You don't have to run out and buy vases; large juice cans are a perfectly good option.

Makes 1 cover.

MATERIALS

Tweed fabric in lemon, sunflower, and marigold shades

Glue Dots

Lengths of 1¾-inch-wide grosgrain ribbon in complementary colors and patterns

1. To determine how much fabric you will need, measure the height and circumference of the vase. Cut a piece of fabric for each vase using the following formula:

height × (circumference + 1 inch)

For example, for a 6-inch-high vessel with a 17-inch circumference, I cut a 6- × 18-inch rectangle of fabric.

2. For the band, bow, and bow band, cut lengths of ribbon using the following formula:

Vase band = circumference + 1 inch

Bow = 2 × desired length of finished bow (the bows pictured are 3 to 5 inches long when finished)

Bow band = 5 inches long for the center.

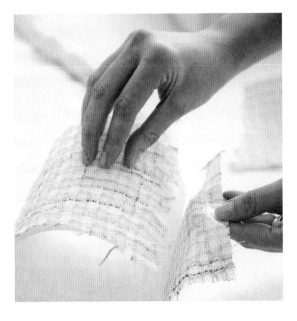

3. Wrap the fabric around the vase, securing one edge to the vase with Glue Dots. Pull the fabric taut, allowing the edges to overlap, and secure other edge with additional Glue Dots.

4. To make the bow, form bow ribbon into a loop with the short edges overlapping slightly and secure the ends with a Glue Dot. Place a Glue Dot on the inside center of the loop where the edges overlap and pinch it together to make two loops. Wrap the bow band around the

center and secure the loose ends with a Glue Dot. Affix the bow to center of the band of ribbon with another Glue Dot.

5. Wrap the band around the middle of the vase, positioning it so that the bow is directly opposite the seam in the fabric cover. Secure one end to the fabric with Glue Dots. Pull the ribbon taut, allowing the edges to overlap, and secure the loose edge with additional Glue Dots.

### ARRANGING RANUNCULUS AND GARDEN ROSES

Ranunculus can be willful! To arrange them and garden roses beautifully, first fill a vase to ¾ full with cold water. Cut each stem (there are several dozen in total of the flowers on this table) about ¾ inch higher than the height of the vase. Blunt each end with a hammer to allow maximum amount of water to travel up the stems. Lay stems in your hand, one by one, until the size of the bouquet exceeds the width of the vessel by about 2 inches. Grasp them as you would a nosegay and slide them into the vase. Arrange as necessary so that the blooms in the middle stand slightly higher than those around the rim.

# Boater Box

Long before she designed her first suit, Coco Chanel was known for her millinery skills, in particular her embellished boater hats. These little take-aways are a sweet reminder of that period. Fill them with a generous mix of lemon and coconut jelly beans, mini yellow chocolate balls, or pastel yellow sugar buttons, and arrange only as many as look pretty on the table. They also make lovely stand-alone treat containers, perfect for a special, shop-till-she-drops girlfriend whose sweet tooth is almost as big as her Chanel wish list.

Makes 1.

MATERIALS

1　4½-inch round craft box (see Find It, page 349)
Cadmium yellow medium acrylic paint
12　inches white silk cord
1　4-inch-wide vintage camellia (see Find It, page 349)
Hot glue or double stick tape
Lemon yellow tissue paper for lining the box

TOOLS

⅛-inch hole punch
All-paints brush, 1-inch wide
Hot glue gun

1. Remove the lid from the box. Using the hole punch, punch two holes 2 inches below the top rim of the box on opposite sides from each other.

2. Squeeze about 3 tablespoons of the paint onto a small plate or piece of scrap cardboard. Paint the outside of the box and lid, squeezing more from the tube as needed, and let dry. Apply another coat if necessary to achieve a completely opaque effect.

3. When the paint is completely dry, thread one end of the cord through one hole from the outside to the in-side of the box. Tie the loose end in a knot on the inside of the box. Repeat with the other end of the cord and the second hole. Using hot glue or double stick tape, affix the camellia to the center of the lid.

4. Line the interior of the box with the tissue paper and fill the box to ¾ with jelly beans. Arrange on the table and give to guests as they say good-bye.

# Pretty Pedestal

I used a cake dummy for this (see Find It, page 348), but there's no reason you can't use two rectangular tissue boxes, a cardboard box, or a stack of books—everyday household items. On some tables I use spongy floral foam, but it doesn't allow for the sharp, clean edges I wanted here.

MATERIALS

1  10-inch-wide × 10-inch-deep × 3-inch-high cake dummy, or boxes, books, etc., put together to make these dimensions
1  yard tweed fabric
1½  yards grosgrain ribbon, 1¾ inches wide
Glue Dots

TOOLS

Dressmaker pins

1. See Pretty Pedestal, page 25, to wrap the cake dummy.

2. Run the ribbon around the pedestal, centering it, and secure it with dressmaker pins as you go. Adjust as needed to make it perfectly horizontal. Affix the ribbon to the pedestal using Glue Dots, removing the pins as you work your way around it. Set it in the center of the table and place the cake stand on it.

# Dessert Tags

Unlike many of the dessert tags in this book, this one is pre-made and embellished with a silk cord.

MATERIALS

6  decorative tags (see Find It, page 349)
3½  yards ⅛-inch silk cord, cut into 8-inch lengths

TOOLS

⅛-inch hole punch

Punch a hole in the center top of each tag. Working with one tag at a time, slide one end of the cord through the hole from the front to the back of the tag. Repeat with the other end. Pull through until a 2-inch loop remains on the front side of the tag.

*Note:* Alternatively, to secure the tags to footed compotes or cake stands, wrap the cord around the stem of the stand and slide the ends through the dessert tag from the front through to the back.

Manner Lemon Wafers, cut into thirds

Yellow malt balls, stacked in a pyramid

Calissons (a delicious French fruit and almond
    candy), arranged in two rows on the diagonal

Rose mints, arranged in rows of alternating yellow
    and white

Butterscotch pillow candies, poured into a small
    bowl with a teaspoon for serving

Lemonade, poured into a clear pitcher and
    garnished with fresh lemon slices

## DISPLAY IT

Forever Size Four Cake

Tailored Tweed Tablecloth

Pretty Pedestal

Couture Vase Cover

Ranunculus and garden roses

Porcelain and glass serving pieces or
    your favorite china

## SWITCH IT

**GROW IT UP:** Serve with your favorite recipe
    for Lemondrop Cocktails.

**GROW IT DOWN:** Serve with lemonade
    garnished with lemon slices and replace the
    ranunculus and garden roses
    with daisies.

**COLOR IT:** Try robin's egg blue and white;
    baby pink and white; sea green
    and white.

# Picnic in the Park

## 2

**O**r in your backyard, on the porch or patio. The truth is, everyone loves a picnic, no matter where it happens. If the living room is your only option, then go for it—serve up the picnic lunches while guests hang out on the sofa! What you're aiming for is an informal vibe; a casual, not-a-care-in-the-world mood. There's nothing like gingham to set that tone—I'm drawn to the classic red and white combination, but you can just as successfully pull off picnic style with the yellow or blue versions. The sweet little check was my starting point for this table, and it led to other traditional red and white patterns—ticking and awning stripes. For the tablecloth, I opted for a classic French ticking in which red predominates, a good way to ground that entire pattern, then added the gingham and striped accents with abandon.

You'll notice that this table doesn't feature a towering centerpiece—a tiered cake or multiple cake stands stacked up to there. I intentionally kept the spread rather low-slung and hung the garland loosely to emphasize the breezy ambience. An unruly but beautiful flowering plant—as opposed to a tight arrangement—does the same. A traditional wicker basket (gingham-lined, of course), filled to overflowing with hearty sandwiches, fruit, and sparkling water, is the focal point, with the sweets spreading out from there. The color scheme makes it easy for me to come up with a menu, since red fruit seems to ooze summer. Cherries figure largely here—they're in the cupcakes, mini pies, and fresh, still-on-the-stem in small bags—because they should! What fruit screams summer more than those super-juicy globes? A strawberry trifle, heavy on the (red) strawberries and (white) whipped cream, is about as fancy as it gets for this picnic, though its assembly is as easy as making a sandwich. Of course, I made those from two "slices" of sugar cookies spread with peanut butter and jelly in between. They're charming and delicious, just like a great picnic should be.

INSPIRATION: Pattern, Destination

PALETTE: Red and white

PERFECT FOR: Graduation party, July 4, family reunion, beach lunch, playdate with kids, plain ole picnic

Mini Cherry Pies

Bake It

# Strawberry Trifle

This is one of those desserts that gives you a lot of visual bang for your buck. Not only is it a lot easier to put together than it looks (especially because I use packaged pound cake!), but it's a ridiculously indulgent combination of dense butter cake, sweetened—and spiked—strawberries, and tons of whipped cream. If you're looking for upping the dessert ante, this is the way to go.

**Fills one 16-cup trifle bowl.**

| | |
|---|---|
| 3 | pints strawberries |
| 4 | tablespoons sugar |
| 6 | tablespoons Grand Marnier |
| 2 | tablespoons lemon juice |
| 1½ | loaves packaged pound cake |
| 4 | cups heavy cream |
| 4 | tablespoons sugar |
| 1 | tablespoon vanilla extract |

1. Set aside 3 perfect strawberries for the trifle garnish. Hull and slice the remaining strawberries into ¼-inch slices. Combine the strawberries, sugar, Grand Marnier, and lemon juice in a large bowl and toss to coat. Cover and refrigerate until the strawberries begin to soften slightly and have soaked in the liquid, stirring occasionally, about 3 hours.

2. Meanwhile, slice the pound cake into 1-inch cubes.

3. Just before you're ready to assemble the trifle, whip the cream in the bowl of a standing mixer fitted with the whisk attachment, on medium speed, until slightly thickened, about 2 minutes. With the mixer running, slowly add the sugar and vanilla. Increase the speed to medium-high and continue to whip the cream until it forms soft peaks, 1 to 2 minutes.

4. Spoon ⅓ of the whipped cream into the bottom of a 16-cup trifle dish. Arrange a single layer of cake cubes over it, using about half the cake. Top with ½ of the strawberries and their liquid. Spoon ½ of the remaining whipped cream over the top of strawberries. Arrange a second layer of cake onto the cream and top with the remaining strawberries. Top with the remaining whipped cream, swirling the top, and garnish with the reserved whole strawberries. Chill for 15 minutes to let cake soak up the juices. Refrigerate until ready to serve.

Style It

Tie your ribbon as you would your shoelaces, allowing the tails to gently spill onto the table, a trick I always use to give ribbons a little movement on a table.

strawberry trifle

# Peanut Butter and Jelly Sandwich Cookies

Yes, I could have gone a more traditional route and piped icing on top of a single sugar-cookie "slice of bread," but it's a lot more fun (and clever) to turn them into real sandwiches. Sometimes turning away from the expected can make or break a table. These are spread with peanut butter and jelly. You can fill them with Nutella Hazelnut Spread or cream cheese and honey, too. My kids love them with those fillings! See the bread slice template on page 336 or use a cutter (see Find It, page 350), or cut freehand if you're feeling brave.

**Makes 8 to 10 cookie sandwiches.**

Sugar Cookie dough, page 12
1 cup creamy peanut butter
1 cup Concord grape jelly

1. Adjust oven racks to upper-middle and lower-middle positions and preheat oven to 325°F. Line 2 baking sheets with parchment paper.

2. On a lightly floured surface, roll out the cookie dough to ⅛-inch thick. Using the bread slice template as a guide, cut out half of the cookies using one side of the template and a sharp knife. Flip the template over and cut out the remaining dough. Re-roll any scraps and continue to cut out cookies. The dough should yield 16 to 20 cookies.

3. Transfer cookies to baking sheets, spacing them evenly 1-inch apart.

4. Put cookies in the refrigerator to chill for at least 30 minutes prior to baking.

5. Bake cookies until light golden, rotating pans from top to bottom and from front to back, 10–12 minutes. Let cookies cool in the pan for 5 minutes, then transfer to a wire rack to cool completely.

6. When cookies are cool, spread 2 teaspoons of peanut butter onto the bottom side of half of the cookies. Spread 2 teaspoons of grape jelly on the bottoms of the remaining cookies. Sandwich the cookies together and serve. Wrap in Gingham Sandwich Wrappers (see Craft It, page 81).

*easy does it* Substitute prepared sugar cookie dough such as Pillsbury Refrigerated Cookie Dough, or purchase Pepperidge Farm Chantilly raspberry cookies.

# Sweet Cherry Pies

What says "picnic" better than a lattice-topped cherry pie? As with most of my desserts, I prefer making this in multiples to create a look of abundance. Don't worry if your lattice isn't perfect; these pies are supposed to look a bit rustic. The filling can be made 2 to 3 days in advance, covered tightly, and refrigerated.

**Makes 4 5-inch pies.**

## Style It

Notice the scalloped edges on the rims of the mini pie plates, the cake stand, and the cherry sacks. This repeated pattern carries the relaxed tone throughout the table.

**ALL BUTTER PIE DOUGH:**

2¼ cups all-purpose flour

1½ teaspoons sugar

1 teaspoon salt

1 cup (2 sticks) cold unsalted butter, cut into ¼-inch pieces

**FOR THE FILLING:**

5 cups frozen sweet, pitted cherries (2 12-ounce bags)

½ cup sugar

⅛ teaspoon salt

¼ teaspoon cinnamon

3 tablespoons cornstarch

2 tablespoons lemon juice

1 egg, lightly beaten

4 teaspoons demerara sugar or sugar in the raw

1. Combine the flour, sugar, and salt in the bowl of a standing mixer fitted with the paddle attachment. Mix on low speed to combine, about 10 seconds. Add the butter and mix on medium-low speed until the mixture is not dry and no chunks of butter remain. It should resemble coarse meal with pieces no larger than a small pea. Drizzle ¼ to ⅓ cup cold water over the mixture and mix on medium-low speed, adding more water as necessary, until the mixture just comes together in a large clump. Transfer the dough to a work surface and shape into two 1-inch-thick disks. Wrap in plastic wrap and chill until ready to use, at least 1 hour.

2. In a large saucepan, combine the cherries, sugar, salt, cinnamon, and cornstarch. Heat over medium heat, stirring constantly, until cherries begin to release their juices, about 5 minutes. Increase the heat to medium-high and stir constantly as the cherries soften, their juices thicken, and the mixture slowly comes to a boil, about 5 more minutes. Remove from the heat and stir in the lemon juice. Set aside to cool.

3. Adjust the oven rack to the lower-middle position and place a baking sheet on the rack. Preheat the oven to 425°F.

4. Take one disk of dough out of the refrigerator. Divide the dough into 4 equal pieces. On a lightly floured work surface, roll out each piece of dough into a 7-inch circle, about ⅛-inch thick. Line each of 4 5-inch pie plates with a circlet of dough, letting it hang over edge.

5. Divide the filling equally among the pies. Roll out the remaining dough into a 12- × 6-inch rectangle. With the long side facing you, cut the dough vertically into ½-inch-wide strips with a chef's knife or pastry wheel, to yield 24 6-inch-long × ½-inch-wide strips.

6. Lay 3 strips, evenly spaced, over the filling of each pie. Place 3 more strips crosswise over them to create a lattice top. Gently press around the edges of each pie to adhere the tops to the bottom crust. Crimp and trim dough with a knife.

7. Carefully brush the lattice top and edges with the beaten egg. Sprinkle 1 teaspoon sugar over each.

8. Line the preheated baking sheet with parchment. Place pies on the baking sheet and bake until the crust is set and begins to turn golden brown, about 20 minutes. Reduce the temperature to 350°F and continue to bake until the filling is bubbling and the crust is a deep golden brown, 10 to 15 minutes more. Let pies cool completely on wire rack.

*easy does it* *Substitute packaged pie dough for the from-scratch version here.*

# Dried Sour Cherry Cupcakes with Simple Glaze

These dense, delicious cupcakes are an ideal picnic treat; they're transportable, and the icing won't slide off. I've also made them for school bake sales and as an after-school treat, with many happy takers.

**Makes 12.**

1¼ cups all-purpose flour

1½ teaspoons baking powder

½ teaspoon salt

6 tablespoons unsalted butter, softened

⅔ cup granulated sugar

2 eggs

½ teaspoon vanilla extract

¼ teaspoon almond extract

⅓ cup sliced almonds, finely chopped

1 cup dried sour cherries, rough chopped

⅔ cup milk

Simple Glaze, page 15

1. Adjust the oven rack to the middle position and preheat oven to 375°F. Spray a nonstick cupcake tin with nonstick spray labeled "for baking." Alternatively, grease and flour the pan.

2. In a medium bowl, combine the flour, baking powder, and salt; set aside.

3. In the bowl of a standing mixer fitted with the paddle attachment, combine the butter and sugar and beat on medium-high speed until light and fluffy, 2 to 3 minutes. Reduce the speed to medium and add the eggs, one by one, beating well after each addition and scraping down the sides of the bowl and the paddle as necessary. Add the vanilla extract, almond extract, almonds, and cherries and mix until combined. Add the milk and mix until combined. Reduce the speed to medium-low and gradually add the dry ingredients, mixing until combined and the batter is smooth.

4. Remove bowl from mixer and stir batter a few times to make sure it's completely combined. Divide the batter evenly in the cupcake tin and bake until the cupcakes are just set and the edges are golden brown, about 17 minutes. Let cupcakes cool in the pan for about 10 minutes, then transfer to a wire rack to cool completely.

5. When the cupcakes are completely cool, drizzle the icing by the tablespoonful over each. Let set. Arrange the cupcakes on a cake stand in a pyramid shape and set on the table.

# Red Zinger Iced Tea with Watermelon Wedges

A colorful and ice-cold drink should always be part of a picnic menu; I wanted to include one that fits the red and white color scheme. Red zinger tea, steeped, chilled, and lightly sweetened, filled the bill. Watermelon wedges make a perfect garnish.

**Makes 2 gallons.**

- 2 gallons Red Zinger tea, chilled
- 1 small watermelon, cut into 2-inch wedges

Divide the tea between two vessels. Just before guests arrive, add the watermelon wedges. Provide a ladle for serving.

## Style It

Swap out everyday glasses for handled mason jars wrapped with frayed strips of gingham fabric.

# Festive Red and White Bunting

I love that this decoration can be customized to reflect any party theme—it's simply scrapbook paper cut into triangles and affixed to a piece of ribbon. Here, I opted for summery stripes and a solid to strike a balance between the many patterns that show up on the table.

**Makes one 14-foot-long bunting.**

MATERIALS

15 sheets 11- × 14-inch scrapbook paper, half solid and half striped

5 yards 1-inch-wide red grosgrain ribbon

Double stick tape

Large red thumbtacks or Command hooks

1. Measure and mark a 12-inch × 12-inch × 8¼-inch triangle on each sheet of paper and cut out.

2. Lay the ribbon on a work surface. Beginning about 12 inches from one end of the ribbon, affix the flags to it. Using double stick tape, affix the right side of the flag onto the ribbon, aligning the top edge of the flag with the top edge of the ribbon. Arrange the flags with a ⅛-inch gap between them.

3. Affix to the wall with large red thumbtacks or suspend from Command hooks.

# DIY (Decorate It Yourself) Lunch Box

Gabled boxes are ideal for putting your personal stamp on something, especially the craft-paper colored versions, which are essentially a blank canvas. For a casual table like this one, all they need is a band of color and a label—you can even add a cute little ladybug that appears as if it's crawling on the box (see Find It, page 349). Invite guests to fill their boxes with the table's offerings before they plunk down on a picnic blanket.

**Makes 1.**

MATERIALS

    1 gabled lunch box, 9½- × 5-inch

    1 30- × 1½-inch strip red construction paper

    Double stick tape

    1 30- × 1-inch gingham ribbon

    1 label sticker (see Find It, page 349)

    Plastic ladybug (see Find It, page 349)

TOOLS

    Hot glue gun

1. Assemble the box. Wrap the band of construction paper around the middle of the box, beginning and ending in the center of a long side, and fasten with double stick tape. Fasten the ribbon to the band with double stick tape in the same manner.

2. Write "Picnic Lunch" on the label and position it in the middle of the band on the side where the seam is. Fasten with double stick tape. Hot glue the ladybug to the top of the box. Arrange the boxes in clusters on the table.

# Gingham Sandwich Wrappers

Inspiration is everywhere, even in the corner deli. I've always loved the way they pull that piece of paper from a giant roll and wrap up a sandwich practically in a single motion. To take the illusion of a real sandwich even further, I wrapped my Peanut Butter and Jelly Sandwich Cookies in gingham tissue paper, tied with ribbon.

**Makes 1.**

MATERIALS

    1 8-inch × 4½-inch rectangle gingham tissue paper

    Double stick tape

    1 8-inch × ¼-inch-wide red cotton curling ribbon

1. Place the tissue paper right side up with the long edge facing you, on a work surface. Fold the top edge onto itself by ¼ inch. Flip the tissue over, with the wrong side facing you. Place the sandwich cookie in the center of the paper so that the top edge of the paper aligns with the indentation in the "bread" of the sandwich cookie. Fold the bottom edge onto the cookie, then wrap the cookie from the sides. Secure with double stick tape.

2. Place the ribbon on a work surface. Position the wrapped cookie on it, seam-side up, so that the ribbon falls just below the folded edge. Secure with double stick tape.

# Pinwheel Favor Boxes

Take a piece of gingham paper, cut it as described below, and you've got a whimsical pinwheel in the making. As with the bunting fluttering over this table, the pinwheels can also be made to suit any theme—just pick the paper pattern accordingly.

**Makes 1 pinwheel.**

MATERIALS

    1 8½- × 11-inch sheet gingham scrapbook paper

    1 5-inch-long lollipop stick

    1 red brad or paper fastener

    1 4- × 3½- × 3-inch red favor box

TOOLS

    Hole punch, ¼-inch

    Hot glue gun

1. Measure and mark a 4-inch square on the scrapbook paper. Cut out. Fold the square in half diagonally and in half again. Unfold. Cut along the creases, stopping about ¼-inch from the square's center, to create four triangles.

2. Using the hole punch, make a hole in the center of the square. Punch a hole in the bottom right point of each triangle. Bring the points with the holes to the center so that they overlap over the center hole. Fasten them with the paper fastener.

3. Hot glue the lollipop stick onto the back of the pinwheel. Fill the favor box with Gummi Twin Cherries and hot glue the pinwheel to the top of the box.

# Scalloped Cherry Sacks

Flat-bottomed penny candy bags make excellent treat containers; rather than leave them as is, I take my scalloped-edged scissors to give them a pretty edge. Another option? Use decorative punches to trim the rim.

**Makes 1.**

MATERIALS

    1 craft bag, 3.5-inch-wide × 2-inch-deep × 6.75-
      inch-tall

    Fresh Bing cherries, washed and dried

    Red and white baker's twine

TOOLS

    Scalloped scissors

Using the scissors, trim 2¼ inches away from the top of the bag to create a decorative edge. Fill the bag to the brim with fresh cherries. Wrap a length of baker's twine about 2 inches below the top edge and double knot it, leaving the tails long enough to puddle on the table.

# Sweet Tags

Simple and yes, sweet, these ridge-sided tags pick up the gingham design elsewhere on the table.

**Makes 1.**

MATERIALS

    1 4½-inch craft stick

    2 2¼-inch-wide sticker labels (see Find It,
      page 350)

Write the name of the sweet on one sticker label. Positioning it about ½ inch below the top of the craft stick, affix it there by backing it with a second sticker label.

## DISPLAY IT

Festive Red and White Bunting banner

Red and white French ticking stripe tablecloth

Wicker picnic hamper

Handled jelly jar drinking glasses

Decorated galvanized tubs

Red and white tablecloth

Large jar for iced tea

Footed cake stand

## SHOP IT

Sandwiches, grapes or other fruit, loaves of
bread, sparkling water, and other favorites
to fill a picnic basket

Fresh cherries

Small, old-fashioned Coca-Cola bottles

Gummi Twin Cherries

## SWITCH IT

**GROW IT UP:** Spike sweet teas with vodka
and garnish with raspberry ice cubes.

**COLOR IT:** Try navy and white or yellow
and white.

# Take Me Away

## 3

**S**hortly after New Year's day, the shop windows in Manhattan undergo a major transformation— out with all the extravagant wintry scenes and mannequins clad in fur-trimmed anoraks sporting fashionable mukluks, and in with tantalizing resort clothes, the kind that give you a tan just by looking at them. As I walk past these windows, covered head to toe in bulky boots, puffy coat, and an oversize scarf, I go into a bit of a trance. Oh, to shed the heavy sweaters, the endless layers . . . to be warm. Of course, I'm mentally packing my bags with beautiful, loose caftans, strappy flats, and flowy pants. Two of my favorite designers, Tory Burch and Trina Turk, seem to capture the spirit of the perfect getaway in every piece of resort clothing they create. Typically a little exotic, a bit bohemian, and slightly preppy, their pieces alone are enough to make me want to book a vacation. Luckily, I can always get my "take me away" fix by designing a table around the idea. You can, too.

The starting point for this table was a bolt of peacock fabric Trina Turk designed and an ikat from one of my favorite sources, Quadrille. The color palette not only evoked "vacation" to me, but the peacock pattern held an exoticism that seemed perfect for a table themed on travel. Rather than using it for a tablecloth, I opted to make two panels to hang on the wall—all the better to truly enjoy it (and no chance of any errant spills staining it!). From there I focused on the centerpiece, a majestic four-tiered cake, imprinted with fondant tiles, that reminded me of the tiles you see in Morocco. I managed to subtly work a yachting reference into the mix, with an aquamarine cake pedestal and nautical navy-wrapped vases tied off in a square knot with bright white rope.

I purposely styled this table to be symmetrical and arranged the platters and vases so that there was an even amount of space between them. Though it sounds very Type A, it makes a big difference if you're going for a light, breezy look. This is not a cluttered, eclectic moment! All of the sweets in the front of the table are low-lying, a styling point that is both practical (no reaching over vertical pieces to get to them) and aesthetically appealing.

Nothing is really more pleasing, though, than the menu here. Though blue is a predominant hue in the palette, you'll notice I steered clear of it when it came to designing the sweets. Blue food, apart from blueberries, just isn't that appetizing! Lime figures largely, not only because it fits the color scheme, but because there are so many fantastic desserts and candies that exploit its refreshing, summery flavor. Key lime bars, cool lime pops, lime wedge jellies—I could go on and on, but then it would be too much of a good thing. But is that ever really true when it comes to getting away?

INSPIRATION: Fashion (Resort Wear), Destination Travel
PALETTE: Sky blue, aqua, lime green, and navy
PERFECT FOR: Bon voyage gathering, boat or beach lover's party, party at the beach, pool party, nautical nuptials, or at-home wedding

# Moroccan Tile Cake

There's nothing like a tiered cake to give a table that all-important vertical element, and there's nothing like a tiled one to instantly whisk you away to Morocco. Unlike on the Chanel table, in which the cake is merely a prop, the third tier of this cake—a rich chocolate layered with unctuous frosting flavored with crème de menthe—is as indulgent as it gets. If you're not a fondant lover, don't discard this recipe. Go ahead and simply make my grasshopper cake without the decoration. Trust me, you will not want to miss out on this moist cake. The design of the cake is courtesy of the extraordinarily talented Wendy Kromer, out of her eponymous specialty cake company.

**Makes 1 8-inch tier.**

3 ounces bittersweet chocolate, finely chopped

1 cup hot coffee

1½ cups all-purpose flour

1 cup cocoa powder

1½ teaspoons baking soda

¾ teaspoon baking powder

¾ teaspoon salt

3 large eggs

1 cup buttermilk

¾ cup vegetable oil

1½ teaspoons vanilla

FOR THE FROSTING:

1½ cups (3 sticks) unsalted butter, softened

4 cups confectioners' sugar

⅛ teaspoon salt

2–3 tablespoons crème de menthe

1 teaspoon vanilla

FOR THE FAKE TIERS:

1 4-inch-deep × 3-inch-high round cake dummy (top tier)

1 6-inch-deep × 4-inch-high round cake dummy (second tier)

1 10-inch-deep × 4-inch-high round cake dummy (bottom tier)

6¾ pounds rolled fondant (1 pound for 4-inch;
1½ pounds for 6-inch; 1¾ pounds for 8-inch;
2½ pounds for 10-inch)

1½ pounds rolled fondant for whole cake or
½ pound for one 8-inch tier (for the tiles)

Sky blue, royal blue, and lime green food coloring gels

TOOLS FOR MAKING TILES:

1 1-inch leaf-shaped cutter

1 ⁵⁄₁₆-inch square cutter

Tape measure

Soft paintbrush, for pastry use only

Toothpick

Nonstick rolling pin

1 1½-inch-wide clean, dry pastry brush

Note: You can replace the rolled fondant for the tiles with gum paste, if you like. Gum paste is more durable and dries faster than fondant.

1. Spray 2 8- x 2-inch round cake pans with nonstick cooking spray and line the bottoms with parchment paper. Adjust the oven rack to the middle position and preheat to 350°F.

2. In a medium bowl, combine the chocolate and coffee. Whisk until the chocolate is completely melted and set aside.

3. Sift the flour, cocoa, baking soda, baking powder, and salt into a medium bowl; set aside. In a large bowl whisk together the eggs, buttermilk, oil, and vanilla until combined. Add the chocolate mixture to the bowl and whisk until combined. Gradually add the flour mixture and whisk until smooth.

4. Divide the batter equally between the two pans. Bake until a cake tester, inserted in the middle, comes out clean, 30 to 35 minutes. Remove cakes from pan and transfer to a wire rack to cool completely.

5. In the bowl of a standing mixer fitted with the whisk attachment, combine the butter, sugar, salt, crème de menthe, and vanilla and mix on medium-low speed until the frosting is smooth. Increase speed to medium-high and beat until light and fluffy, about 4 minutes. Keep covered until ready to use.

6. Once the cakes are completely cooled, if frosting only, see Crumb Coating, page 19. Follow with a second layer of frosting. If using fondant, see Decorating a Cake with Fondant, pages 18-20, for leveling and filling, rolling out the fondant, and assembling and covering.

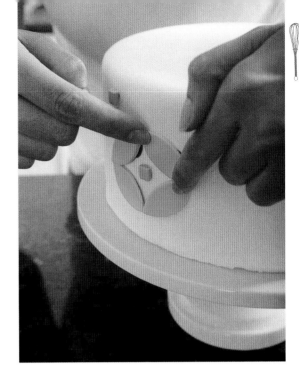

1. While the fondant on the cake is still soft, measure and mark the sides of the tiers to determine how many leaf circles you will need for each one. On the cake pictured, each circle is 1.5 inches wide. Bear in mind that you may have to space the circles slightly inconsistently to avoid overlap. Lightly mark the fondant with a toothpick at each point where a new circle starts. If you are decorating a tier that is 4 inches high, you will need 2 sets of circles. If you are decorating a cake that is 3 inches high, you will need 1 set of circles.

2. Tint ¾ of the fondant for the tiles with a mix of the sky and royal blue food coloring gels to achieve Mediterranean blue. Set the remaining rolled fondant aside.

3. Roll ¾ of the Mediterranean blue fondant to ⅛-inch thickness. Using the leaf-shaped cutter, cut as many leaves from the strip as you need to make the circles on the tier. Each circle is made up of 4 leaves. If you are decorating more than one tier, continue rolling and cutting the blue fondant until you have the desired number. Keep the leaves on a tray covered with plastic wrap as you work, so that they stay soft.

4. Using the paintbrush moistened with water, paint the undersides of four leaves, then affix them to the tier, at the toothpick markings, arranging them on an angle so that their points touch at the tips. Repeat with remaining leaves.

5. Roll the remaining Mediterranean blue fondant out to ⅛-inch thickness and cut as many squares with the cutter as there are circles on the cake, plus additional squares for placing between the rows of circles.

6. Using the paintbrush moistened with water, lightly paint the back side of each square with water, and then attach it to one of the tiers.

7. Tint the remaining rolled fondant for the tiles lime green. Using your fingers, roll the lime green rolled fondant into ⅛-inch balls, then brush them with water and attach to the cake as pictured on page 91.

# Limeade Popsicles

Pour this bubbly lime-infused drink into prosaic little Dixie cups, and in a few hours you have the most beautiful sea-glass green frozen pops. They're beyond easy!

**Makes 5 popsicles.**

1½  cups plain seltzer
Juice and zest of ½ lime
1  tablespoon sugar

1. Combine the seltzer, lime juice, and sugar in a blender and mix for 30 seconds. Add the lime zest and pulse 5 seconds more. Divide the liquid among 5 Dixie cups. Place on tray and freeze for 5½ hours, inserting lollipop sticks into the center of each 1½ hours after putting them in the freezer.

2. Remove the paper cups from the pops and arrange them, upside down, on a tray lined with decorative paper (see Template Index, page 336, and download template at http://blog.amyatlas.com).

I used paper cups to keep things simple here, but if you want to give these pops a decorative edge, freeze them in fluted tins or other, more elaborate molds. Keep in mind that the tops must be flat in order to set them on a tray.

# Tile Cookies

A super-embellished sugar cookie can be a beautiful thing, especially when it mimics a design that recalls a spectacular place. My tried-and-true sugar cookies are decorated here with a Moroccan design courtesy of Christine Mehling of Better Bit of Cookies, one of my favorite cookie decorators. These pretty little squares are mini works of art, an offering your guests will truly appreciate.

**Makes 20 2-inch square cookies.**

Sugar Cookies, page 12
1 pound rolled fondant
Royal Icing, page 15
Food coloring gel, sky blue and turquoise

SPECIAL TOOLS:

1 2-inch square cookie cutter
1 1-inch leaf-shaped cutter
1 ⁵⁄₁₆-inch square cutter
Smoothing tool
Palette knife
Small rolling pin
Small paintbrush, for pastry only

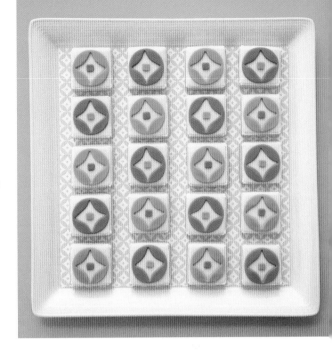

1. Using the 2-inch square cookie cutter, stamp out cookies from dough and bake at 350°F for 12 minutes. Cool completely on a wire rack.

2. Meanwhile, roll out half the fondant (8 ounces) to ⅛-inch thickness. Cut out squares of fondant using the 2-inch square cookie cutter. Working with one cookie at a time, use a teaspoon to drizzle a thin stream of the Royal Icing on the top of the cookie. Place a square of fondant over the icing, aligning the edges. Smooth the fondant with your hands or the smoothing tool to make the surface as even as possible. Using a palette knife, straighten the four edges of the cookie.

3. To 4 ounces of white fondant, add sky blue food coloring gel to achieve desired color. Repeat with 4 ounces of turquoise food coloring gel. Working with the sky blue fondant first, roll it out to ⅛-inch thickness and cut out leaves with the leaf cutter, four for each cookie. Roll out the turquoise fondant to ⅛-inch thickness and use the ⁵⁄₁₆-inch square cutter to cut out one square for each cookie.

4. Using a paintbrush moistened with water, brush the back sides of the leaves and squares and apply to the fondant, positioning the leaves on an angle so the tips touch one another. Place the square in the center of the leaves. Arrange the cookies on a platter lined with decorative paper (see Template Index, page 336, and download template at http://blog.amyatlas.com) and serve.

# Pistachio Cupcakes

The deliciously subtle flavor of pistachios—not to mention the gorgeous sea-glass green hue of these cupcakes—is achieved by grinding pistachios into a flour. It's a wonderful technique for adding nutty flavor to batter.

Makes 12.

½ cup shelled, unsalted pistachios
1¼ cups all-purpose flour
1½ teaspoons baking powder
½ teaspoon salt
6 tablespoons unsalted butter, softened
¾ cups granulated sugar
2 eggs
⅔ cup milk
1 teaspoon vanilla
¼ teaspoon almond extract
2 cups Quick Vanilla Buttercream, page 14

1. Adjust the oven rack to the middle position and preheat to 375°F. Line a standard cupcake tin with white cupcake liners.

2. Combine the pistachios and flour in the bowl of a food processor and pulse until pistachios are finely ground, 15 to 30 seconds. Transfer the mixture to a medium bowl and stir in the baking powder and salt; set aside.

3. In the bowl of a standing mixer fitted with the paddle attachment, combine butter and sugar and beat on medium-high speed until light and fluffy, 2 to 3 minutes. Reduce the speed to medium and add the eggs one at a time, beating well after each addition and scraping down sides of bowl and paddle as necessary. Add the milk and extracts and mix until combined. Reduce the speed to medium-low and gradually add the flour mixture to the bowl, mixing until combined.

4. Give the batter a few stirs by hand to make sure it's completely combined. Divide batter among the cupcake cups and bake until just set and the edges are golden brown, about 17 minutes. Let cupcakes cool in pan for 10 minutes, then remove from the pan to cool completely on wire rack.

5. Fill a pastry bag or resealable plastic bag fitted with a star tip (Wilton Star Tip #21) with buttercream and pipe 8 stars on the top of each cupcake, pulling up the pastry bag as you pipe each one to elongate it vertically.

Try to make all of the stars the same height. Arrange the cupcakes on a pair of rectangular trays lined with decorative paper (see Template Index, page 336, and download template at http://blog.amyatlas .com). Replenish them as necessary.

# White Chocolate-Mint Bark

It practically melts in your mouth, this milky white and mint green swirled candy. It always looks best piled high—and somewhat randomly—on a footed serving dish.

Makes about 24 2-inch pieces.

16 ounces white chocolate, finely chopped
    and melted (see How to Melt Chocolate,
    page 16)
¼ teaspoon peppermint extract
Green food coloring gel

1. Line a baking sheet with foil. Stir the peppermint extract into the melted chocolate. Transfer half of the chocolate to a separate bowl and stir in 2 or 3 drops of the food coloring until desired shade of green is achieved.

2. Spoon the green white chocolate onto the pan and spread to ⅛-inch thick. Randomly spoon white chocolate over it and use a chopstick to swirl the colors into each other, keeping the thickness to ⅛ inch. Tap the pan on the counter to settle chocolate and smooth the top.

3. Chill in the refrigerator until set, about 1 hour. Cut into pieces and stack on a footed cake stand. Serve immediately.

# Key Lime Bars

Here's a perfect example of how you can turn a pie into a bar, simply by changing out the shape of the pan and cutting the results in a specific way. Skip the pie tin and the triangle slice and bake these in a square pan, then cut them in precise squares. Use the template on page 336 for the serving tray liner.

**Makes 16.**

- 2 cups graham cracker crumbs
- 4 tablespoons granulated sugar, divided
- 12 tablespoons unsalted butter, melted
- 1 14-ounce can sweetened condensed milk
- 5 large egg yolks
- ½ cup fresh key lime juice
- 1 teaspoon key lime zest
- Green food coloring gel
- 1 cup heavy cream, chilled
- 2 limes, each cut into 8 thin slices, for garnish

1. Adjust the oven rack to the medium position and preheat oven to 375°F. In a medium bowl, combine the graham cracker crumbs, 2 tablespoons sugar, and butter and stir until the crumbs are thoroughly moistened. Press crumbs into 9- × 9-inch baking pan. Bake until crust is just set and beginning to turn gold, about 12 minutes. Set aside to cool slightly. If the crust puffs up, use the back of a measuring cup to gently press it back into place.

2. In a large bowl, whisk together the condensed milk, yolks, lime juice and zest until smooth. Add in 3 to 4 drops of the food coloring or enough to achieve desired green color. Pour the mixture into the shell and bake until the edges of the custard are set and the center jiggles slightly, about 15 minutes. Let cool completely.

3. In the bowl of a standing mixer fitted with the whisk attachment, whip cream and remaining 2 tablespoons sugar on medium-high speed to medium peak. Spoon a teaspoon of the whipped cream onto each bar, then garnish with a slice of lime. Arrange the bars on a square rimmed platter lined with decorative paper (see Template Index, page 336, and download template at http://blog.amyatlas.com). Leave an equal amount of space between the bars.

***easy does it*** *Skip the bars and make pudding instead! Pistachio Jell-O Instant Pudding and Pie Filling is the most gorgeous green, tastes excellent, and is available at your local supermarket. Chill it in tiny votives or other small glasses big enough to hold a few spoonfuls.*

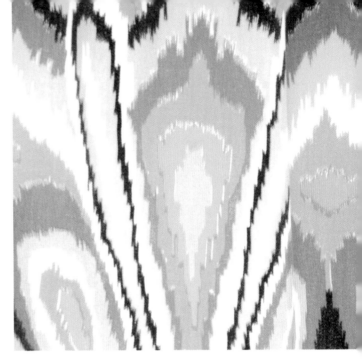

# Cabana Curtains

Full and loose, these fabulous panels perfectly frame the table's focal point (the cake). A pair of fabric panels is not hard to find—you can certainly purchase them if time is an issue. But the truth is, making your own is inexpensive and easy. There's really nothing more to it than stitching the edges to finish them. Choose a cotton or cotton/linen blend; they are both easy to work with and suit the summery sensibility of this table. Avoid slippery fabrics such as satin or silk.

**Makes 2 panels.**

MATERIALS

    Yardage of desired fabric

TOOLS

    Fabric scissors
    Straight pins
    Sewing machine (optional)

1. Cut the fabric to desired size; mine measured 9 yards long × 5 yards wide with a 2-inch allowance for finishing the edges and a 1-inch allowance for the rod pocket.

2. Place the panels on a work surface wrong side up. Turn all the edges onto themselves ½ inch. Pin and press. Turn the edges onto themselves again ½ inch. Pin and press. Stitch around all four sides of the panel to make finished edges.

## Style It

A vacation is a time to loosen up, so why not do the same when choosing patterns for a resort table? Take chances on this one— mix bold patterns but keep the palette limited and vary the size of the graphics. A mix of ethnic-inspired textiles, no matter where they hail from, can work if you keep these design principles in mind.

3. Working with one panel at a time on a work surface, with the wrong side facing up, fold 1 inch of the top edge onto itself. Pin and press. Stitch across the panel to make the rod pocket.

4. Slide a rod through the panels and hang.

# Aquamarine Cake Pedestal

A four-tiered cake on a footed cake stand just wasn't enough! I had to raise that glorious tower just a little bit higher, which is why I slid this fabric-wrapped pedestal, one of my favorite table props, underneath it. Use the purest aquamarine cotton or linen fabric you can find. Wrap with cotton rope for a nautical vibe.

MATERIALS

1 10-inch-wide × 10-inch-deep × 3-inch-high cake dummy, or boxes, books, etc., put together to make these dimensions

1 yard aquamarine cotton or linen fabric

1½ yards white cotton rope

Cognac leather scraps, cut into two 2- × 3-inch rectangles

Double stick tape

TOOLS

Dressmaker pins

1. See Pretty Pedestal, page 25, to wrap the cake dummy.

2. Wrap the rope around the pedestal so that the rope ends meet in the center. Secure the rope with a square knot and spread the tails to either side of the pedestal.

3. Wrap a leather rectangle around one end of the rope and secure with double stick tape. Repeat on the other end.

# Crepe-Covered Cylinders

I love the texture and flexibility of crepe paper, especially if I need to cover a round item, like a vase. Crepe paper reminds me of jeans with a little bit of stretch—even the slightest amount of give makes the difference between a great fit and a so-so one. Crepe comes in rolls of varying widths; I used a 20-inch-wide roll and cut it to the height of my vase, which was 12 inches. Just like on the cake pedestal, page 101, the rope ends are finished in leather—a seasonal touch that echoes the details on resort totes.

Makes 1 cover.

MATERIALS ,

Navy blue crepe paper

Double stick tape

Length of ½-inch-thick white cotton rope

Cognac leather scraps, cut into two 2- × 3-inch
   rectangles

1. Measure the circumference of your vessel and cut a piece of crepe accordingly, adding about ½ inch for overlap to the width. Beginning at the bottom of the vase, wrap the crepe around it, securing with double stick tape.

2. Cut a length of rope that is about 2½ times the circumference of the vase. Tie the rope around the vase's middle, securing it with a square knot.

3. Wrap a leather rectangle around one end of the rope and secure with double stick tape. Repeat on the other end.

# Take Me Away Take-aways

You can print anything you want on the label;
I thought my line, with its double meaning, was quite clever!

*Makes 1 bag.*

## MATERIALS

1 5- × 7-inch piece white card stock

Double stick tape

1 Kelly green favor bag, 3½-inch-wide ×
    2-inch-deep × 6¾-inch-tall

Lime and blueberry jelly beans

8-inch length navy blue cotton cord

## TOOLS

Hot glue gun

1. See the Template Index, page 336, download template at http://blog.amyatlas.com, and print the label onto the card stock. Using double stick tape, affix the label onto the front of the bag about 3 inches from the bottom, centering it.

2. Fill the bag half-full with the jelly beans and fold about 1 inch of the top down onto itself. Run your fingers along the top to make a sharp crease and then unfold.

3. Using an 8-inch length of cotton cord, hot glue one end to the bag at the crease. Press down on the flap to secure it. Repeat on the other side.

# Crinkle Candy Wraps

This crepe paper reminds me of the gauzy crinkle scarves that can give any resort outfit a stamp of personal style. Somehow *anything* seems more special if it's wrapped, even candy that comes in its own wrapper!

Makes 1 wrapper.

MATERIALS

20-inch-wide roll navy blue crepe paper

Saltwater taffy

Lime green sour rope gummy strings

Cut a 5- × 4-inch rectangle of crepe paper. With a long side facing you, center the piece of taffy on it lengthwise, then wrap the long edges around it. Twist the ends to close them up. Tie a length of gummy slice into a knot around each end. Arrange the candies so that the knots show.

# Ready-to-Wear Drink Flags... and Candy Bags

I used the same patterned paper for these that I did on the Take Me Away gift bag labels and vessel liners to subtly carry the patterned theme through the table. It's not necessary, but I find that it gives the table a cohesive look.

See instructions for Drink Flags and Decorative Candy Bags on page 29 and the ready-to-wear patterned template on page 336.

Saltwater taffy, for wrapping in crepe paper

Aqua M&M's, for filling candy bags

Green Sunny Seed Drops, for filling candy bags

Green jelly beans, for filling candy bags

Lime green sour rope gummy strings

Green ribbon candy, piled pyramid-style on
a footed cake stand

Lime and blueberry jelly beans, for filling
Take Me Away Take-away bags

Green jelly candies, placed on rectangular platter

Seltzer Water, served in small clear glasses

Fresh limes, cut into half-moon slices for
drink garnish

## DISPLAY IT

Cabana Curtains

Lime green cotton/linen tablecloth

Green young hydrangeas

Square and rectangular white-rimmed platters
lined with decorative paper

White cake stands

Fabric-covered vases and pedestal

## SWITCH IT

**GROW IT UP:** Serve with your favorite recipe for
grasshoppers.

**GROW IT DOWN:** Serve seltzer with lime or make
limeade. Pour it into glasses with rims small
enough to set a mini powdered donut on
them. Cut three thin strips from a fruit roll-up
and drape over donut in a triangle shape to
mimic a life preserver.

**COLOR IT:** Substitute classic nautical red and navy
or chic orange and navy.

# Ribbon Candy

*"We elves try to stick to the four main food groups:
candy, candy canes, candy corns, and syrup."*

—BUDDY, AS PLAYED BY WILL FERRELL, IN *Elf*

As for the rest of us, that suggestion could indeed be true around the holidays, when it seems every dish and jar beckons with glistening towers of sweet stuff. None conjures the magic of the season quite like ribbon candy, the whisper-thin, fragile-as-glass loop-de-loops flamboyantly colored to indicate their flavors. I have distinct memories of the fluted white hobnail compote my grandmother piled pieces of it into—and how I always wanted the clove-flavored piece that was inevitably on the bottom of the stack. The longer the candy sat in the dish, the stickier it got, until it eventually welded itself into one fabulously intricate piece that looked like sculpture.

In fact, making ribbon candy *is* a bit like making sculpture. When F. B. Washburn, a Brockton, Massachusetts–based candy-maker found success with his coconut bar cookie in 1856, he turned his talent to candy-making and the first ribbons—as well as sour balls, peppermint starlights, and lollipops—were born. What inspired Washburn to shape slabs of sugar into graceful, looped ribbons? We may never know why, but how he did it is perhaps more fascinating. How *did* he get those colorful, reed-thin stripes into the ribbon? Back then, the entire process was done by hand, and in the case of several high-quality candy-makers today, it still is.

Picture a huge mound of molten sugar—sugar, corn syrup, water, and cream of tartar heated to a blistering 310°F in an enormous copper bowl—poured onto a cool marble-top table. From this point, turning a sticky pool of hot sugar into glistening ribbons is a race against the clock for two candy-makers. As it oozes out to the surfaces' edges, one adds flavoring—anise, clove, cinnamon, bubble gum, lime, peanut butter, you name it—while the other scrapes the lava-like mixture onto itself using a dough scraper. The flavoring must be incorporated very quickly or it will evaporate. Wearing welding gloves to protect their hands, the candy-makers mix and gather the dough repeatedly until the flavoring is infused throughout. The sugar now has a taffy-esque consistency. A portion of

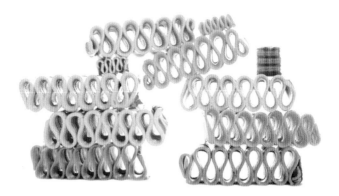

the candy is cut away, tinted with food coloring, and placed in front of a heater to keep it pliable. It will eventually be cut into strips to create the ribbon candy's stripes.

While one candy-maker is coloring a piece, the other is "hanging" the base batch on a giant hook and pulling it over and over—hook, pull, unhook, hook, pull, unhook—until it turns white. All in all, it takes about 5 minutes for the amber slab to turn creamy white. Amazing! Next, while working in front of the heater, the stripes are pressed into the base color, which is loosely shaped like a boule. All of the pieces are still so hot that the stripes melt right into the base color. Then comes the truly tricky part. One candy-maker, the puller, pulls a ribbon-width piece out of the amorphous blob, patting and stretching it as thin as possible. At this stage, the puller is wearing cotton gloves, which give the candy its lustrous sheen. He or she then shapes it into the candy as we know it and must do so in 6 to 8 seconds to form each piece, or it will harden. Shaping it is a bit like learning how to crimp the edges of a pie; the index and middle fingers on the right hand "walk" the ribbon around themselves, while the thumb on the left hand pushes the whole thing forward to keep the width consistent. Not all candy-makers shape the ribbons by hand; some use crimping machines to do the job for them. In fact, some ribbon candy is entirely machine-made, right down to the pouring of the sugar onto the marble slab. But little else has changed over the more than 150 years that ribbon candy has symbolized the sweetest season of all.

Not that I limit myself to using it in the waning months of the year. Not at all! There's no other candy that stacks quite like it—or takes guests right back to a nostalgic time and place. I've been known to use it strictly as decoration, packed akimbo into a domed cake stand or as a tray liner for a dessert that needs a little boost. My favorite go-to source is Hammond's. Their ribbon candy comes in dozens of captivating colors and flavors and is the perfect year-round option on any sweets table.

LITTLE DEBBIE
CAKES

MOON
PIES

MINI BLOOD
ORANGE
CHEESECAKES

SUGAR
COOKIES

# Mad for Zigzag

## 4

I was a charter subscriber and complete junkie for the interior design magazine *Domino.* When it folded a few years ago, I was crushed. Where would I get my David Hicks–meets–sheepskin rugs–meets–Lucite table fix every month? And where was I ever going to find the genius that was one of their best features: "Turn This Outfit into a Room"? There really wasn't anything quite like that in shelter magazines until *Domino* came along. And I could totally relate; I had been turning fashion into sweets tables in the same way for, like, ever!

Case in point: Back when I was practicing law, I walked home from the office every night. Sometimes it would take me twice as long as it should. I'd stop to look in every shop window along the way, turning the displays into candy fantasies.

Once, in a rare impulsive moment, I bought myself a Missoni scarf, a zigzag-laden piece of luxurious cashmere—a total indulgence. I figured I would wear it, of course, and I rationalized that it was essential inspiration for my future career—I'd get a ton of mileage out of that scarf. And I have.

This table is one interpretation of those Missoni chevrons, pared down in palette, overblown in pattern, and totally vibrant and playful. It has an obvious graphic vibe, one that I convey more through the styling of the desserts than through the sweets themselves. Though you can pipe meringue through a star tip to create pleats, make a sugar cookie zig and a MoonPie zag, it's the pleated cake stand skirt and eye-popping jagged backdrop that really help to get your groove on. Once you've done that, it's hard to stop. Notice that the serving pieces pick up the zigzag theme: V-shaped candy dishes, square trays placed on the diagonal, rectangular ones arranged symmetrically, fluted cake plate rims, and a candlestick (yes, that's a candlestick-turned-cake-plate-stem holding the bowl of orange slices) with notched, zigzag stems. Subtle, maybe, but the cumulative effect works perfectly. Of course, I couldn't ignore orange rickrack, which grows right up into a striking embellishment when tied around a bright white ramekin or a sharply dressed Hershey's candy bar. And then there's the hint of black. Whether in an interior, in fashion, or on a table spread with desserts, it gives the table just the right amount of style cred.

INSPIRATION: Fashion

PALETTE: Orange and white

PERFECT FOR: Almost *any* occasion—bridal shower, engagement party, office party (especially to celebrate the end of a crazy busy season or special project), birthday party

# Carrot Cupcakes

These are among the most popular sweets I've had on my sweets menus, probably because they are so familiar and homey. To make them pop for a table like this, pipe the cream cheese frosting on about ¼-inch-thick and top with an orange starlight candy.

*Makes 12.*

1 cup all-purpose flour

1¾ teaspoons baking powder

1 teaspoon ground cinnamon

½ teaspoon salt

½ teaspoon nutmeg

¼ teaspoon ground cloves

2 eggs

½ cup granulated sugar

⅓ cup light brown sugar

¾ cup vegetable oil

1½ cups grated carrots

⅓ cup raisins

1 teaspoon vanilla

Cream Cheese Frosting, page 14

1. Adjust an oven rack to middle position and preheat oven to 375°F. Line a standard cupcake tin with white cupcake liners. Sift together the flour, baking powder, cinnamon, salt, nutmeg, and cloves into a medium bowl.

2. In a large bowl, whisk together the eggs and sugars until combined and the mixture is light yellow. Whisk in oil until smooth. Stir in the carrots, raisins, and vanilla until combined. Gradually stir in the flour mixture until just combined.

3. Spoon the batter into the cupcake liners and bake until the cupcakes are set and golden brown, about 20 minutes. Let cool in pan for 10 minutes, then remove the cupcakes to cool completely on a wire rack.

4. Spoon the buttercream into a pastry bag or resealable plastic bag fitted with a Wilton Round Tip #1A. Pipe onto each cupcake in graduated circles. Top each with a starlight candy and arrange on a pedestal, reserving extra to replenish as guests help themselves.

*easy does it* Betty Crocker makes a delicious boxed carrot cake mix that can be substituted for home-baked cupcakes.

# Meringue Sandwiches

A creamy stripe of orange curd comes between two delicate meringue bites for the sweetest little kiss ever in these one-bite treats. The recipe for this curd is a soft orange and it is great on its own; if you want a more vibrant hue as in the photo, stir in a few drops of orange food coloring gel. Make the curd when you need a Zen moment, as it requires constant stirring to prevent it from going grainy.

**Makes 12 sandwiches.**

FOR THE CURD:

   Juice and zest of 1 orange
   Juice of ½ lemon
   ½  cup sugar
   3  large eggs, beaten
   ½  cup (1 stick) butter

FOR THE MERINGUES:

   2  large egg whites
   ¼ teaspoon cream of tartar
   ½  cup granulated sugar

1. Combine the juices, sugar, and eggs together in a heavy-bottomed saucepan. Heat over medium heat, stirring constantly, until the mixture comes to a simmer. Add the butter and continue to stir until the mixture begins to thicken, 5 to 10 minutes. Remove from the heat and pour through a strainer into a medium bowl. Stir in the orange zest. Seal with plastic wrap to prevent a film. Refrigerate until set, at least 3 hours but preferably overnight.

2. Adjust the oven racks to the lower-middle and upper-middle positions and preheat the oven to 175°F. Line 2 baking sheets with parchment paper.

3. In the bowl of a standing mixer fitted with the whisk attachment, whisk egg whites and cream of tartar on medium-high speed until foamy, about 30 seconds. Increase the speed to high and slowly add the sugar. Continue to whisk until the meringue holds stiff peaks, about 3 minutes.

4. Using a rubber spatula, transfer the meringue to a pastry bag fitted with a star tip (Wilton Star Tip #22). Pipe 1½-inch rosettes onto the prepared sheets, spacing the rosettes 1 inch apart. Using an offset spatula, tamp down the peaks on half of the meringues; these will be used for the bottom half of the sandwich cookies so the cookies can sit flat on the tray.

5. Bake until crisp but still white, about 2½ hours. Transfer pans to wire racks and let meringues cool completely on pan. The meringues will keep, tightly covered, at room temperature up to one week.

6. To assemble the kisses, place 2 teaspoons of curd on top of the tamped down meringue rosettes. Top with a peaked rosette. Arrange the kisses on a footed cake stand and set on the table.

***easy does it*** *Skip the orange curd and instead put a small scoop of blood orange sorbet between the meringues. Use a small melon baller to scoop a perfect amount of sorbet—and serve immediately!*

# Cheesecake Mousse with Blood Orange Gelee

These little pots of unctuousness make perfect one-off dessert for a small dinner party as much as they make one of many offerings on an elaborate table. And they're *soooo* easy. Don't let the gelee intimidate you; it's just gelatin and blood orange juice mixed together. Make the cheesecakes the day before you're planning to serve them, then top them off with the luminous gelee on the day of the gathering.

**Makes 6 4-ounce servings.**

FOR THE MOUSSE:

- 2 cups heavy cream
- 16 ounces cream cheese
- ⅔ cup confectioners' sugar
- 1 teaspoon lemon juice
- 1 teaspoon vanilla extract
- ½ teaspoon salt

FOR THE GELEE:

- ½ cup blood orange juice or pulp-free orange juice
- 1 teaspoon unflavored gelatin
- 2 teaspoons sugar
- 1 small blood orange, cut into six slices

1. In a medium bowl, whisk the heavy cream until stiff peaks form, then cover and refrigerate. In the bowl of an electric mixer fitted with a paddle attachment, beat the cream cheese and confectioners' sugar until combined. Add the lemon juice, vanilla, and salt and continue to beat until light and fluffy. Using a rubber spatula, fold in ⅓ of the whipped cream. Fold in the remaining whipped cream, making sure to incorporate air into the mixture as you fold. Fill a pastry bag or resealable plastic bag fitted with a large round tip (Wilton Round Tip #1a) with the mousse and pipe an equal amount into each of six ramekins. Cover with plastic wrap and chill at least 1 hour.

2. Meanwhile, prepare the gelee. Pour half of the orange juice into a small bowl. Sprinkle the powdered gelatin over it and let sit for about 5 minutes, stirring occasionally. In the meantime, combine the remaining juice and the sugar in a saucepan and bring to a boil. Add the gelatin mixture to it and stir with a rubber spatula until completely dissolved. Remove from the heat.

3. Place a blood orange slice on each chilled mousse. After you have placed the orange slices on the chilled mousse, pour the gelee mixture to the rim of the ramekin. Note that the gelee mixture shouldn't be boiling when you pour it on top, but you shouldn't cool it completely or it will set before you pour it.

4. Chill for at least ½ hour before serving, or cover with plastic wrap and refrigerate for 2 to 3 days. When ready to serve, embellish ramekins with rickrack (see Rickracked Ramekins, page 124), arrange on a rectangular tray lined with white sanding sugar, and place on the table.

# Zigzag Squares

Rolled and cut cookies are the chameleons of my dessert tables. Shape, color, and frost them in whatever way you want to suit the theme. Here, I flooded them with royal icing and piped a minimalist zigzag pattern on them, then set them on the diagonal on a tray lined with orange rock candy crystals. Use a 2-inch square cookie cutter to cut out the sugar cookies.

**Makes about 20 2-inch square cookies.**

Royal Icing, page 15
Orange food coloring gel
Sugar Cookies, page 12, cut with
   2-inch square cutter

1. Place ½ cup of the Royal Icing in a small bowl. Place remaining Royal Icing in another bowl. Stir in a few drops of the orange food coloring, adding more until desired shade is achieved. Wrap tightly with plastic wrap and set aside.

2. See Outlining and Flooding Cookies with Royal Icing, page 17, to cover the Sugar Cookies in the white Royal Icing. Let dry overnight.

3. Spoon the orange icing into a pastry bag fitted with a plain pastry tip (Wilton Round Tip #2). Pipe 3 zigzag lines on each cookie, spacing them evenly apart. Let dry completely, 1 to 2 hours more.

4. Line a rectangular rimmed platter with orange rock candy crystals. Arrange the cookies on them on the diagonal, overlapping one another.

# Pleated Pedestal Skirts

Card stock, folded this way and that to make a zigzag pattern, could not be an easier way to outfit a tower of plain cake dummies or gift boxes of various sizes, a little couture moment on a fashion-inspired table. This tower is one of my favorite alternatives to a sky-high cake when I need to add a vertical element to the table.

MATERIALS

1 6-inch-square ×
4-inch-high cake
dummy or box

1 10-inch-square ×
4-inch-high cake
dummy or box

1 14-inch-square ×
4-inch-high cake
dummy or box

2 yards orange
cotton fabric

Glue Dots or
double stick tape

Dressmaker pins

9 12-inch-square
sheets orange-
and-white-striped
card stock

4 yards ⅛-inch
orange silk cord

TOOLS

Hole punch with
⅛-inch punch

1. See Pretty Pedestal, page 25, to cover the cake dummies.

2. To make the pleated skirt for the bottom tier, cut 12 4-inch-wide strips from the striped card stock. Using a bone folder, fold each strip crosswise like an accordion with 1-inch folds.

3. Collapse each strip into the width of a single accordion fold and, using the hole punch, punch a hole in the center of the strip.

4. Using Glue Dots or double stick tape, attach the strips together, right sides facing and lining up the center holes.

5. Thread the silk cord through every hole in the skirt. Wrap the skirt around the tier, securing it in the back with dressmaker pins.

6. Make the pleats for the remaining two tiers in the same way, using 8 4-inch strips for the middle tier and 4 4-inch strips for the top tier.

# Peaks and Valleys Wall Decoration and Table Runner

I am always amazed by what I can do with simple card stock or construction paper. Among the dozens of ways I've used it—sealing off candy bags, making dessert tags, trimming a cupcake tower and cake stands, lining serving trays—the wall decoration has got to be the simplest to draw all eyes upward. These instructions are for an 8- × 3-foot table, but they can easily be adjusted to suit the size of your table. Just add or take away pieces of card stock to lengthen or shorten it.

MATERIALS

12 15-inch-long × 4-inch-wide pieces orange card stock (see Find It, page 351, for extra-long card stock)

Double stick tape or Glue Dots

12 15-inch-long × 4-inch-wide pieces white card stock

Reusable adhesive

1. Working with two pieces of orange card stock at a time, arrange them into a V and bind with double stick tape or Glue Dots. Glue the remaining pieces of stock together this way to make six Vs that span the length of the table.

2. Repeat with the white card stock and set aside.

3. Using the reusable adhesive, affix the orange zigzag to the wall, so the top of the Vs are 48 inches above tabletop.

4. Lay one of the white zigzags vertically two feet to the left of the center of the table and the other two feet to the right of the center of the table.

**Style It**

Notice that I stuck with a clean cotton duck tablecloth here—no pattern or fussy material is necessary, because the zigzag pattern does all of the design work.

# Chic Candy Bar Wraps

The simplest details—a length of cotton herringbone twill and a strand of rickrack—can turn a prosaic bar of candy into a totally fashionable take-away. I love the stark contrast between the orange and white—so sharp and graphic.

Makes 1.

MATERIALS

Orange card stock

Length of 1-inch-wide white cotton twill

Double stick tape or Glue Dots

Length of ¼-inch orange rickrack

1. To make the wrapper, see Custom Candy Bar Wrappers, page 27.

2. For the white band, cut a piece of ribbon in the following length: (2 × length of candy bar) + ½-inch

3. For the rickrack appliqué: (2 × length of candy bar) + ½-inch

4. Center the twill band on the candy bar wrapper and secure in the back with double stick tape or Glue Dots. Center the rickrack on the band and secure in the back with double stick tape or Glue Dots.

# White Chocolate—Rimmed Soda Glasses

How cool is this? Like fabulous topstitching on a jacket, melted white chocolate rims the outside of these drinking glasses. It's painted on with a paintbrush, a technique that's applicable to almost any pattern and any table. I use the least expensive chocolate chips I can find.

Makes enough for 12 glasses.

MATERIALS

4 ounces white chocolate chips

TOOLS

1 ¼-inch all-paints paintbrush

1. Melt the chocolate (see How to Melt Chocolate, page 16).

2. Remove the melted chocolate from the heat. Working 1 inch below the rim, paint a zigzag pattern around the glass. Refrigerate until ready to serve.

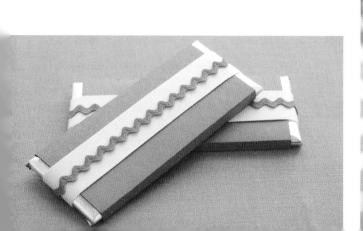

# Private Label Dessert Tags

I prefer using card stock for these, but standard printer paper is fine. See the Template Index on page 337, download it at http://blog.amyatlas.com, and follow the instructions below.

*Makes 1.*

MATERIALS

White card stock or printer paper
1  6-inch length of ½-inch-wide orange grosgrain ribbon
Glue Dots

Print the dessert tag on the card stock. Cut it out and affix the ribbon to the back with a Glue Dot. Fasten the tag to the top of the table with a second Glue Dot, positioning it so that the tag hangs 2 inches below the edge of the table. Place a serving tray over it to cover the Glue Dot.

# Zig and Zag Favor Box

One box zigs, the other zags. Just switch the angle of the card stock strip to alternate their orientation, then arrange the boxes on the table so that together they zigzag.

*Makes 1.*

MATERIALS

1  3¼-inch-long × 2¼-inch-wide × 2¾-inch-high electric orange favor box
1  3-inch-long × 1-inch-wide piece white card stock
Double stick tape or Glue Dots

Affix the strip of card stock to the box on a diagonal with double stick tape or Glue Dots, trimming the corners away so that the edges are flush with the box. Alternate the direction in which the strip is affixed so that when you arrange the boxes on the table, they create a zigzag pattern.

### Style It

Break it up! All of those jagged edges might look harsh if I hadn't thrown a few rounded ones in the mix. Here, the size and shape of the gerbera daisies contrast nicely with the wall and table decor. On the table itself, the circular dessert vessels (ramekins, glasses, the cupcakes themselves) get along nicely with the pair of pleated rimmed cake stands and the tall, faceted stem of the third one.

# Rickracked Ramekins

It is remarkable how the addition of a simple piece of ribbon can turn a plain Jane presentation into something so much more appealing. Think of these little rickrack ringlets as the tennis bracelets of the sweets styling world.

MATERIALS

1 10-inch-long piece
¼-inch-wide orange rickrack
Glue Dot

Wrap the rickrack ribbon around the middle of the ramekin and secure with a Glue Dot. Trim away any excess.

Don't want to purchase V-shape candy dishes like the ones on page 109? Be creative with what you own. Take plain ole rectangular white dishes and place them on the diagonal to achieve a similar look.

Little Debbie Zebra Cakes, arranged on a bed of orange jelly beans

Orange MoonPies, cut into 1- × 2-inch pieces, each topped with an orange M&M and arranged diagonally to make a zigzag pattern on a bed of orange and white barberpoles

Orange M&M's, enough to generously fill a shallow V-shaped tray

Orange pillow mints, enough to generously fill a shallow V-shaped tray

Orange jelly beans, arranged in a tray as a bed for Little Debbie Zebra Cakes

Orange fruit wedges, arranged in a generous pyramid on a super-tall, footed cake plate

Orange bark, piled onto a low cake plate

Orange striped pillow mints, enough to generously fill a shallow tray

Orange barberpoles, a bed for MoonPies

Orange rock candy, a bed for the Zigzag Squares

Orange sanding sugar, a bed for the Cheesecake Mousse with Blood Orange Gelee

Orange soda, enough to fill at least 12 8-ounce glasses

## DISPLAY IT

Orange gerbera daisies, sparingly tucked into narrow-necked vases

Peaks and Valleys Wall Decoration and Table Runner

Pleated Pedestal Skirts

Orange cotton/linen tablecloth

White trays and vessels with black accents

## SWITCH IT

**GROW IT UP:** Serve with mimosas.

**GROW IT DOWN:** Serve with orange creamsicles.

**COLOR IT:** Substitute pink and red or yellow and white.

# Pastel Pretty

## 5

Creating this table gave me the opportunity to indulge my lifelong obsession with soft greens, pinks, yellows, blues, and lavenders. As I was planning the design and the menu, it became clear that many of the sweets that I was attracted to—and that suited this palette—were of a certain vintage. Ribbon candy, saltwater taffy, Necco Wafers, Jordan almonds, and pillow mints all hark back to a different era, one that came long before sours and gummies and gourmet-flavored jelly beans. Blessed with so many candies to play with, I started with the only one I knew that contained every pastel hue in one pack: Necco Wafers. By turning these retro favorites into a runner (Yes, you read that right!), I brought them into the twenty-first century.

# All of those dots

running in rows of random links read like a digital printout. On the other hand, I put it together the old-fashioned way, with a gaggle of my girlfriends, as if we were part of a quilting bee. The truth is, gluing all of those pretty disks down is easy, but it does take some time. It's well worth it, as the effect is stunning. I love how graphic the circular Necco Wafers look when they are brought together in a large scale.

I chose a solid sea green tablecloth to set everything on, and then served up sweets, most of which have a dreamy texture (think éclairs, marshmallows, thickly frosted cupcakes), primarily in pink hues. Setting them on clear and glossy pink serving pieces only adds to the ethereal effect. By arranging various items in solid blocks of color, the spread never becomes too cluttered or chaotic. That said, such a soft palette is very forgiving when multiple patterns and shades are in the mix. I used several here; don't be afraid to experiment. You'll notice that no one shade dominates, which is another key to the success of a pretty pastel table. And then there's the backdrop, which is nothing more than a few lengths of the prettiest mohair yarn dotted here and there with glassine flowers. It's as delicate as the billowy cotton candy it frames. Those gossamer threads beautifully play up the sweets here: vanilla cake, banana cupcakes, pound cake bites, sugar cookies, and pink frosted éclairs. For someone who prizes pastels as much as I do, it's positively celestial.

INSPIRATION: Color
PALETTE: Petal pink, lavender, sea green, pale and aqua blue
PERFECT FOR: Baby shower, Mother's Day, Easter

# Pretty in Pink Vanilla Butter Cake

If I could put a towering fondant-covered cake on every sweets table in this book, I would. But my goal all along has been to give you as many ideas and recipes as possible so that you can choose them à la carte, so to speak, and create your own signature tables. I can't see doing this particular pastel spread any other way, though, than with a gorgeous tiered cake as the centerpiece. But rather than suggest you make all three tiers (which would serve 100 people), I've supplied the recipe for the middle tier, enough to serve around thirty guests, and used fondant-covered cake dummies for the top and bottom tiers. Jill Adams, the genius cake designer behind the Cake Studio NYC, provided the decorating technique that blankets my vanilla cake. A big thank-you to you, Jill!

Makes two 9-inch round layers for one 9-inch tier.

Vanilla Butter Cake, page 11, doubled, plus
    additional ½ cup milk
2¼ cups Quick Vanilla Buttercream, page 14

FOR THE FAKE TIERS:

   1  6-inch-deep × 4-inch-high round cake dummy
   1  12-inch-deep × 4-inch-high round cake dummy

TO DECORATE THE CAKE:

6½  pounds rolled fondant (1½ pounds for 6-inch
    round; 2 pounds for 9-inch round; 3 pounds for
    12-inch round)
Pink food coloring gel
Necco Wafers, about 100 (3 2-ounce rolls)
Soft paintbrush, for pastry use only
Royal Icing, page 15

1. Spray two 9-inch round baking pans with nonstick cooking spray and line the bottoms with parchment paper. Adjust the oven rack to the middle position and preheat to 350°F.

2. Divide batter between the pans and bake until golden, or a cake tester inserted in the center comes out clean, 25 to 30 minutes. Remove cakes from pan and transfer to a wire rack to cool completely.

3. Once the cakes are completely cooled, see Decorating a Cake with Fondant, page 18, for assembling and covering with fondant, and add pink coloring gel as directed on page 19.

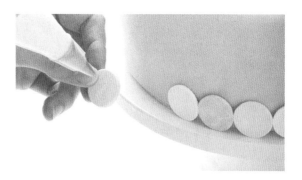

4. To apply the Necco Wafers to the cake, moisten the paintbrush with water or a dot of Royal Icing and affix the logo side of the wafer to the bottom rim(s) of the layers. To make the clustered Necco flowers, arrange 5 Necco Wafers in an overlapping circle and "glue" them together with Royal Icing. Make sure the logo sides face down. Affix the flowers to the cake with more Royal Icing.

# Pastel Sugar Cookie Rounds

Royal Icing has that luminous quality that a beautifully decorated Easter egg does. These are my chameleon cookies; they can be frosted or iced to complement the palette of any table. What's more, they're the perfect hostess gift. Take note: A little dab of food coloring goes a long way in Royal Icing. Begin tinting the icing with just a speck of it and go from there.

**Makes about 2 dozen 2-inch round cookies.**

Sugar Cookies, page 12
Royal Icing, page 15
Yellow, green, and blue food coloring gel
Pink and purple food coloring gel

1. Using a 2-inch round cookie cutter, stamp out the circles from the dough and bake as directed.

2. Divide the icing among 5 small bowls. Add a speck of one food coloring per bowl and stir to thoroughly incorporate. Continue to add the coloring in tiny amounts until desired shade is reached. Cover the bowls with plastic wrap until ready to use.

3. Follow the instructions for Outlining and Flooding Cookies with Royal Icing, page 17, to cover the cookies.

*Style It*

Subtle ruffled touches appear throughout this table, a detail that may not be obvious at first, but by repeating it in small ways, it adds up to make a statement. Notice the "ruffled" rims of the cookie platter and éclair wrappers, page 135; the ribbon candy shape; and the swirled frosting on the cupcakes, page 139.

# Pink Éclairs

Almost anything can be tweaked to suit a table theme, but I have to admit I was hesitant to fiddle with a time-honored, beloved classic like chocolate éclairs. But that feeling passed—quickly. If you've never made your own éclairs before, start now. They're a revelation. See Find It, page 353, for the rectangular treat cups.

Makes 12 to 14 4-inch éclairs.

FOR THE VANILLA PASTRY CREAM:

- ½ cup sugar
- 3 tablespoons cornstarch
- ⅛ teaspoon salt
- 5 egg yolks
- 1 cup whole milk
- 1 cup half-and-half
- 1½ teaspoons vanilla extract
- 4 tablespoons unsalted butter

FOR THE PÂTE-À-CHOUX:

- 4 tablespoons unsalted butter, cut into ½-inch pieces
- 1 teaspoon sugar
- ½ teaspoon salt
- ½ cup plus 2 tablespoons all-purpose flour
- 3 large eggs

FOR THE GLAZE:

- 1½ cups confectioners' sugar
- Pink food coloring gel

1. In a medium bowl, whisk together the sugar, cornstarch, and salt. Add the egg yolks and whisk until combined; set aside.

2. Combine the milk and half-and-half in a medium saucepan and heat over medium-high heat until it simmers. Whisk half of the hot milk into the egg mixture. Return egg-milk mixture to the saucepan and cook over medium heat, whisking constantly, until mixture thickens and two or three large bubbles appear on the surface. Whisk in the vanilla and butter. Pour the mixture into a heatproof bowl and cover with plastic wrap. Chill in the refrigerator until set, at least 3 hours.

3. Adjust an oven rack to the middle position and preheat oven to 450°F. Line a baking sheet with parchment paper. In a medium saucepan, combine ¾ cup water, butter, sugar, and salt over medium-high heat and cook, stirring, until the mixture just comes to a boil. Quickly stir in the flour and continue to stir until the mixture comes together and pulls away from the sides of the pan. Reduce the heat to medium and continue to stir for 2 minutes more (a film may form on the bottom of the pan—this is okay).

4. Transfer the mixture to the bowl of a standing mixer fitted with the paddle

attachment and beat on medium speed until the mixture cools slightly and the steam disappears, about 3 minutes.

5. Slowly add the eggs, one at a time, mixing to completely incorporate after each addition. Stop mixer and scrape down the sides of the bowl and the paddle as necessary.

6. Spoon the batter into a pastry bag or resealable plastic bag fitted with a round tip (Wilton Round Tip #1a). Pipe 12 to 14 straight 4-inch lines, spaced 2 inches apart, onto the baking sheet.

7. Bake for 15 minutes; do not open the oven door. At this point, the éclairs will be puffed and golden brown. Reduce the heat to 350°F and bake until éclairs appear dry and are a deep golden brown, 15 to 20 minutes more. Do not underbake; this may cause the éclairs to collapse. Let cool completely on pan.

8. When éclairs have cooled, use a small skewer to poke a hole in either end of each one. Gently move the skewer around inside the éclair to clear a space for the cream.

9. Spoon the cooled pastry cream into a pastry bag or resealable plastic bag fitted with a Wilton Round Tip #230. Fill éclairs with pastry cream from both ends, taking care not to overfill.

10. In a medium bowl, combine the confectioners' sugar and 1 to 2 tablespoons of water until smooth. Stir in a few drops of pink food coloring until the desired color is achieved. Hold an éclair over the bowl of glaze, spoon the glaze over it, and spread to coat the top. Place the éclairs in individual rectangular treat cups and arrange on a rectangular platter in a single layer. Replenish platter as necessary.

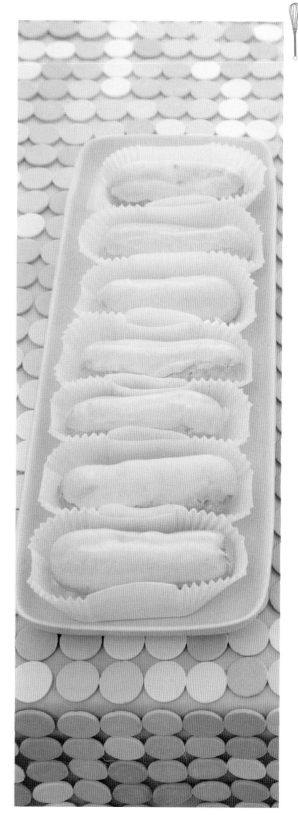

# Tickled Pink Pound Cake Bites

What can I say? A buttery, dense cake cloaked in creamy (pink!)
white chocolate. So much perfection in such a tiny package.

Makes 24 1-inch square bites.

2 loaves store-bought pound cake

12 ounces good quality white chocolate

Pink food coloring gel

White pearlized sprinkles or sugar pearls

1. Prepare a baking sheet with parchment and
   set a rack over it. Set aside. Using a serrated
   knife, trim the crust from the pound cakes
   on all sides. Slice the pound cake into
   1-inch square pieces, using an exaggerated
   sawing motion to get a smooth cut. Place
   the squares on the rack.

2. Meanwhile melt the chocolate (see How to
   Melt Chocolate, page 16). Add a few dabs of
   the food coloring gel and mix thoroughly,
   adding more as necessary to achieve desired
   color.

3. Using a teaspoon, drizzle the pink
   chocolate over each square, then patch
   the exposed parts on the sides with more.
   Using offset tweezers, place a single pearlized
   sprinkle in the center of each bite. Let set
   for at least 1 hour. Carefully remove the
   squares from the rack using a small kitchen
   knife. Arrange, spaced evenly apart, in a
   single layer on a rice paper—lined platter and
   set on the table. The squares will keep, stored
   in an airtight container, up to 2 days.

# Pink and Whites

Make these cool, creamy smoothies just before guests arrive—and offer them each one as they walk through the door.

Makes 4 12-ounce drinks.

- 1½ quarts vanilla ice cream, softened
- 2 cups milk
- 1½ quarts strawberry ice cream, softened
- 5 large strawberries, hulled and chopped
- 4 dollops of cotton candy (see Find It, page 353)

Confetti sprinkles (optional)

Put the vanilla ice cream and 1 cup of the milk in a blender and blend until smooth, about 1 minute. Divide the mixture equally among 4 12-ounce glasses. Place the glasses in the freezer (for no more than 5 minutes) and rinse out blender. Repeat with the remaining milk, strawberry ice cream, and strawberries. Spoon the strawberry mixture into the glasses, on top of the vanilla mixture. Place the glasses in the freezer for 5 minutes more. Top each with a dollop of cotton candy and confetti sprinkles.

# Banana Cupcakes with Cream Cheese Frosting

Okay, some girls get excited about a new handbag, a chic pair of shoes, or the latest restaurant. Me? Candy is my muse. So when Koppers began making their version of classic Good & Plenty in a rainbow of pastels, I couldn't use them enough. They are just soooooo pretty. Keeping in mind how the tiny candies can give your jaw a workout, I resisted covering the entire top of these cupcakes. A sweet little circlet strikes just the right note.

*Makes 12.*

1 stick (½ cup) unsalted butter, at
    room temperature
1 cup granulated sugar
2 eggs
½ cup sour cream
2 ripe medium bananas, roughly chopped
1½ cups all-purpose flour
1 teaspoon baking soda
½ teaspoon cinnamon
Pinch of salt
½ teaspoon vanilla extract
Cream Cheese Frosting, page 14
Licorice pastels (or any pastel candy or sprinkles)

1. Preheat oven to 350°F. Line a cupcake pan with pastel paper liners. In the bowl of an electric mixer fitted with a paddle attachment, beat the butter and sugar until light and fluffy. Scrape down the sides of the bowl with a rubber spatula and continue to beat, adding one egg at a time until thoroughly combined. Add the sour cream and bananas and mix until combined.

2. In a medium bowl, sift together the flour, baking soda, cinnamon, and salt. Add flour mixture to the mixer and beat until just smooth, 1 to 2 minutes. Add the vanilla and beat until just combined.

3. Fill each cup about ⅔ of the way full with the batter and bake, rotating halfway through, until the cupcakes are golden and a cake tester inserted in the middle comes out clean, 18 to 20 minutes. Let cupcakes cool in the pan for 5 minutes, then transfer to a wire rack to cool completely before frosting.

4. Spoon about 2 tablespoons of the frosting onto each cupcake. Using an offset spatula and holding the cupcake in your hand, spread the frosting on in swirls by turning the cupcake in your hand. Ring each cupcake with licorice pastels. Serve immediately or store in an airtight container and refrigerate up to three days.

# Necco Wafer Runner

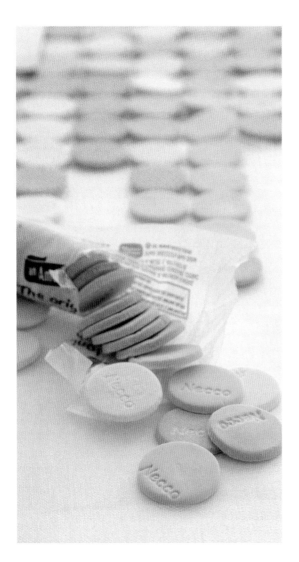

First, a little background on the prosaic little Necco Wafer, an acronym for the New England Confectionery Company, which was created more than 160 years ago. Would you believe that Admiral Byrd hauled 2½ tons of the little disks to the South Pole and that the U.S. government requisitioned a major portion of them for its troops during World War II? The Necco Wafer is practically indestructible, which is good news if you make a table runner out of it (which will give you candy cred for a lifetime)! You might want to approach this project as if you're hosting a quilting bee—invite a few friends over, heat up the glue guns, and start "quilting." I used an Omnigrid straight edge (see Find It, page 352), a tool quilters use to make perfect squares.

MATERIALS

Waxed paper

1  5- × 3-foot-wide piece of neutral netting or tulle

72  2-ounce rolls Necco Wafers, brown and black
   separated out

TOOLS

Gridded ruler mat with 1-inch markings, such as
   an Omnigrid

Hot glue gun

1. Lay sheets of waxed paper on a gridded ruler.

2. Spread the tulle or netting on top of the waxed paper. Measure and mark the tulle 6 inches from each edge to create a frame. You will be gluing the wafers in strips inside the frame.

3. Using the gridded ruler as your guide, hot glue the wafers to the tulle, logo side down, in strips in a rainbow pattern. Vary the lengths of the strips (see Template Index, page 337, and download the template at http://blog.amyatlas.com). You will be creating 48 strips. Make certain the glue is dry before proceeding to step 4.

4. With the help of a friend, flip the runner over so that the waxed paper is facing up. Gently peel away the waxed paper from the tulle. Flip the runner over again so that it is Necco Wafer side up.

5. Position the runner in the center of the table. To store, place the runner between two sheets of packing paper and roll into a log. Place in a plastic bag and store at room temperature.

***easy does it*** *Use a piece of fabric with multicolored pastel polka dots, or white dots on a pastel background. Ideally, the dots should be at least 1 inch wide. Alternatively, you can sprinkle inexpensive confetti dots or Necco Wafers over a solid-colored fabric. Kids love to sprinkle these around; invite them to help you.*

# Ethereal Yarn "Curtain"

I don't knit much, but it doesn't stop me from visiting Purl, a wonderland of gorgeous yarns in Manhattan's SoHo neighborhood. The shop is organized floor-to-ceiling by color, which means I can find my favorite pastels quickly, then stand and stare at them for what seems like hours (wait... it *is* hours). The effect of hanging yarn in strands to make a whimsical curtainlike back-drop is not only dreamy, it's timeless and easy.

MATERIALS

1 skein each mohair yarn in light blue, pink, and yellow

1 8½- × 11-inch sheet glassine in pink, lavender, and yellow

Command hooks

Fishing line

Double stick tape

TOOLS

Round scalloped punch, 3 inches

1. Cut the yarn into 6-yard lengths, stack like colors together, and set aside. Cut out three flowers from each piece of glassine using the scalloped punch.

2. Mount two Command hooks on the wall behind the table, positioning them at least 5 feet above the table and 1 foot beyond either end of the table. Suspend a length of fishing line from the Command hooks.

3. Hang the lengths of yarn over the fishing line in clusters of the same color, leaving spaces between them. Using double stick tape, affix the scalloped flowers to the yarn in a haphazard fashion.

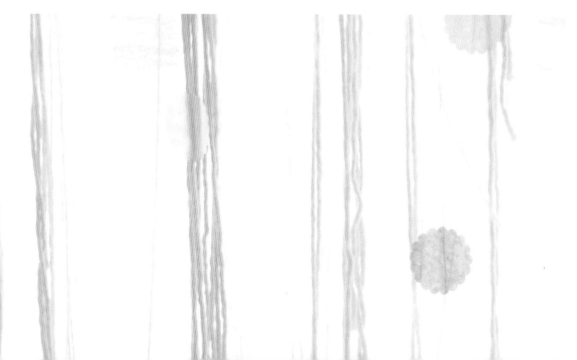

# Colorful Cotton Candy Sticks

The aroma of cotton candy is as enticing as the fluffy stuff itself, and it has a bit of a Proustian effect on me. Yes, I was the daughter who begged, pleaded, and *insisted* that I get a stick of it at the amusement park. Adults, I can say with 100 percent certainty, love cotton candy as much as little kids. To add your own touch to the white sticks, cover them with pretty pastel rice paper. See the Template Index, page 337, download the template at http://blog.amyatlas.com, print and cut it out.

Makes 1 cover.

MATERIALS

1 small piece pastel tissue or rice paper
1 cotton candy stick, see Find It, page 352
Double stick tape

Using the template, trace it onto the rice paper and cut out. Wrap it around the cotton candy stick and secure with double stick tape. Make one for each guest.

# Cotton Candy Server

Here's a styling trick that turns out to be a great way to present any cone-shaped item on a serve yourself table.

Makes 1 server.

MATERIALS

Styrofoam or floral foam, cut ¼ inch smaller on all
    sides than the interior dimensions of your tray and
    ½ inch deep
Pastel pink nonpareils

1. Measure and mark the foam with ¼-inch Xs where you want to make the holes to hold the cotton candy sticks. Be sure to leave enough space between the Xs to accommodate the clouds of cotton candy that will be on the sticks.

2. Using a utility knife, cut holes ¼ to ½ inch in diameter and ½ inch deep. Slide the foam into the tray.

3. As you make the sticks for the cotton candy, set one into each hole. Top each with purchased or homemade cotton candy. Fill the serving tray with enough of the nonpareils (or other desired candy) to cover the foam by ¼ inch.

# Polka Dot Party Bags

Clear candy bags open up all kinds of creative possibilities—they can be topped with a theme-related paper closure (see Decorative Candy Bags, page 29) or embellished on the inside, as I've done here.

*Makes 1 bag.*

MATERIALS

1 piece ivory card stock, 7⅛-inch-long × 3-inch-wide

1½-inch polka-dot stamp

Pastel ink pads in green, aqua, blue, yellow, and lavender

1 cellophane bag, 3-inch-wide × 1¾-inch-deep × 6¾-inch-high

Double stick tape

Length pastel pink yarn

Pink and yellow pillow mints

Sea green taffy

TOOLS

Bone folder

1. Measure and mark the card stock along its length at 4¼ inches and 5⅞ inches. Using the bone folder, fold the paper crosswise at the marks to create creases.

2. Place the paper on a work surface with the two creases at the bottom. Fold the paper at the bottom crease and mark it with pastel dots. Fold it onto itself at the second crease. Mark the unfolded portion of the paper with pastel dots starting at the top and moving one-third of the way down.

3. Unfold the card stock and slide it into the cellophane bag so that it fits snugly into the bottom of the bag. Fill the bag with the candies up to where the dot design begins. Fold the top of the cellophane bag onto its back side and secure with double stick tape. Wrap the yarn around the bag lengthwise and finish with a simple bow.

Pastel cotton candy, set atop sticks and presented in a candy-filled Lucite tray

Marshmallow Blocks (raspberry, lemon, strawberry), stacked in a pyramid on a footed glass
cake stand

Little Debbie pink cakes, cut into thirds crosswise
and each topped with a lavender Sunny
Seed Drop

Pink and yellow mini marshmallows in a footed
glass compote

Pink pillow mints in a super-tall footed compote

Pastel striped ribbon candy, arranged on pretty
serving plate

Pastel saltwater taffy in a small-footed
glass compote

Matte pastel dragées in a low-footed
glass compote

## DISPLAY IT

Necco Wafer Runner

Ethereal Yarn "Curtain"

Sea green silk taffeta tablecloth

Glass cake stands and compotes

Lucite boxes filled with nonpareils

Pastel serving plates

## SWITCH IT

**GROW IT UP:** Serve pink ladies garnished with a
sprig of lavender.

**GROW IT DOWN:** Serve pink and whites or
pink lemonade.

**COLOR IT:** Choose one pastel color—seafoam
green, robin's egg blue, lavender—for a
dreamy monochromatic look.

# Darling Dots

## 6

**D**o dots rock your world? As I was putting this table together, the phrase "connect the dots" kept running through my head. It's both a metaphor for linking ideas to see the big picture and one of my favorite puzzle games from childhood. It's no surprise that this super-playful pattern puts a smile on even the grumpiest face. Walt Disney styled up one of his most beloved characters, Minnie Mouse, in a cheery, bright red and white polka-dot dress. For decades, fashion designers have trotted out the dots particularly during prosperous and carefree times: Think especially the 1950s and 1980s, when economic growth fueled consumer confidence and retail and department stores soared. To this day, I'm loving dots of all sizes—polka, Swiss, whatever—which is why

# I put them front and center on this birthday

sweets table (though happy dots are perfect for so many occasions).

You'll notice that I've resisted plastering them on every visible surface, Roy Lichtenstein–style; a pair of candy boards covered in red polka dots is enough to announce the table's theme. Elsewhere, they pop up somewhat subtly—on slender ribbons, adorning cupcakes and sugar cookies, topping candy favors, and shimmering on ice cream cone–shaped rice crispy treats. By opting for grounding solids in the pink tablecloth and pink and white serving dishes, the scheme could handle even more, though subtle, pattern—stripes and florals show up in the candy bags, on the candy bars, and in the candy itself (see barberpoles). Rather than hang a banner as I do elsewhere in this book, I ran yummy pink and red iced "Take a Sweet" cookies in an arch-shape right on the table to invite one and all to come on over and dig in.

So what are you waiting for?

**INSPIRATION:** Pattern, Color

**PALETTE:** Pink and red

**PERFECT FOR:** Birthday party, Valentine's Day, baby shower, bridal shower

# Bake It

# Pinwheel Cupcakes

These are the bull's-eyes of the table. The eye is drawn directly to the jaunty little disks set into chubby bubble-gum-pink swirls of buttercream on these vanilla cupcakes. You can make the fondant disks in advance and store them, covered, in a cool, dry place.

**Makes 24.**

Vanilla Butter Cake, page 11, doubled
Confectioners' sugar
  1  pound white rolled fondant
⅓  cup Royal Icing, page 15
Red food coloring gel
Pink food coloring gel
Quick Vanilla Buttercream, page 14

1. Adjust the oven rack to the middle position and preheat the oven to 350°F. Line two cupcake tins with liners.

2. Divide the cake batter among the cupcake liners. Bake until the cupcakes are golden and a toothpick inserted in the center comes out clean, 16 to 18 minutes. Transfer the pan to a rack and let cupcakes cool for 5 minutes. Remove from the pan and cool completely.

3. Meanwhile, make the fondant disks. On a work surface lightly dusted with confectioners' sugar, roll out the fondant

to ⅛-inch-thick. Using a 1¾- or 2-inch round cutter, stamp out 24 disks. Place them on the work surface and let dry, about 1 hour.

4. Place Royal Icing in a small bowl and tint with drops of red food coloring. Stir, adding more coloring until desired shade is achieved. Spoon the icing into a small pastry bag fitted with a round tip (Wilton Round Tip #1).

5. Pipe tiny dots in a circle in the center of each disk. Pipe larger dots around the outer rim of the disk. Let dry completely, about 3 more hours.

6. Tint the buttercream with drops of pink food coloring. Stir, adding more coloring until desired pink is achieved. Fill a pastry bag or resealable plastic bag fitted with Wilton Round Tip #1a with the buttercream and pipe in graduated circles. Top each with a fondant disk placed at an angle.

7. Stack three graduated cake stands on top of each other. Arrange the cupcakes on each tier. Place a footed compote in the center of the top cake stand and fill with mixed hard candies.

## SWAP IT OUT

### DIY Paper Circles

If you are fondant-fearful, you can substitute these paper disks made from scrapbook paper. However, I guarantee that by the time you finish this book, you'll fall for fondant.

**Makes 1.**

MATERIALS
1 piece 12- × 12-inch dotted scrapbook paper
Double stick tape or Glue Dots
1 lollipop stick

TOOLS
1 2-inch circle punch cutter or scissors

1. Using the circle punch cutter or scissors, cut the scrapbook paper into 2 2-inch circles.

2. Apply one strip of double stick tape or a Glue Dot lengthwise to the back side of one of the circles. Affix the lollipop stick lengthwise to the adhesive. Apply another strip of double stick tape or another Glue Dot lengthwise to the back side of the remaining circle. Adhere to other side of lollipop stick. Place the lollipop stick into cupcake at an angle.

Style It

## BUILD HEIGHT WITH GRADUATED CAKE PLATES

When there's no multitiered cake or soaring flower arrangement in my design scheme, I get stacking. The focal point on this table is made from stacking three separate cake stands in 6-inch, 10-inch, and 12-inch sizes, plus a small compote on top. Round, square, oval—it doesn't matter as long as they are graduated in size. First line each one with scrapbook paper (here they match one of the candy bar wrappers), then glue one stand to another with hot glue: Run a bead of hot glue around the base of the 10-inch stand and immediately center it on top of the 12-inch stand. Repeat with the 6-inch stand. Finally place a small compote at the top. Let dry thoroughly before placing the stack on the table. To take the stands apart, use an adhesive remover such as Goo Gone to dissolve the glue.

# Take a Sweet Cookies

Sometimes when I serve a sweets table, guests are hesitant to dig right into the sweets. I thought nothing could be more inviting than an actual sign that says "Take a Sweet." Letter cookie cutters open up unlimited messaging possibilities. If you don't have them, see the Template Index on pages 344–345 and download the template at http://blog.amyatlas.com to make this charming edible invitation to indulge.

**Makes one "Take A Sweet" banner.**

Sugar Cookies, page 12
Royal Icing, page 15
Red and pink food coloring gel

1. Using the template or cookie cutters, cut out the letters to spell "TAKE A SWEET."

2. To decorate the cookies, see Outlining and Flooding Cookies with Royal Icing, page 17. Make sure to tint one bowl of royal icing red and one bowl pink.

3. Arrange in an arched shape on the front center of the table.

# Strawberry Truffles

A delicious variation on the traditional chocolate bonbon, these pretty little treats look like dots in 3-D when piled into a small bowl. If your hands get sticky while rolling the truffles, wash your hands and resume rolling.

**Makes about 30.**

2⅔ cups white chocolate chips, melted (see How to Melt Chocolate, page 16)

¼ cup (½ stick) unsalted butter, cut into ¼-inch pieces, softened

½ cup plus 2 tablespoons strawberry preserves

1 cup pink sanding sugar or pink dusting sugar

1. Stir the softened butter and strawberry preserves into the melted chocolate until combined. Cover in plastic wrap and chill until firm enough to scoop, about 1 hour.

2. Scoop flat tablespoons of the truffle mixture and, using your hands, roll the truffles into balls. Place on the baking sheet and chill again until firm.

3. Put the sanding sugar on a dinner plate. Roll the chilled truffles in the sugar. Arrange the truffles in a bowl and place on the table.

## SWAP IT OUT

**Attention: Chocolate Lovers!**

To make dark chocolate strawberry truffles, swap out the white chocolate chips for the same amount of bittersweet chocolate chips.

# Meringue Kisses

These treats are so light and sweet. Resist the temptation to make them too tall or they'll fall over in the oven. Worse, the tips will burn.

**Makes 24 kisses.**

    4  large egg whites
    ½  teaspoon cream of tartar
    1  cup granulated sugar
    Pink food coloring gel

1. Adjust the oven rack to the middle position and preheat the oven to 175°F. Line a baking sheet with parchment paper.

2. In the bowl of a standing mixer fitted with the whisk attachment, combine the egg whites and cream of tartar and whisk on medium–high speed until peaks form, about 2 minutes. Increase speed to high and add sugar gradually. Continue to whisk until the meringue is glossy and forms stiff peaks, about 2 minutes. Whisk in a drop of pink food coloring, or as much as needed to turn the meringue pale pink.

3. Transfer the meringue to a pastry bag or resealable plastic bag fitted with a small star tip (Wilton Star Tip #22). Pipe 12 kisses, each about 1½ inches wide at the base and 2 inches high, onto the prepared baking sheet. Pipe them 2 inches apart.

4. Bake until crisp but still pale pink, about 2½ hours. Do not let the meringues brown. Transfer the pan to a wire rack to let meringues cool completely.

5. Arrange on a footed cake stand lined with pink patterned scrapbook paper.

# Never-Melt Crispy Rice Ice Cream Cones

Diamonds, stars, squares, circles, triangles—and ice cream cones? Absolutely. Like brownies and sugar cookie dough, crispy rice treats can be cut into almost any shape. The fun part is dipping the top into melted white chocolate to make the "ice cream."

**Makes 8 to 10.**

Crispy Rice Treats, page 13

6 ounces white chocolate chips, melted
   (see How to Melt Chocolate, page 16)

Pink food coloring gel

Red nonpareils

1. Using the ice cream cone template (see Template Index, page 338, and download the template at http://blog.amyatlas.com) or a cookie cutter, cut the cones from the pan and set aside on waxed paper.

2. Add a few drops of coloring gel to the melted white chocolate to get the desired shade of pink and stir until the color is thoroughly incorporated.

3. Working with one "cone" at a time, dip only the scoop of ice cream into the pink chocolate and return the cone to the waxed paper. Sprinkle with nonpareils. Repeat with remaining cones. Let dry thoroughly.

4. Arrange in 2 layers on a white platter lined with decorative paper and set on the table.

# Dots and Lines Sugar Cookies

It's back to grade school art class with these fun-to-make lined and dotted sugar cookies! Keep the bowls of Royal Icing covered with plastic wrap when you're not using them; the icing tends to dry very quickly.

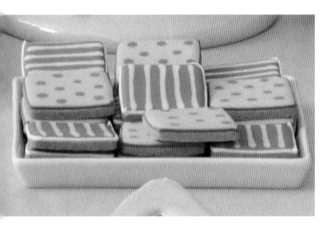

**Makes 20 2-inch-square cookies.**

Sugar Cookies, page 12

Royal Icing, page 15

Red and pink food coloring gel

1. Adjust the oven racks to the upper-middle and lower-middle positions and preheat the oven to 350°F. Line 2 baking sheets with parchment paper. Using a 2-inch square cookie cutter, cut out cookies from dough and bake as directed.

2. To decorate, see Outlining and Flooding Cookies with Royal Icing, page 17, to cover half of the cookies with red and the remaining half with pink. Let dry completely. Pipe pink parallel lines about ⅛ inch apart on the cookies iced with red icing. Transfer cookies to a wire rack and allow icing to dry completely. Pipe red dots on the cookies iced with pink icing. Transfer cookies to a wire rack to dry completely. Arrange on a rimmed platter, stacking the cookies in random single and double layers.

***easy does it*** *Frost the cookies with canned frosting and use candy dots rather than piping dots onto the iced cookies. Licorice ropes work well for the striped cookies.*

# Pretzels in Pink

They're so pretty you almost don't want to eat them, but what a waste if you don't! The combination of white chocolate and salty pretzels is to die for. My boys love to make them because they are so easy and they get to poke the holes in egg cartons for the drying technique.

**Makes 20.**

12 ounces good-quality white chocolate, such as Callebaut or Ghirardelli, finely chopped and melted (see How to Melt Chocolate, page 16)
Pink food coloring gel
20 8-inch pretzel logs

1. Place the bottom of an egg carton wrong side up on a work surface and poke rod-size holes in each egg holder (see photo, page 325). This will be to hold your pretzel rods while the chocolate is drying, so you won't get a foot on one side of the pretzel. Set aside. Alternatively, if you don't mind the foot on one side of the pretzel, line a sheet pan with a piece of parchment.

2. In a medium bowl, stir pink food coloring gel, a tiny dab at a time, into the melted chocolate, until desired shade of pink is achieved.

3. Working with 1 pretzel rod at a time, hold the pretzel by one end over the bowl and spoon chocolate over it, turning the pretzel, coating it to within 1 inch of either end. Use the back of the spoon to scrape off excess back into the bowl. If you like, drizzle the chocolate back and forth to create a drizzle pattern.

4. Place one of the uncoated ends of the rod into a hole in the egg carton or lay the pretzel on the parchment. Repeat with remaining pretzel rods. Chill in the refrigerator until completely set, about 30 minutes.

5. Once the pretzels are set, arrange the rods, in several discrete log piles, on a platter and set on the table.

# Dotted Swiss Candy Boards

The big polka-dot statement on this table, a pair of these is all you need for an eye-popping backdrop. I particularly love the size and scale of this pattern; not too timid, not too loud.

**Makes 1.**

MATERIALS

1 yard red and white polka-dot cotton fabric

1 30- × 20-inch ½-inch-thick piece foam core

Double stick tape

1½ yards 3-inch-wide light pink double faced satin ribbon

Fabric scraps, cut into 2½-inch-wide × 3-inch-long strips, enough for 12 bags

12 clear candy bags (see Find It, page 348)

12 red corsage pins

Dressmaker pins

Thumbtacks

1. Place the polka-dot cotton wrong side up on a work surface. Center the foam core on it. Trim the fabric, leaving a 2-inch border on all sides. Fold the fabric onto the foam core and secure with double stick tape, beginning on a long side, then the opposite side and the remaining short sides. Pull taut but not so much that the fabric buckles.

2. Tie the ribbon in a bow with 4-inch-wide loops and 18-inch tails. Attach the tails to either side of the back of the top of the candy board with the dressmaker pins.

3. Using the fabric scraps and clear candy bags, follow the instructions for Decorative Candy Bags on page 29. Attach the candy bags to the board with the dressmaker pins. Arrange the candy board on the table so that it leans against the wall. Attach the ribbon to the wall with thumbtacks.

## Style It

Don't throw away those scraps of fabric! I find I'm always going back to my box of castoffs to tie around drink stirrers or seal the top of candy favors.

# Sweet Favor Boxes

These trim little boxes are just the right size for one or two truffles; encourage guests to help themselves for a sweet party memento. You might want to write each guest's name on a sticker, or leave it blank as I've done here.

**Makes 1.**

MATERIALS

1 red linen box, 3¼ inch × 3 inch × 2¼ inch

12 inches × ¼-inch-wide pink satin ribbon

1 2- × 1½-inch decorative sticker
   (see Find It, page 353)

Assemble the box and place a truffle or two or other desired candies in it. Wrap the ribbon around the box from front to back, and tie in a bow on the top. Affix the sticker to the center front of the box. Assemble as many boxes as there are guests. Arrange them on the table before guests arrive.

# Mix and Match Chocolate Bars

I used a selection of patterned scrapbook paper for these and chose a different one for the white, milk, and dark chocolate.

See instructions for Custom Candy Bar Wrappers on page 27. After wrapping the bar, place a 2½-inch-wide × 1-inch-high label, centered, on the scrapbook paper (see Find It, page 353).

Marshmallow ropes, tied in a knot and arranged on a platter

Pink and white marshmallows, piled three high on a platter

Pink jelly beans; saltwater taffy; red malt balls; cherry gummy slices; pink Necco wafers; pink, red, and white Good & Plenty; red and pink malt balls; pink, red, and white ribbon candy; pink, red, and white M&M's; pink pillow mints; red Jordan almonds for the candy favor bags

Striped barberpoles, piled horizontally on a platter

Hershey chocolate bars

Candy favor boards hung with wide ribbon

Pink milk glass cake stands in graduated sizes stacked on top of one another and trimmed with ribbon around the rim and stem

Small pink compote

Square and rectangular white platters

Pink tablecloth

## SWITCH IT

**GROW IT UP:** Spike the Pink and Whites, page 137, with strawberry or raspberry liquor or serve a pink lady.

**GROW IT DOWN:** Serve pink lemonade or cherry soda.

**COLOR IT:** Substitute orange and red or yellow and red.

# Honey, I Love You

**E**very now and then I have a client who wants a table designed around a particular flavor: peanut butter, chocolate, even pomegranate, which presented particular challenges! My personal favorite happens to present a zillion possibilities for a sweets table. I've been crazy about honey for as long as I can remember, but it wasn't until just before my first wedding anniversary that I found myself designing this dessert table in my head. Seriously, is there a better word than *honey* for a candy lover *in love*? Not only is the stuff oozy, gooey, and drool-worthy delicious, but it's beautiful, too (okay, right there it meets the criteria for making it onto my table). *Honey* brings to mind so many other words to visually riff on—bees, hives, combs, wax— my brain doesn't stop buzzing with ideas.

7

First there's the hive, with its totally unique shape. The beehive cakes, made using an easy-to-get mold, really set the stage for this table. Bake just one of these for any special gathering and you'll feel like a queen bee. (Sorry!) A graduated swirl of meringue looks like a hive, too—and becomes an unexpected topping on a moist chocolate cupcake. I couldn't resist a glass hive-shaped drink dispenser (who could?) filled with a cooling amber brew of peach iced tea sweetened with, well, honey. And because I love a theme, I serve it in pretty dessert wineglasses shaped like upended hives.

Can you guess the pattern on stroopwafels, those Dutch wafer cookies found in every supermarket? It resembles honeycomb. So do the graphics on many pretty gift wraps—they're perfect tray liners. Hexagons cut from simple translucent paper and attached to one another become a super-size honeycomb backdrop that looks like sculpture, but you don't need an art degree to make it. I swear. And then there are the sheets of real beeswax that are typically rolled into candles. I love the texture and it is incredibly malleable, which means you can cover just about *anything* with it—and I say go for it. The cake pedestal, dessert tags, and chocolate bar wrappers on this table all incorporate beeswax, but there's no need to stop there—use them to line the serving trays, too!

Along with the bee design baked right into the cakes, I had to add some buzzers on the table, their bodies made from colored marzipan, their wings from almond slices. I resurrected that grade school staple, pipe cleaners, and simply twirled them around my index finger to make fuzzy little creatures to cinch gift bags shut. There are silk bees, too, purchased from the craft store. Of course, it wouldn't be right to leave out the yummy honey in its most pure form, which is why jars of honey (fill them yourself or just buy them that way) capped in decorative paper and stylishly arranged on the table do double duty—as pretty props and delicious mementos for guests. My feeling is, if honey is the food of gods, heroes, seers, and poets, then there couldn't be a more perfect table inspiration for someone you're crazy in love with.

INSPIRATION: Flavor

PALETTE: Yellow, black, and stone

PERFECT FOR: Milestone wedding anniversary, engagement party, child's birthday party

honey
panna cotta

# Honey Beehive Cake

This is such an amazingly comforting cake—a little sweet, a little dense, a little banana-y. I like it so much I made three for this table, but one works fine—just surround it by jars of golden honey. A layer of Quick Vanilla Buttercream spread between the two halves of the hive is the "glue" that holds it together. Set the marzipan bees into the Royal Icing before it dries, just after you drizzle it on the cake. For those that are buzzing on the bare cake, attach them with a dab of Royal Icing. See Find It, page 355, for the beehive cake mold.

**Makes one 16-inch-high, 7-inch-diameter cake from a mold.**

FOR THE CAKE:

- 1 cup (2 sticks) unsalted butter, at room temperature
- 1½ cups sugar
- 4 eggs
- ⅔ cup milk
- ¼ cup honey
- 2 tablespoons lemon juice
- Zest of 1 lemon
- 1 teaspoon vanilla extract
- 1 medium banana, mashed
- Pinch of salt
- 1½ teaspoons baking powder
- 1 teaspoon ground cinnamon
- 2¾ cups all-purpose flour

FOR THE HONEY GLAZE:

- ½ cup honey
- ¼ cup sugar
- 2 tablespoons lemon juice
- Pinch of salt

FOR THE DECORATION:

- 2 cups Quick Vanilla Buttercream, page 14
- 1¼ cups Royal Icing, page 15
- Marzipan Bees, page 181

1. Preheat the oven to 325°F. Prepare a beehive cake mold by greasing with butter or spraying with nonstick spray and dusting with flour. In the bowl of a standing mixer fitted with a paddle attachment, beat the butter and sugar to combine. Beat in one egg at a time to combine. Scrape down the sides of the bowl with a rubber spatula. Beat in the milk, honey, lemon juice, lemon zest, vanilla, and banana. In a medium bowl, sift together the salt, baking powder, cinnamon, and flour. Add flour mixture to the mixer and beat until a smooth batter forms.

honey beehive
cake

2. Divide the batter between the halves of the cake mold and bake for 45 to 50 minutes or until a cake tester comes out clean. Invert onto a cooling rack and cool, outside of the hive up.

3. Meanwhile, prepare the honey glaze. Combine the honey and sugar in a small pot and bring to a boil. Add the lemon juice and salt and stir to combine. Using a pastry brush, brush the glaze all over both halves of the cake while the cake is still warm, allowing the glaze to soak in. Refrigerate for at least 30 minutes.

4. When the cake is cool, use a serrated knife to trim and flatten the flat sides of the cakes. Use a small offset spatula to cover one flat side of the cake with the butter-cream. Sandwich with the other half and stand the cake upright. Refrigerate for at least 30 minutes or until the cakes are solidly stuck together.

5. Once the cake is chilled, transfer it to a cake stand and drizzle the Royal Icing over it. Place one or two marzipan bees around the crown and rim of the hive. Affix additional bees to the cake itself by using a dab of Royal Icing as the "glue." The cake will keep, tightly covered, for up to three days in the refrigerator. To serve, take the cake(s) into the kitchen, cut in half at the seam and lay flat, then cut crosswise into 1-inch slices.

### DISPLAY IT

Haute Honeycomb backdrop

Honey linen tablecloth

Silk bees

Stroopwafels, for lining trays

Gift wrap tray liners

Honey grahams, for lining trays

Domed pedestals

White platters

Hive-shaped glasses

Beehive lemonade dispenser

Ribbon bows on cake stands

"Honey I Love You" garland

### Style It

When a tall, tiered cake isn't a possibility, you can achieve an equally powerful impact with several smaller ones, each placed on its own cake stand and all of them clustered in the center of the table. Put one on a pedestal to vary the heights.

# Honey, I Love You Cookies

These sunny yellow treats say it all.

Makes 1 Honey, I Love You banner.

Sugar Cookies, page 12
Royal Icing, page 15
Yellow food coloring gel

1. See the Template, Index pages 344–345, and download the template at http://blog .amyatlas.com or, using 3-inch letter cookie cutters, cut out the letters to spell "HONEY I LOVE YOU" from the sugar cookie dough. Proceed with baking instructions.

2. Decorate by following the instructions for Outlining and Flooding Cookies with Royal Icing, page 17.

3. See Those Four Little Words, page 180, for instructions for the table banner.

# Bee Macaroons

Here's a ridiculously easy way to create something playful out of a sophisticated sweet. It's the kind of transformation I live for—turning a macaroon into the pudgy little body of a bumblebee with a few stripes of chocolate and almond-slice wings.

Makes 24.

1½ cups dark chocolate chips, melted (see How to Melt Chocolate, page 16)

24 honey or vanilla macaroons

48 almond slices, toasted (see next page)

1. Place the macaroons on a rack set over a piece of waxed paper and set aside. Transfer the melted chocolate to a small piping bag fitted with a Wilton Round Tip #2 or a small resealable plastic bag with a corner snipped. Pipe three stripes of chocolate equidistant from one another across the top of each macaroon. Tuck a toasted almond slice into the macaroon filling, followed by a second one directly opposite it.

2. Line a platter with gift wrap cut to fit it. Arrange the bumblebees in rows on it and place on the table. Replenish the bees as necessary.

TO TOAST ALMONDS FOR BEES' WINGS:

Remove broken or chipped pieces from the sliced almonds. Preheat oven to 350°F. Spread the almond slices in a single layer on an ungreased shallow cookie sheet. Toast, stirring occasionally, until golden, 10 to 15 minutes. Transfer to a plate to cool.

***easy does it*** *Use Nilla Wafers piped with chocolate stripes or fudge stripe cookies in place of the macaroons.*

Layer store-bought cookies, like stroopwafels and graham crackers, onto serving platters. It's a fun styling element and acts as a barrier from wrapping paper that is not food safe.

# Chocolate Beehive Cupcakes

Nothing makes me happier than a meringue moment, especially when it serves as a visual pun! These indulgent cupcakes easily take center stage when you want to elevate a simple chocolate cupcake to spectacular status. They even taste delicious up to 2 days after making. The meringue topping seeps into the cupcake, like a simple syrup, yet it retains its beehive shape.

Makes 12.

1 cup all-purpose flour
½ cup cocoa
¾ teaspoon baking soda
¼ teaspoon salt
¾ cup granulated sugar
⅔ cup buttermilk
7 tablespoons vegetable oil
1 large egg
1 large egg yolk

FOR THE HONEY-MERINGUE TOPPING:

2 large egg whites
1 cup sugar
1 teaspoon honey
1 tablespoon corn syrup
2 teaspoons vanilla extract

1. Adjust the oven rack to middle position and preheat oven to 350°F. Line a standard cupcake tin with cupcake liners. Sift together the flour, cocoa, baking soda, and salt in a medium bowl; set aside.

2. In another medium bowl, whisk together the sugar, buttermilk, oil, egg, and yolk until combined. Add the flour mixture and whisk until smooth.

3. Divide batter evenly among the cupcake liners and bake until just set or a toothpick inserted in the center comes out clean, 17 to 19 minutes. Let cupcakes cool in the pan for 5 minutes, then remove from the pan and cool completely on a wire rack.

4. Meanwhile make the meringue. In the bowl of a standing mixer, whisk together the egg whites, sugar, ¼ cup plus 1 tablespoon water, honey, and corn syrup until combined. Set the bowl over a pan of simmering water and cook, whisking constantly, until the mixture registers 160°F on a candy thermometer.

5. Immediately place the bowl on the mixer fitted with the whisk attachment and whisk on high speed until mixture is thick and glossy, about 3 minutes. Add vanilla and whisk until combined.

6. Spoon the meringue into a pastry bag or resealable plastic bag fitted with a plain tip (Wilton Round Tip #2a). Pipe a beehive-shaped topping on each cupcake, making gradually smaller circles as you create a peak.

7. Using a crème brûlée torch or a small blowtorch, gently brown the "hives." Line a serving platter with honeycomb-patterned gift wrap followed by graham cracker halves set on the diagonal. Arrange a cupcake on each of the graham crackers, then place the platter on the table. Alternatively, store the cupcakes in an airtight container up to 2 days.

# Honey Panna Cotta

Take me to the land of milk and honey any day! These sweet, smooth, creamy little confections are nothing more than cooked cream (and a little bit of yogurt) capped with a luminous band of honey-flavored gelatin. Tell the kids it's pudding; call it panna cotta if it's an adult celebration. No matter the name, it's amazing.

Makes 8 4-ounce glasses.

4 tablespoons milk
2¼ teaspoons (1 envelope) gelatin
2 cups heavy cream
1 vanilla bean, split, seeds scraped
⅓ cup honey
⅓ cup sugar
2 teaspoons lemon juice
2 cups good quality plain Greek yogurt, such as Fage

FOR THE HONEY GELEE:

1 teaspoon gelatin
⅓ cup honey
8 toasted almond slices, for garnish

1. Put the milk into a small bowl and sprinkle the gelatin over it. Stir and set aside for 5 minutes.

2. Combine the cream, vanilla bean seeds, honey, and sugar in a medium pan and bring to a boil. Remove from the heat and let cool slightly. Add the gelatin-milk mixture to the pan and stir until completely dissolved. Add the lemon juice and stir. Whisk in the Greek yogurt. Divide the mixture evenly among 8 4-ounce glasses,

leaving about ½ inch of space between it and the rim. Chill at least 3 hours in the refrigerator.

3. To make the gelee, combine 2 tablespoons of water and the gelatin in a small bowl and stir. Set aside for 5 minutes.

4. Meanwhile, combine 1 cup of water and the honey in a pan and bring to a boil, stirring constantly. Remove from the heat and let continue to cook for a few seconds. Add the gelatin mixture to it and stir until it is completely dissolved.

5. Divide the gelatin mixture over the panna cotta evenly among the glasses. Chill until set, at least one hour. Garnish each with a single toasted almond slice inserted into the center of the gelee.

6. To serve, line a platter with patterned gift wrap followed by a layer of stroopwafels arranged on the diagonal. Place a glass on each stroopwafel and set the platter on the table. Alternatively, leave off the toasted almond slice, cover the panna cotta in plastic wrap, and refrigerate up to 3 days. Garnish just before serving.

**easy does it** *Swap out the Panna Cotta with Honey Gelee for a cup of vanilla Greek yogurt topped with a swirl of honey.*

# Tupelojitos

I served peach iced tea, sweetened with honey, in the hive-shaped drink dispenser. But for adult gatherings, you may want to try this delicious drink that beekeeper Ted Dennard, owner of the Savannah Bee Company, was generous enough to share with me. His tupelo honey is to die for—I highly recommend ordering it to make these golden amber drinks. See Find It, page 354.

**Makes 3 quarts.**

20  ounces tupelo honey
 1  small bag ice cubes
Juice of 10 medium limes
Handful of mint sprigs
½  cup Light rum (optional)

Combine the honey with 1½ cups warm water in a medium bowl. Stir until the honey has completely dissolved. Place the ice cubes in a 2-gallon pitcher. Pour the honey mixture over the ice. Fill the pitcher with cold water. Add the lime juice and the mint sprigs and stir. Add the rum and stir. Add more honey, lime, or water to taste. Pour into clear glasses and arrange on the table.

# Haute Honeycomb

One bee eats more than 8 pounds of honey to make a single pound of wax for the comb, but I say don't go it alone. I made this beautiful backdrop with a handful of girlfriends and turned the whole process into a self-styled quilting bee. With a little help, you can "stitch" it together (jump rings and a hole punch replace needle and thread) in very little time. Notice that there are bits and pieces missing, an intentional move to make it more interesting. Each cell has 3¾-inch sides; scale yours up or down to suit the size of your table.

## MATERIALS

Translucent yellow and
stone vellum
½-inch copper jump rings
Fishing line, for hanging
Command hooks, for hanging
Silk bees

## TOOLS

Hole punch with a ⅛-inch punch
Glue Dots

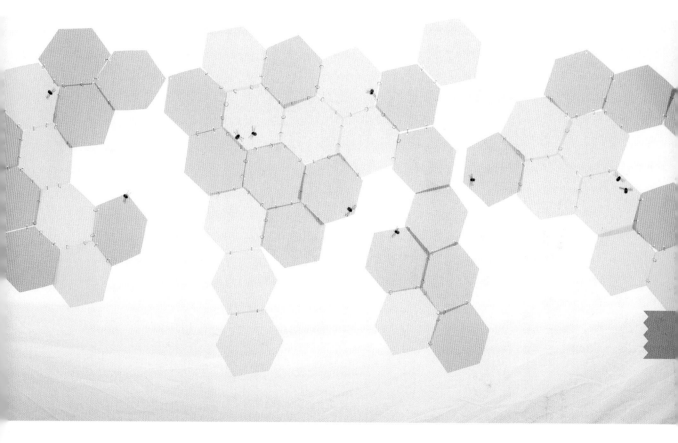

1. Use the hexagonal template (see page 338 and download and print it from http://blog .amyatlas.com). Cut out cells. Place cells on vellum, trace, and cut. Punch a hole ½-inch in from the edge of every corner of the hexagon. To connect the cells, open a jump ring from front to back (don't pull it apart from side to side at the seam or you won't be able to pinch it back together nicely) and thread it through a hole on one cell and the corresponding hole on another cell. Continue connecting the cells this way, alternating the cell colors here and there, until you are happy with the way the backdrop looks. We made this one in four sections that do not connect.

2. To hang the honeycomb, tie fishing line to the jump rings on the topmost cells. Either affix to a window casing or suspend from the ceiling fitted out with Command hooks. Once it's hung, step back to determine where to place the silk bees. Affix them to the comb with the Glue Dots.

# Those Four Little Words

... and there's nothing else to say!

MATERIALS

Letter cookies to spell out "HONEY I LOVE YOU,"
    page 169
5 yards ½-inch-wide gold silk ribbon, divided into
    2-yard and 3-yard lengths
Marzipan Bees, opposite page

TOOLS

Hot glue gun
Masking tape

1. Lay the shorter piece of ribbon right side up on a work surface. Place the cookies to spell "HONEY" in the center of the ribbon so that the tops of the letters are flush with the top of the ribbon. Hot glue each one to the ribbon. Let dry thoroughly. Repeat with the longer ribbon, placing the cookies to spell "I LOVE YOU" on it.

2. Hang the ribbons on the front of the table, affixing each end to the underside of a platter with masking tape. Hot glue a marzipan bee on each of the Os, positioning them so that they face each other.

# Beeswax Pedestal

The great thing about beeswax is that it easily conforms to any shape you want it to. I wrapped the sides of a cake dummy round with it, then set a pretty disk of textured paper on top. Floral foam works just as well as Styrofoam, and you can also get a similar look with a square made from shoe or tissue boxes.

*Makes 1 pedestal.*

MATERIALS

1 10-inch-deep × 3-inch-high round cake dummy,
    Styrofoam, or floral foam
1 10-inch circle cut from yellow scrapbook paper
Double stick tape or Glue Dots
1 12- × 12-inch sheet golden beeswax
Dressmaker pins

TOOLS

Very sharp scissors

Affix the scrapbook paper to the top of the form with double stick tape or Glue Dots. From the piece of beeswax, cut 3 3-inch-wide × 12-inch-long strips. Affix the strips to the side of the pedestal, securing them with the pins. Trim where necessary so that the top and bottom edges are flush with the edges of the pedestal.

# Marzipan Bees

Marzipan is like Play-Doh for grown-ups, except that it's edible. Made of almond paste (ground almonds and sugar), powdered sugar, and a moistening agent, it takes well to food coloring gel, and you can sculpt it into just about anything. These cute little guys are nothing more than alternating rounds of yellow and black colored marzipan, smooshed together into the capsule shape of a bee. Almond slices are fragile and can easily break when you're inserting them into the marzipan. Have extra on hand in case your wings fall apart.

*Makes 16.*

### MATERIALS

¼ cup marzipan

Yellow and black food coloring gels

2 tablespoons (about 32) sliced almonds, toasted
  (see page 171)

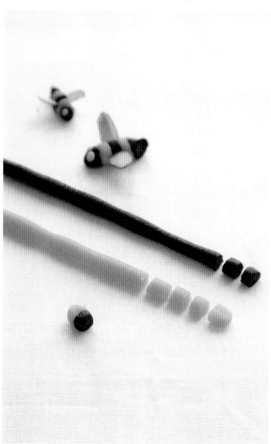

1. Divide the marzipan into two equal portions. Add yellow gel to one and black to the other. Knead the paste to incorporate the color, adding more if necessary to achieve desired shade.

2. Roll each portion of colored marzipan into a ⅛-inch-thick rope. Cut each rope into ⅛-inch slices. Stack five slices of marzipan horizontally, alternating colors, beginning and ending with black. Shape the head so that it is rounded and the tail so that it is slightly torpedo shaped. From another slice of yellow, make two small balls for eyes and affix them on the head. Insert a sliced almond into either side of the bee for wings. Repeat with remaining marzipan and almonds. The bees will keep, in a rigid, tightly covered container, up to one week.

# Honey, Take Me Home

Kids may go for the candy bags as favors, but a pretty jar of honey—with a wooden spinner—is all about the adults. It's probably the easiest take-away to put together.

MATERIALS

Lidded jelly or canning jars in various sizes
Various flavors honey, from dark to light
Gift wrap in patterned yellows, ambers, stones
Waxed cotton string or twine
Wooden honey spinners

Fill the jars with honey to within ⅛ inch of the rim and screw the lids on tightly. Cut the gift wrap into squares with dimensions that are 3 times the diameter of the lid. Cover the lid with the wrap, pleating it around the rim so that it is relatively smooth. Secure it with a length of string, wrapping it around twice for good measure. Arrange the jars on the table with the spinners artfully placed nearby.

# Beeswax Belly Bands

In all of the years that I've been creating sweet tables, I've never found a chocolate bar uneaten or left behind after the last guest has said good-bye. There's something about a custom wrapper that makes a piece of chocolate sweeter than it already is. A belt of real beeswax is the special touch here.

Makes 12.

MATERIALS

Gold and amber sheets of card stock
1 8- × 16-inch sheet natural beeswax
Chocolate bars, such as Hershey's
Glue Dots

Make the Candy Bar Wrappers, page 27, with the card stock. Cut the beeswax sheet into 1- × 16-inch strips. Wrap them horizontally around the middle of each chocolate bar so that the seam is on the back. Let the wax overlap by ⅛-inch or so and press the strips into each other. Trim away excess. If the comb refuses to stick, use a Glue Dot to secure it. Arrange the chocolate bars on a rimmed tray and place on the table. Decorate with extra marzipan bees.

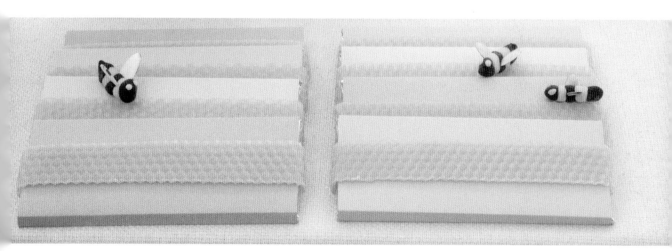

# Golden Gift Bag

**Makes 1.**

### MATERIALS

2 black pipe cleaners, 1 cut in half

1 yellow pipe cleaner

1 small yellow bag, 6¼-inch-high × 3½-inch-wide × 2-inch-deep

Bit-O-Honey pieces, for filling

Length ⅜-inch-wide black ribbon

Glue Dots

### TOOLS

Hole punch with ½-inch punch

1. Hold a black and the longer yellow pipe cleaner side by side. Beginning at the top knuckle of your index finger, wrap them around the tip of your finger three times.

2. Separate the yellow from the black and, using the yellow, make the wings by shaping the pipe cleaner into 2 loops in the shape of an 8. Secure the wings by looping the black pipe cleaner twice around the center of the 8.

3. To shape the head, tightly wind the remaining black around itself, in front of the wings, until 2 inches remain.

4. Center the remaining black pipe cleaner under the head and wrap it around itself to secure. Fold each end onto itself to create the antennae.

5. Fill the bag to 3 inches with the candy. Fold 1½ inches of the top onto itself and punch a hole through all layers with the hole punch. Slide the 2-inch length of remaining black pipe cleaner through the hole from front to back so that the bee sits on the front of the bag. Bring the pipe cleaner back to the front and wrap it around itself to secure.

6. Wrap the length of black ribbon around the bottom of the bag, about 2 inches from the bottom, and affix with Glue Dots.

# Beeswax Dessert Tags

If I could wrap the table in beeswax, I would (Hey, why not?). I love how easy it is to work with and how it gives this table such cool texture. So rather than just use a basic dessert tag, I couldn't help but back it with a cute little honeycomb cell.

Makes 1.

MATERIALS

2 8½- × 16-inch sheets golden beeswax
Ivory card stock
Glue Dot

See the templates on page 338 and download them at http://blog.amyatlas.com. Print, trace, and cut out a hexagon from the beeswax. Print the rectangular beeswax tag onto the cardstock and cut it out to fit in the center of the hexagon. Write the name of the dessert on the tag, then affix to the honeycomb hexagon with a Glue Dot. Repeat for remaining desserts.

## SHOP IT

Jordan almonds, to fill ¾ of a domed pedestal

Stroopwafels, for lining trays

Honey in the comb, cut into small rectangles, and stacked on a beehive-shaped domed plate

Lemon Bark, to fill ¾ of a domed pedestal

Peanut butter malt balls, arranged in "hive style," four on bottom, one on top, in honey paper cupcake liners and set on a gift wrap–lined tray

Honey sticks, set in a beeswax-wrapped vessel

Bit-O-Honey pieces, placed inside gift bags

Chocolate bars, customized

Honey grahams, for lining trays

Unsweetened iced tea (I chose peach), sweetened with honey while it's hot

## SWITCH IT

**GROW IT UP:** Serve Tupelojitos (see page 177) or stinger cocktails.

**COLOR IT:** Use primary yellow and black (for kids), milk chocolate and amber (for adults).

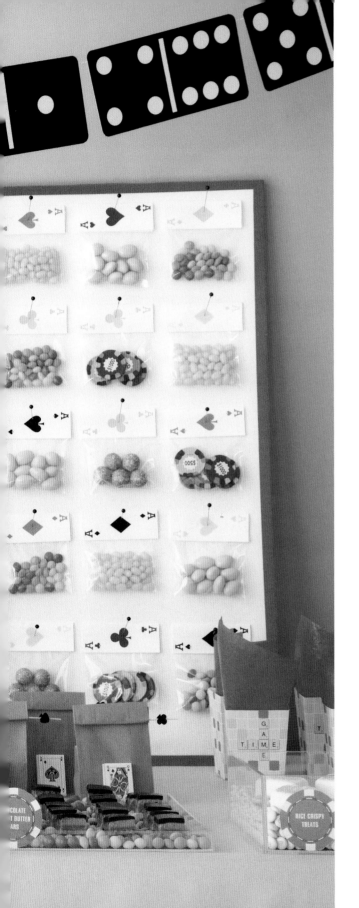

# Game Night!

I'm traditionally known for my tailored and monochromatic style. Bringing a candyland of colors into my table designs can sometimes be a challenge, but it is well worth the reward if it works. Often, multicolored palettes work when there is a playful theme. Since my husband and I often spend Friday nights playing board games with our sons, I thought I'd take a turn with incorporating a playful palette into a game night dessert table.

My sons, Zach and Josh, love dominoes, checkers, any games that involve throwing dice, and mostly Monopoly Junior. I remember my older brother, Jonathan, challenging me to never-ending rounds of the original game; I always went for the green, yellow, and orange properties, most likely because I loved the color combination.

8

# Bingo!

I brought all of those saturated hues together in this super-colorful table—and it works because I grounded them with complementary shades of lighter yellow (on the table) and blue (on the backdrop). Of course, I always like to put my own spin on things, so I took liberties with traditional game colors: a yellow and white checkerboard, multicolored aces, and rainbow-hued Scrabble-inspired boards. The beauty of a game night theme is not only that it gives you the freedom to go wild with color (think Parcheesi, Sorry!, Trouble, Chinese checkers), but that it's a generation spanner. Children, teenagers, coeds, parents, grandparents—every age can get into this gathering. There are sweets for all of them, too—cheesecake on a stick, my grandmother's famous rocky road cake-cum-cupcakes, blondies, crispy rice cereal treats, marshmallows. Of course, I couldn't help but turn them into game-themed symbols. Diamond-shaped cookie cutters helped, as did white chocolate chips for creating dominoes, and M&M's and Sunny Seed Drops for a self-styled checkerboard. Like any classic board game, once you get into it, it's hard to stop!

INSPIRATION: A passion

PALETTE: Orange, green, yellow, periwinkle, black-and-white accents

PERFECT FOR: All-ages birthday party; special slumber party; school fund-raiser or themed bake sale; family reunion; bridge, poker, mahjong, or bunko night

# Grandma Dotty's Rocky Road Cupcakes

As I mentioned in the introduction, my mom isn't much of a baker (but a very good cook), so when I visited my grandmother's house, it was a very special treat for me. Baking was my time to bond with Grandma. Grandma always let me frost the cake with her caramel frosting (the way my kids do when we're baking together). I still love to bake this the way she did—in a round pan—but for a special occasion, turning the batter out into individual cupcakes allows me to arrange them on one tier of a stack of cake stands, and you know how I feel about vertical elements on a table! Don't wait to create an entire table to make these; they're runaway hits for any day of the week.

**Makes 12.**

FOR THE CAKE:

- 1 cup all-purpose flour
- ½ teaspoon baking powder
- ¼ teaspoon salt
- ¼ teaspoon baking soda
- ½ cup sour cream
- 1 teaspoon vanilla extract
- 6 tablespoons unsalted butter, softened
- ½ cup granulated sugar
- 1 egg
- ¾ cup bittersweet chocolate chips, chopped, or mini semisweet chips
- 1½ cups Marshmallow Fluff
- Mini marshmallows, for garnish

FOR THE CARAMEL BUTTERCREAM:

- 1¼ cups granulated sugar, divided
- ¼ cup heavy cream
- 12 tablespoons unsalted butter, divided, softened
- 2 large egg whites
- 2 pinches salt
- 1 teaspoon vanilla extract

1. Adjust the oven rack to the middle position and preheat oven to 350°F. Line a standard cupcake tin with cupcake liners. In a small bowl, whisk together the flour, baking powder, salt, and baking soda until combined; set aside. In a small bowl, combine the sour cream and vanilla and stir.

2. In the bowl of a standing mixer fitted with paddle attachment, cream butter and sugar on medium-high speed until light and fluffy, about 4 minutes, scraping down sides of bowl as necessary. Add the egg and beat until completely incorporated. Reduce the speed to medium-low and gradually add the flour mixture, alternating with the sour cream mixture, until combined. Add the chocolate chips and mix until combined.

3. Divide the batter equally among the cupcake cups and bake until just firm and a toothpick inserted in the center comes out clean, 16 to 18 minutes. Let cupcakes cool in pan 5 minutes, then transfer to a wire rack to cool completely.

4. Using a paring knife, slice a 1-inch-wide by ½-inch-deep piece off the top of each cupcake. Fill area of cupcake with a rounded teaspoon of marshmallow fluff. (If some spills out of the top, that's okay.) Replace the top of cupcake to cover the marshmallow. Set aside.

5. To make the caramel buttercream, combine ¾ cup of the sugar and ¼ cup water and heat over medium-high heat until the sugar has dissolved. Brush down the sides of pan with water to wash off sugar crystals. Bring mixture to a boil and continue to cook, not stirring, until it turns the color of deep amber. Remove from heat and immediately whisk in the cream and 3 tablespoons of the butter. Transfer to a bowl and let caramel cool to room temperature, about 30 minutes.

6. In the bowl of a standing mixer, whisk together the egg whites, salt, and remaining ½ cup sugar until combined. Place the bowl over a pan of simmering water and cook, whisking constantly, until the mixture registers 150°F on a candy thermometer.

7. Immediately put bowl on the standard mixer fitted with the whisk attachment and whip on medium-high speed until thick, glossy, and the consistency of shaving cream, 3 to 4 minutes. Reduce the speed to medium, add remaining 9 tablespoons of butter, and mix until creamy and light. Add the vanilla and whip until creamy.

8. Stop mixer and add the caramel. Mix on medium-high speed until combined and light and creamy, scraping down the sides of the bowl as necessary. If buttercream seems too loose at this point, chill for about 20 minutes and whip again.

9. Spoon the buttercream into a pastry bag or resealable plastic bag fitted with a Wilton RoundTip #1a. Pipe onto each cupcake in graduated circles. Top each with a mini marshmallow and arrange on a cake stand.

MARSHMALLOW DICE

***easy does it*** There are many wonderful gourmet marshmallows available. See Find It, page 356.
for my favorites.

# Marshmallow Dice

Obvious! I'll be honest, though. Before I came up with this, I tried to figure out how to get dots inside Jell-O cubes. This is the curse of a confectionista! Anyway, these could not be simpler.

**Makes 16 2-inch cubes.**

- 2 cups confectioners' sugar, divided
- 2 tablespoons plus 2½ teaspoons unflavored gelatin
- 2 cups plus 2 tablespoons granulated sugar, divided
- ½ cup light corn syrup
- 2 large egg whites
- 1 tablespoon vanilla
- Candy dots
- Canned vanilla frosting, for adhering dots

1. Prepare an 8- × 8-inch baking pan with vegetable oil, rubbing it on the bottom and sides. Place ⅓ cup of the confectioners' sugar in the pan and tilt and tap to coat.

2. Place ½ cup of water in a small bowl and sprinkle the gelatin over it. (If there is any dry gelatin on the top, sprinkle a bit of water over the top and gently stir so all of the gelatin will soften.) Let mixture sit until gelatin has softened, about 10 minutes.

3. In a medium saucepan, combine ½ cup water with 2 cups of the granulated sugar and the cup corn syrup. Stir over medium-high heat until sugar has dissolved. Using a pastry brush, brush sides of pan to return any sugar crystals to the mixture. Cook, without stirring, until syrup registers 240°F on a candy thermometer.

4. Remove from the heat and gently whisk in the softened gelatin until dissolved. In the bowl of a standing mixer fitted with the whisk attachment, whip egg whites on medium-high speed until frothy. Add the remaining 2 tablespoons of sugar and continue to whip until eggs whites form stiff but not dry peaks; transfer to a small bowl. Immediately rinse and dry mixer bowl and whisk attachment, and return these to the mixer.

5. Pour the syrup mixture into a very clean mixing bowl and whisk on high speed until it is thick, white, glossy, and the consistency of shaving cream, about 5 minutes. Reduce the speed to medium and mix in vanilla.

6. Using a rubber spatula, gently fold in whipped egg whites until completely combined. Immediately spread the mixture into the prepared pan and lightly smooth top. Sift ⅓ cup of the confectioners' sugar over the top. Let marshmallows set at room temperature, at least 3 hours.

7. Place the remaining confectioners' sugar in a medium bowl. Using a greased knife, cut marshmallows into 16 2-inch squares. Toss marshmallows in sugar, one at a time, to coat.

8. To make the dice, arrange the candy dots on one side of each marshmallow in patterns mimicking those on dice. Affix them to the marshmallows with a dab of vanilla frosting. Arrange the dice in a rimmed tray filled with colored candy and place on the table.

# Butterscotch Domino Blondies

A home-baked classic—with an artful interpretation of one of my favorite games. These can be made one day in advance and kept in a covered container.

**Makes 32 2- × 1-inch rectangles.**

- 1 cup plus 1 tablespoon all-purpose flour
- 1 teaspoon baking powder
- ¼ teaspoon baking soda
- ½ teaspoon salt
- ¾ cup butterscotch chips
- ½ cup (1 stick) unsalted butter, melted
- 1 packed cup brown sugar
- 1 egg
- 1 egg yolk
- 2 teaspoons vanilla extract

White chocolate chips for decorating the top of dominoes

- 4 ounces white chocolate chips, melted (page 16)

1. Adjust the oven rack to the middle position and preheat the oven to 350°F. Spray a 9- × 9-inch baking pan with nonstick cooking spray. Sift the flour, baking powder, baking soda, and salt into a bowl; set aside. In a small bowl toss ½ cup of the butterscotch chips in 1 tablespoon flour and set aside.

2. Combine the butter with the brown sugar. Add the egg, egg yolk, and vanilla and mix until incorporated. Gradually add the flour mixture, stirring until mixture is smooth. Stir in the flour-coated butterscotch chips until combined.

3. Transfer the batter to the prepared pan. Scatter the remaining butterscotch chips evenly over the top of the batter. Bake for 20 minutes or until just set. Let cool in pan. Cut into 2- × 1-inch rectangles. Press the white chocolate chips, pointed side down, into the blondies in domino patterns.

4. Spoon the melted chocolate into a pastry bag fitted with a small round tip. Pipe a line of chocolate crosswise at the half point on each bar. Let dry. Arrange the bars in a rimmed tray filled with colored candy and set on table.

## Style It

Blondies/brownies are notoriously tough to cut cleanly, but with a little practice—and a silicone bench scraper (aka baker's helper)—I've arrived at a solution for those shredded edges. First, let the blondies cool in the pan. Then use the long straight edge of the bench scraper to cut vertically into the blondies. Don't drag it across the pan! Use the short straight edge to separate the pieces from the pan.

# Crispy Rice Diamonds

These small-scale treats are ideal for learning how to work with rolled fondant (the curve of which is not steep, trust me!). Try these before you move on to your friend's birthday cake or any of the tiered centerpieces in this book. What's so great about beginning here is that the intrepid among you can also try your hand at coating hearts, spades, and clubs that you've cut out with a cookie cutter.

**Makes 17 3-inch-long diamonds.**

Crispy Rice Cereal Treats, page 13
Confectioners' sugar
1 pound rolled fondant
Yellow sanding sugar

1. Using a 3-inch diamond-shaped cutter, make an impression in the block of crispy rice treats. Using a knife, cut along the outlines to get about 17 diamonds.

2. Dust a work surface with confectioners' sugar. Roll the fondant out on the work surface to ⅛-inch-thick. Using a 4-inch round cutter, cut out I round at a time from the fondant. Drape it over a diamond crispy rice treat, gently fitting it along the sides and pressing it to adhere. Trim the edges with a sharp knife. Sprinkle sanding sugar in the center of each. Arrange these on a rimmed tray filled with colored candy and place on the table.

# Twister Cheesecake Pops

If you ask me, the only thing better than New York cheesecake (okay, I'm not impartial) by the slice is the kind that requires no utensils at all. A two-bite-size serving is just perfect, especially when there are more sweets to try. Kids love these (of course, they're on a stick!) and they charm adults. I chose to embellish them with my two favorite colors on the Twister board.

**Makes 30 to 35.**

24 ounces (3 8-ounce packages) cream cheese, at room temperature
1 cup sugar
½ cup sour cream
2 teaspoons lemon juice
¼ teaspoon salt
2 eggs lightly beaten with 2 egg yolks
¼ cup all-purpose flour
16 ounces good-quality white chocolate
20 lollipop sticks
Blue and yellow sanding sugar

1. Adjust the oven rack to the middle position and preheat oven to 375°F.

2. In a standing mixer fitted with the paddle attachment, whip the cream cheese on medium speed until soft. Add the sugar and beat until combined. Add the sour cream, lemon juice, and salt. Slowly beat in the egg mixture. Add the flour and mix until just combined.

3. Pour the batter into a 9-inch round pan and bake until the top of the cake begins to brown, 40 to 50 minutes. Cool and refrigerate for at least four hours.

4. Melt 2 ounces of the chocolate (see How to Melt Chocolate, page 16) and set aside. Using a small ice-cream scoop, scoop up some of the cake and roll it into a ball, about 1½ inches in diameter. Place the ball on a parchment-lined baking sheet. Repeat until all of the cake is used.

5. Dip the top of each lollipop stick into the melted chocolate, then push each stick into a ball of cake. Freeze for at least 2 hours.

6. Meanwhile, pour enough of each of the sanding sugars into bowls so that they are about ½-inch deep. Set aside. Melt the remaining chocolate as above. Dip each cheesecake pop into the chocolate to cover it entirely. Let excess drip back into a side bowl or pan to prevent a big chocolate foot on the bottom. Immediately dip the pops into the sanding sugar to cover them by half and alternating between the yellow and blue, so that the bottom resembles circles on a Twister board.

7. Arrange on a cake plate, stick-side-up and ½ inch apart. Place on the table.

# Chocolate Peanut Butter Bars

*Mmmmmmmmmm.* Quite possibly the most genius combination of ingredients—ever. Give me chocolate and peanut butter in any shape or form, and I am good to go. It is my absolute favorite flavor combo; a perfect after-school treat or casual dinner party dessert. The bars hold their shape best if they are chilled until just before serving.

**Makes 32 1-inch squares.**

- 2 cups graham cracker crumbs
- 18 tablespoons unsalted butter, divided into 12 tablespoons melted and 6 tablespoons softened
- 1 tablespoon granulated sugar
- 1 cup peanut butter
- 1 cup confectioners' sugar
- 1 teaspoon vanilla extract
- ⅜ teaspoon salt
- 4 ounces good-quality semisweet chocolate such as Ghirardelli, finely chopped
- ⅜ cup heavy cream

1. In a medium bowl, combine the graham cracker crumbs, the 12 tablespoons of melted butter, and the granulated sugar and stir until the crumbs are thoroughly moistened. Firmly press into bottom of a 9- × 9-inch baking pan. Use the bottom of a measuring cup to help press the crust down.

2. In the bowl of a standing mixer fitted with the paddle attachment, mix the peanut butter, confectioners' sugar, vanilla, salt, and the 6 tablespoons of softened butter until completely combined. Spread over graham crust and smooth the top with an offset spatula. Chill until set, at least 1 hour.

3. Meanwhile, heat the chocolate and cream in a medium microwave-safe bowl, stirring with a whisk every 30 seconds, until chocolate is melted and the mixture is smooth. Pour the chocolate over the peanut butter filling and evenly spread with an offset spatula. Jiggle the pan to smooth out the chocolate. Chill until set, about 1 hour. Using a hot, wet knife, cut into 1-inch squares and arrange on a rimmed tray filled with multicolored candy.

# Cheery Checkerboard

Yes, make as much out of candy as you can. Dice? Check. Dominoes? Check. A checkerboard? Absolutely! Admittedly, this project is not for the time-challenged or those with short attention spans. But it is an oddly soothing endeavor, one that will win raves from game night guests.

**MATERIALS**

1    15-inch-square piece hot yellow heavy card stock

16-inch-square tray or platter

1½   pounds hot yellow M&M's

½    pound white Sunny Seed Drops

24   foiled Oreos or whatever round candy you prefer

**TOOLS**

Metal ruler

Hot glue gun

1. Measure and mark a ½-inch rim around the card stock. Measure and mark 2-inch squares inside the rim; you should have 7 squares across and seven down. Place on the serving tray.

2. Using a hot glue gun, fill every other square with M&M's; each square will accommodate 4 M&M's across and 4 down. Fill the remaining squares with Sunny Seed Drops; cover the area with hot glue and scatter the Sunny Seeds in it, then gently shake off the excess.

3. Arrange your round, checkered desserts (we used foiled Oreos here) on the checkerboard in desired pattern and place on the table.

*easy does it* Use two different-colored Starbursts or black and white chocolate-covered graham crackers to make fast work of crafting a checkerboard. Even easier? Use boards from those games tucked away in the attic, the ones that are missing some of their pieces! Use foiled Oreos and red licorice wheels, for example, for the "pieces" on a real checkerboard.

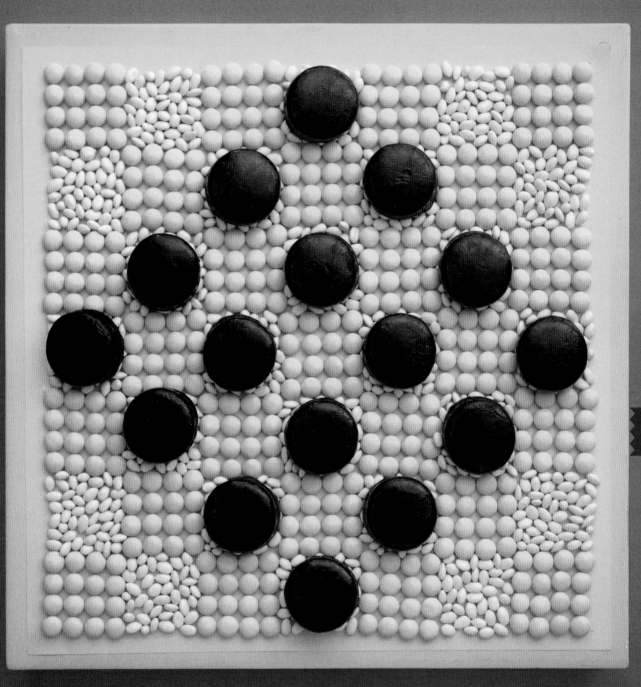

# Gaming Purse

I couldn't help but figure out a way to use the cute suit toothpicks that adorn these take-aways. A simple toothpick can dress up a plain ole paper bag.

**Makes 1.**

MATERIALS

- 1 cup aquamarine M&M's
- Glue Dot or hot glue
- 1 small orange paper bag, 6¼-inch-high × 3½-inch-wide × 2-inch-deep
- 1 specialty toothpick with club or spade tip (see Find It, page 355)
- 1 chocolate "card" (see Find It, page 355)

1. Pour the M&M's into the bag and fold the top over twice. Secure with a Glue Dot or hot glue. Slide the toothpick into the seam.

2. Make as many favor bags as there are guests. Arrange them on either side of the stacked cake stands on the table. Lean the chocolate card on the center front of the bag.

# Game Time Candy Cups

Instead of plates, I prefer cleverly designed candy cups for eating from; guests can fill them with the treats they want to taste and walk away from the table to enjoy the party. See the Template Index, on page 339, and download and print the template from http://blog.amyatlas.com, to make this Scrabble-inspired game night version.

**Makes 1 box.**

MATERIALS

    Candy Cups, page 28

    2 small sheets orange waxed paper or food-safe tissue paper (see Find It, page 355)

Assemble the Candy Cup. Line it with the waxed paper and place on the table. Make as many cups as there are guests at the party. Invite them to use the cup as their "plate" at the party; they can fill it with a few treats to nibble on while they mingle.

# Domino Streamer

Could it be the graphic black-and-white palette that's so appealing? Or memories of endless rounds of dominoes with my brother Jonathan when we were kids? He always wanted to set up the tiles like soldiers and flick one with his finger to watch the rest fall. I, on the other hand, loved the shiny white dots. Oversize and hung end-to-end, they make a great, grand statement for this table. See the templates on page 339, and download and print them from http://blog.amyatlas.com, to make the individual dominoes.

**Makes 1 10-foot streamer.**

MATERIALS

    12 sheets 11- × 14-inch white card stock

    5 yards yellow and white cotton twine

    2 transparent Command hooks

TOOLS

    Hot glue gun

1. Print the dominoes onto the card stock or printer paper. Cut them out with sharp scissors; trim the corners to round them.

2. Lay the dominoes, wrong side up, on a work surface, short end to short end, leaving a 1-inch space between them. Working with two dominoes at a time, run a bead of hot glue along the top edge of each. Lay the twine in the glue, leaving a 12- to 16-inch tail of twine on each end for tying it up on the wall. Let dry. Repeat with remaining dominoes.

3. Affix the Command hooks on the wall about 4 yards above the table and 1 foot beyond the ends of the table. Tie the garland to the hooks at either end, letting the middle of the garland hang lower than the hooks.

# Coming Up Aces Candy Boards

One is great, two even better. Symmetry is always pleasing to the eye, especially when it involves clear bags of colorful candy! These boards are totally easy to make and they're reusable; simply re-cover them in fabric that suits the color palette of your party.

**Makes 1.**

MATERIALS

1 yard white cotton linen

1 30-inch × 20-inch piece ½-inch-thick foam core

3 sheets 11½- × 14-inch orange card stock (or use ribbon), cut into 1½-inch-wide × 14-inch-long strips

20 Ace Candy Bags, page 206

20 Black corsage pins

TOOLS

Bone folder

Hot glue gun

1. Place the fabric wrong side up on a work surface. Center the foam core on it. Trim the fabric, leaving a 2-inch border on all sides. Fold the edges of the fabric onto the back side of the foam core and secure with double stick tape, beginning on a long side, then doing the opposite side and the remaining short sides. Pull taut but not so much that the fabric buckles.

2. Using the bone folder, make creases at ½-inch intervals along the short side of each strip of card stock to make the trim. Hot glue the trim around the rim of the board, overlapping the pieces slightly. To make clean corners, trim the paper on the diagonal at the corners before hot gluing.

3. Attach the candy bags to the board with the corsage pins. Arrange the candy board on the table so that it leans against the wall.

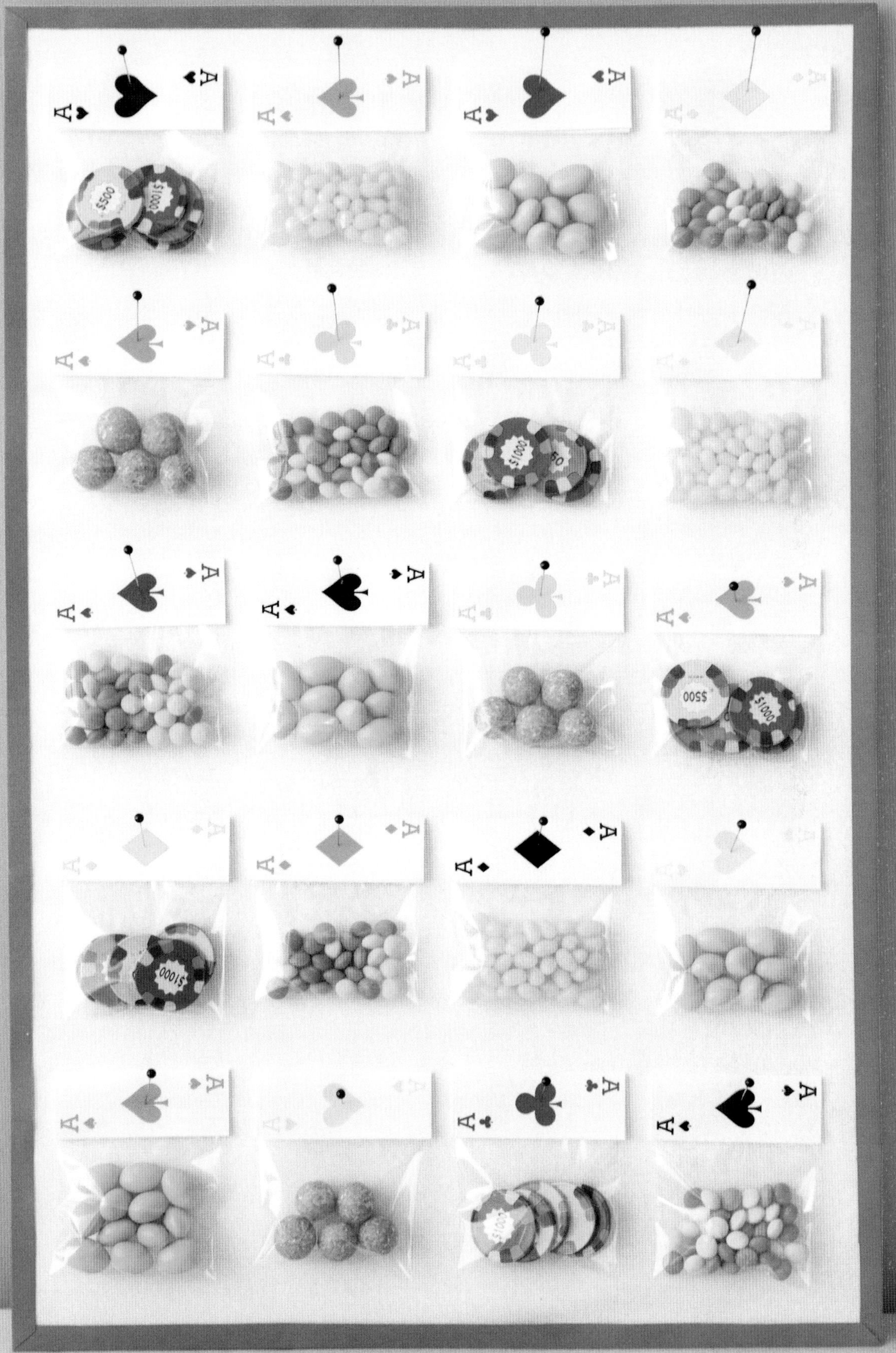
$500
$1000
50

# Ace Candy Bags

# Poker Chip Dessert Tags

Rather than sticking strictly to the traditional black and red playing card palette, I chose colors that complemented this multihued table—green, orange, yellow, light blue—and a little black and red for good measure. Remind guests that these little bags are for the taking; they're secured with easy-to-remove corsage pins. Use the template on page 339 for the toppers. Simply download and print from http://blog.amyatlas.com.

**Makes 1.**

MATERIALS

¼ to ½ cup colorful candy such as malt balls, Lemonheads, Skittles, M&M's, foil-wrapped poker chips, Jordan almonds

See Decorative Candy Bags, page 29, to make the candy bags using the template.

I chose to make these for only those sweets arranged along the front of the table.

**Note:** Use the Template Index and instructions on page 339 and refer to Dessert Tags, page 33, to make as many as you like for your own table.

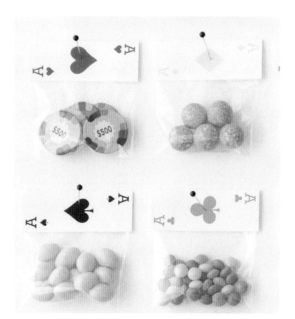

Dice Lollipops, arranged on a footed cake stand, stick side up (see Find It, page 356)

Various colored candy (we used jujubes, lime green Sixlets, aquamarine M&M's, multicolored Skittles), for lining trays

Chocolate cards, placed on gaming purse favors

Various candy for filling Ace Candy Bags (foil-wrapped poker chips, jelly beans, Jordan almonds, malt balls)

Foiled Oreos, Sunny Seed Drops, M&M's for Cheery Checkerboard

## SWITCH IT

**GROW IT UP:** Serve with your favorite recipe for Joker cocktail:
2 parts gin, 1 part whiskey, pour over ice and strain into a martini glass.

**GROW IT DOWN:** Serve with Orangina.

**COLOR IT:** Try black, red, and white.

## DISPLAY IT

Coming Up Aces Candy Boards

Lemon yellow cotton tablecloth

Domino Streamer

Crossword puzzle drinking glasses (see Find It, page 356)

Glass-footed cake stands

Lucite boxes, deep and shallow

Game pieces such as Scrabble-inspired tiles, chess pieces, and dice

# A Trip Down Rocky Road

**G**oogle *"rocky road"* and you'll find more than 1.6 million entries. Square, cup, sheet, bundt, pop—the irresistible chocolate treat with the surface that resembles a Vermont back road during mud season can be baked in every shape imaginable. But most, if not all, rocky road goodies have two ingredients in common: marshmallows and chocolate. And who can resist *that* pairing? Depending on what country you're in, though, this ultimate Willy Wonka-esque concoction can include a bunch of other add-ins. In the U.S., we're somewhat reserved as compared to British and Australian bakers. Walnuts and almonds are typical here, while Down Under, coconut, glacéed cherries, and Turkish delight, a nut-and-dried-fruit confection, are part of the mix. In the U.K., glacéed cherries and raisins show up, along with a dusting of powdered sugar on top.

It's not clear how a popular ice cream flavor came to top brownies, cupcakes, bars, chocolate cakes, and cupcakes. Indeed, long before Ben & Jerry's raised mix-ins to an art form (Chunky Monkey, anyone?) rocky road had become one of America's favorite ice creams, a combination of chocolate ice cream shot through with marshmallows and nuts. Before it showed up in all of its gooey glory, Americans chose from among just three flavors: vanilla, chocolate, and strawberry, and they were never served as naked scoops, but as the key ingredient in sundaes. That all changed in 1929, when William Dreyer and his business partner and confectioner, Joseph Edy, added walnuts (which they later replaced with almonds) to their chocolate ice cream. But they didn't stop there. As the

story goes, Edy added marshmallows made bite-size by snipping a batch with his wife's sewing scissors, and rocky road was born. The name, which most people associate with the sweet cream's rutted appearance, is actually a double entendre. The Dreyer-Edy duo decided the moniker was fitting for the times; the Great Depression had hit and the pair wanted to give people something to smile about. Today, you can find ice cream labeled "rocky road" that might start with vanilla ice cream or is packed with chocolate chips, streaked with fudge or caramel, or even studded with biscuits.

From its beginnings in the icebox, rocky road has spawned incarnations in the form of fudge, clusters, brownies, and of course, cake. Then there's the Annabelle Candy Company Rocky Road candy bar. Marshmallows, cashews, and a thin covering of chocolate are the primary ingredients in the bar with the bright red wrapper, the brainchild of Sam Altshuler, a Russian immigrant who arrived in the U.S. in 1917, founded the candy company in 1950, and spent years perfecting his Rocky Road candy bar recipe. It's still available on the West Coast, where it enjoys a cult-like following; the rest of us looking for a fix have to exercise a little delayed gratification by ordering it online.

Determining just when the combination of marshmallows, chocolate, and nuts migrated from ice cream and candy bars to brownies and cake is difficult. But it makes perfect sense. And in true American spirit, there are as many variations as there are bakers. My family loves rocky road in any form. But I'm a smooth-surface kinda girl, so I stud my cake batter with chocolate chips, fill the inside with marshmallow spread, and top the whole thing with a caramel buttercream. In other words, I took the smooth road, because that's what puts a smile on my—and I hope your—face.

# Apple of My Eye

**T**his table was inspired by one I did years ago for a client's husband whose birthday happened to fall in October. This man and woman so very clearly adored each other that it seemed a shame not to exploit the season *and* the saying. Here, I grew-it-down a little to make it more child-friendly. As I began to plan the table's elements—color palette, vessels, and menu—I realized that almost everything I needed was conveniently located at the Union Square farmer's market, one of the most inspired places in all of New York City, especially in the fall. The variety—and sheer volume—of apples is mind-blowing (and there are always samples to taste). I was instantly drawn to the brightest green ones because they are so cheery (fall tables so often look brown and drab).

9

They served as the starter for my color choices, not to mention the primary flavor inspiration.

To look at the produce stands, you'd think the farmers themselves were moonlighting stylists. I took my cues directly from them—right down to the utilitarian crates and baskets they use to cart their produce. My brain's "sweet wheels" began to turn, and I zeroed in on malt balls. They come in red, gold, and Granny Smith green and can be piled into crates and containers like so many apples. Perfect! I also couldn't resist foiled caramel-filled chocolates wrapped to look like shiny apples (stem and all). But for all its sweetness, the candy alone didn't entirely satisfy me, because visions of apple pies wouldn't stop dancing around in my head. The problem is, a single pie is too flat to be a centerpiece, so I made several mini pies and arranged them at the front of the table. Along with Cinnamon-Raisin-Bread Pudding Bites, for which I took the same approach, and tiny caramel lady apples, I introduced as much rusticity in the desserts as I did in the display pieces. The chunky wooden cake stands offer up red-domed apple cupcakes—and gave me that all-important vertical element. I made the pedestals myself, just one of a handful of crafts here that brought me right back to my middle-school shop and art classes. An easy-as-pie apple print tablecloth (that I created with my son) and a simple but sentimental garland conjured an unmistakable back-to-school spirit, yet another part of the season's ambience.

INSPIRATION: Flavor

PALETTE: Red, yellow, granny apple green

PERFECT FOR: Autumn birthday or anniversary, school bake sale, teacher appreciation, Harvest Day celebration, engagement party

# Delicious Apple Cupcakes

The beauty of cupcakes is that you can fill the paper liners to various depths to get a certain effect. Here, I filled them to the brim to get that domed-top apple shape. Topped with red sanding sugar, pretzel stems, and Sour Patch candy leaves to look truly apple-y, they are always a hit and perfect for a school bake sale.

Makes 12 cupcakes.

1½ cups all-purpose flour

⅜ teaspoon baking soda

¾ teaspoon baking powder

½ teaspoon salt

½ teaspoon cinnamon

⅛ teaspoon nutmeg

7 tablespoons unsalted butter, softened and cut into ½-inch pieces

¾ cup granulated sugar

2 large eggs

1 cup unsweetened applesauce

Red sanding sugar

½ recipe (2 cups) Quick Vanilla Buttercream, page 14

12 2-inch-long thin pretzels

12 green Sour Patch candies, each cut into the shape of a leaf with kitchen shears or a leaf cutter

1. Adjust the oven rack to middle position and preheat oven to 350°F. Line a standard cupcake tin with cupcake liners. In a medium bowl, combine the flour, baking soda, baking powder, salt, cinnamon, and nutmeg; set aside.

2. In a bowl of a standing mixer fitted with the paddle attachment, combine the butter and sugar and beat on medium-high speed until light and fluffy, about 3 minutes. Scrape down bowl with a rubber spatula as necessary. Add eggs, one at a time, stopping the mixer and scraping down the bowl as necessary. Reduce the speed to medium-low and gradually add the flour mixture, alternating with the applesauce, until just combined. Stir the mixture with a rubber spatula a few times to make sure the batter is combined. Divide evenly among the cupcake cups.

3. Bake until the tops are golden and just firm to the touch, 16 to 18 minutes. Let cupcakes cool in pan for 5 minutes. Remove cupcakes from pan and allow to cool completely on a wire rack.

4. Put the sanding sugar on a dinner plate. Coat the top of each cupcake with 2 tablespoons of the buttercream, smoothing it with an offset spatula. Roll the cupcake around in the sanding sugar to coat it entirely. Slide a pretzel stick in the center of each cupcake and tuck a Sour Patch leaf next to it. Arrange the cupcakes on footed cake stands and place on the table.

# Mini Apple Pies

You can't let the fall go by without making at least one apple pie, but six little ones are even better! There are some desserts that should never be fiddled with and this is one of them. Lots of cinnamon and a super-flaky crust. Classic.

Makes 6 5-inch pies.

All Butter Pie Dough, page 77, doubled

2 pounds Granny Smith apples, peeled, halved, and cored

¾ cup granulated sugar

2¾ teaspoons cornstarch

1 teaspoon ground cinnamon

4 teaspoons lemon juice

1 egg, beaten

6 tablespoons cold unsalted butter, cut into ¼-inch cubes

3 teaspoons sugar

Small circular cookie cutter

1. Prepare the All Butter Pie Dough, and shape into 2 1-inch-thick disks as directed.

2. Adjust the oven racks to the middle and bottom positions and place 2 sheet pans on the racks. Lightly grease 6 5-inch pie plates. Preheat oven to 425°F.

3. Slice apple halves into ¼-inch slices, and then slice horizontally in half. Combine the apples, sugar, cornstarch, cinnamon, and lemon juice and toss to coat.

4. Lightly flour a work surface. Divide one disk of pastry into six equal pieces. Work with one piece at a time and keep the remaining pieces of dough refrigerated. Roll out each into a ⅛-inch-thick, 7-inch circle. Fit one into each pie plate, allowing dough to overhang edge. Divide the filling equally among the pies and dot each with a cube of the butter.

5. Divide the remaining disk of pastry into 6 pieces, again keeping those pieces you are not working with refrigerated. Roll into 6 7-inch circles, ⅛-inch-thick. Lightly brush the edges of the bottom dough with beaten egg to help the top adhere. Place the dough over the filling and gently press edges together to seal. Trim the excess dough with a sharp knife. Use the tines of a fork to seal the edges. Chill pies in the refrigerator for 30 minutes.

6. Using a small circular cutter, stamp a hole in the center of each pie. Brush pies with remaining beaten egg and sprinkle ½ teaspoon of sugar over the top of each one. Bake until golden, apples are tender, and juices bubble, 30 to 35 minutes, rotating pans from top to bottom and front to back halfway through baking. Let pies cool on wire racks. Arrange them on the table on either side of the cupcake centerpiece. I placed four pies on my table and saved two for replenishing.

# Cinnamon-Raisin Bread Pudding Bites

Make these the morning of the party and your guests will be greeted by the aroma before they walk through the door. There's nothing like a little cinnamon to get into a fall frame of mind! Creamy and cakey, what could be bad about a few bites of bread pudding?

*Makes 12.*

8 ounces challah bread, cut into ½-inch cubes

3 tablespoons melted salted butter, plus extra for greasing pan

⅓ cup plus 2 tablespoons granulated sugar

5 large egg yolks

1 cup heavy cream

1 cup whole milk

1⅛ teaspoons ground cinnamon

⅓ teaspoon salt

⅓ cup golden raisins

1. Set the oven rack to the upper-middle position and heat oven to 350°F. Butter a standard-size 12-cup muffin tin. Spread the bread cubes onto a rimmed baking sheet and, using a pastry brush, dab with the melted butter. Bake until just lightly toasted, 8 to 10 minutes. Remove from oven and cool in the pan on the wire rack.

2. Whisk together ⅓ cup of the sugar and the 5 yolks in a large bowl until combined. Whisk in cream, milk, 1 teaspoon of the cinnamon, and salt until combined. Gently fold in the bread cubes and raisins. Let mixture rest for 10 minutes.

3. Divide the pudding mixture equally among the cupcake cups. Let mixture rest for 10 more minutes so bread can fully soak up liquid. In a small bowl, combine the remaining 2 tablespoons of sugar and remaining ⅛ teaspoon of cinnamon until combined. Sprinkle evenly over the pudding mixture. Bake until the tops are golden and the pudding is just set, 16 to 18 minutes.

4. Let the puddings cool in the pan on a wire rack. Run a sharp knife around each cup to release each pudding. Arrange the puddings on a tray and place at the front of the table.

**ATTENTION: CHOCOLATE LOVERS!**

# Pumpkin–Chocolate Bread Pudding Bites

Pumpkin and chocolate are one of my favorite seasonal combinations. For the chocoholics in the crowd, these do the trick!

*Makes 12.*

- 8 ounces challah bread, cut into ½-inch cubes
- 3 tablespoons melted salted butter, plus extra for greasing pan
- ½ cup granulated sugar
- ¼ cup packed light brown sugar
- 4 large egg yolks
- 1 large egg
- 1¼ cup pumpkin puree
- 1 cup heavy cream
- ½ cup whole milk
- 2 teaspoons ground cinnamon
- ¼ teaspoon ground nutmeg
- ¼ teaspoon ground cloves
- ¾ teaspoon ground ginger
- ¼ teaspoon salt
- ¾ cup chopped bittersweet chocolate

1. Set oven rack to upper-middle position and heat oven to 350°F. Butter a standard-size 12-cup muffin tin. Spread bread cubes onto a rimmed baking sheet and, using a pastry brush, dab with the melted butter. Bake until just lightly toasted, 8 to 10 minutes. Remove from the oven and let pan cool on a wire rack.

2. Whisk together the sugars, yolks, and egg in a large bowl until combined. Whisk in the pumpkin, cream, milk, cinnamon, nutmeg, cloves, ginger, and salt until combined. Gently fold in the bread cubes and chocolate chunks. Let mixture rest for 20 minutes.

3. Divide pudding mixture equally among the cupcake cups. Let the mixture rest for 10 more minutes so the bread can fully soak up liquid. Bake until the tops are golden and the pudding is just set, around 30 minutes.

4. Let pan cool to room temperature on a wire rack. Run a sharp knife around each cup to release pudding. Arrange the puddings on a tray and place at the front of the table.

# Caramel Lady Apples

I loved the lacquered red version of these when I was a kid; I remember working so hard to take that first bite into the sticky candy coating! For this table, it seemed only right to downsize to a smaller apple guests and children could easily get their mouths around. Dipped in caramel, each one is three bites of gooey indulgence. Take care when working with caramel syrup—it gets very hot. If caramel begins to harden before you've finished the apples, gently heat it over medium heat until liquefied.

Makes 12.

12 8-inch skewers or lollipop sticks
12 lady apples
 1 cup granulated sugar
 ¼ cup light corn syrup
Green construction paper
Double stick tape

1. Hold each apple firmly on a work surface and carefully press a skewer through the stem end; set aside. Lightly spray a baking sheet with nonstick spray; set aside.

2. In a small saucepan, combine the sugar, corn syrup, and ½ cup of water and cook over medium-high heat, gently stirring just until the sugar dissolves. Brush sides of pan with water to eliminate sugar crystals.

Bring to boil and cook, without stirring, until syrup is a light golden color and registers 350°F on a candy thermometer, brushing sides of pan as necessary if small crystals form.

3. Immediately remove the caramel from the heat and, working quickly, tilt the pan, dip one apple at a time into the caramel, and swirl to coat. Place each apple on the prepared baking sheet and repeat with remaining apples, working briskly. Let cool to harden, about 15 minutes. Add a paper leaf, cut from green construction paper (see the Template Index, page 340, and download and print the template from http://blog.amyatlas.com). Attach the leaf to the skewer with double stick tape.

*easy does it* If you don't have time to melt caramel, use Hammond's Candy Apples from Hammond's Candies (see Find It, page 357).

# Brownie Apples

Who wouldn't want to bite into an apple, only to have it taste like a fudgy brownie? Like crispy rice treats, brownies are ideal for cutting into myriad shapes, including a shiny red Macintosh apple. See the Template Index, page 340, for the brownies' shape, and download and print the template from http://blog.amyatlas .com, or use a cookie cutter (see Find It, page 357).

Makes 8.

Fudge-y Brownies, page 13
Quick Vanilla Buttercream, page 14, ½ recipe
Red sanding sugar
½ cup Royal Icing, page 15, colored
   with green food coloring gel

1. Using the template or cookie cutter, outline the apples on the brownies. Using a sharp knife, cut them out.

2. Spread the tops of the brownies with a thin layer of buttercream, leaving the stem brown. Smooth with an offset spatula.

3. Put the red sanding sugar on a dinner plate. Plunge one brownie, frosting side down, into the sanding sugar to coat it entirely. Repeat with the remaining brownies.

4. Fill a pastry bag or resealable plastic bag fitted with a Wilton Leaf Tip #352 with the green Royal Icing. Pipe a stem pair of leaves on each apple. Arrange the brownies on a tray lined with decorative paper and place on the table.

# "Apple of My Eye" Banner

Who doesn't want to be the apple of someone's eye? And why not announce it?
I designed this scalloped banner to subtly recall pie tins—and to send a not-so-subtle
message to a loved one. See the Template Index on page 340 for the banner.

MATERIALS

12 8½- × 11-inch pieces white card stock

8 yards red and white baker's twine

TOOLS

Hot glue gun

Utility knife

Command hooks or tape

1. See page 340 for reference and download and print the fluted template from http://blog.amyatlas.com. Cut out with a small utility knife to get precise edges.

2. Lay the letters in "APPLE" right side up next to each other on a clean work surface. Hot glue a length of baker's twine to the back of the letters, affixing it about ¼ of the way from the top, and leaving about 2 inches of space between the letters.

3. Repeat with the rest of the letters in "OF MY EYE," making sure to leave ample space between the words. Hang the garland using Command hooks or tape.

## SWAP IT OUT

Spell it out in Sugar Cookies, if you like. Follow the instructions for making the Take a Sweet Cookies on page 152, using red and light green food coloring gel. Attach the letters to red and white baker's twine with a glue gun. See the Template Index, pages 344–345, for the letters (which you can download and print at http://blog.amyatlas.com) or use cookie cutters.

## Style It

There's nothing like a bountiful table, especially during the harvest season. But you don't need to wipe out the local farmer's market to make your table seem abundant.
Fill the apple baskets and crates with tissue paper or paper towels first, then pile the fruits and sweets on top, making sure to cover the filler so only you will know!

# Apple Print Tablecloth

This is a fantastic project for a little helper; my son, Zach, is just old enough now to give me a hand with my table crafts and is particularly happy when paint is involved. Even easier than the classic potato printmaking, in which you have to carve a shape from the potato, a halved apple is as graphic as you need to run with the motif.

MATERIALS

White or ivory cotton canvas tablecloth
1 Granny Smith apple, halved lengthwise, seeds removed
Light green acrylic paint
Titanium white acrylic paint
Cadmium yellow light acrylic paint

TOOLS

Painter's tape
All-paints paintbrush, ¼-inch

1. Drape the tablecloth over the table, positioning it in desired place. Run a strip of painter's tape along the length of the top front edge of the cloth.

2. Place the tablecloth on a clean work surface (you can even use your sweets table). Run a second strip of tape along the length of the cloth 3 inches below the first strip. Affix the tape so that the bottom edge is at the 3-inch mark.

3. Squeeze equal amounts of green and white paint and less of the yellow paint onto one plate and mix them together for one shade of green. On another plate, squeeze and mix just green paint for the second shade of green.

Using one half of the apple, either dip it flat side down into one of the paint plates or paint it with a paintbrush.

Press the apple down on the cloth just above the bottom piece of tape. Continue making apple prints along the edge of the tape, alternating paint colors as desired and working from left to right. Using your paintbrush, paint apple stem and fill in the apple-half prints with extra paint if necessary. Let dry.

4. Remove the bottom piece of tape. Spread the cloth on the table, aligning the remaining piece of tape with the front edge of the table. Remove it and get styling!

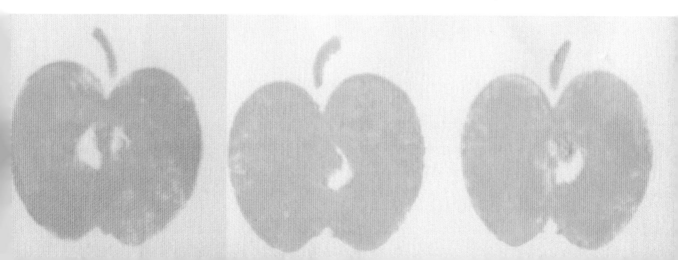

# DIY Wooden Cake Stands

Seriously, make your own! These are as easy to put together as that childhood classic, Tinker Toys. No, maybe easier—you just have to drill a few holes and screw some pieces of wood together. All of the pieces may be available pre-cut at the hardware store but if not, see Find It, page 357, for a supplier.

**Makes three 12-inch cake stands of varying heights.**

### MATERIALS

3 12-inch-diameter × ¾-inch-thick solid pine disks
3 6½-inch-diameter × ¾-inch-thick solid pine disks
1 10-inch-long × 1-inch-diameter dowel
1 6-inch-long × 1-inch-diameter dowel
1 4-inch-long × 1-inch-diameter dowel
6 2-inch-long × ⁵⁄₃₂-inch-diameter flat head screws

### TOOLS

Hand drill fitted with ⅛-inch-diameter drill bit
Screwdriver

1. Measure and mark the center on one side of each pine disk. Using the hand drill, drill a hole completely through each pine disk at the mark.

2. Measure and mark the center of each end of the dowels. Using the hand drill, drill a ½-inch-deep hole into each end of the dowels at the mark.

3. Using the screwdriver and working with one 12-inch disk and one 6½-inch disk at

a time, screw a flat head screw through the hole in each disk and into the ends of the dowel. Tighten securely. Repeat with remaining disks and dowels.

***easy does it*** *HOW TO FIND THE CENTER: Trace the wooden disk on a piece of paper and cut out each circle. Fold each paper circle in half and then in half again. Unfold the paper and place it on top of the wooden disk. Lightly poke a hole through the paper into the wooden disk at the intersection of the creases in the paper. You have found the center of the disk!*

# U–Pick Goody Bag

These plump golden delicious and Macintosh apple bags make for sweet picking. I put them in a bushel basket by the door so that guests can help themselves on their way out. You can add green bags (Granny Smith!), too, of course. See the Template Index, page 340, for the leaf.

*Makes 1.*

MATERIALS

1 mini craft bag (6¼-inch-tall × 3½-inch-wide × 2-inch-deep) in red, gold, or apple green

Candy, as desired

Floral tape

Apple green double crepe paper

TOOLS

Hot glue gun

1. Fill the craft bag ¾ full with candy. Twist the top of the bag into a stem. Pull a length of floral tape from the roll, stretch it, and wrap around the stem, beginning at the top and working your way down it. Set aside.

2. Download the leaf template at http://blog .amyatlas.com, and cut a leaf from the crepe paper. Hot glue the leaf to the stem of the apple.

# Seed Bag of Sweets

I love putting a little bag of treasures on the table, a gift guests must open to see what's inside. These rustic pouches with a tiny apple attached are perfect for a fall harvest table.

*Makes 1 bag.*

### MATERIALS

1 piece apple-patterned scrapbook paper
(see Find It, page 357)
1 3- × 5-inch drawstring burlap bag
(see Find It, page 357)
Apple jelly beans and apple sours

### TOOLS

Hot glue gun

Cut out individual apples from apple-patterned paper for tags. Fill the burlap bag to ¾ full with the candy. Cinch the bag and tie the strings in a double knot. Hot glue the apple tag underneath the strings. Arrange in clusters on the table.

# Marzipan Macintosh Apples

A pretty little embellishment propped here and there on the table, these apples are adorable—and, best of all, edible. Note the worm coming out of the apple on the cake stand! Marzipan is available in specialty food stores and in some supermarkets. Just add food coloring.

*Makes 1 apple, with worm.*

### MATERIALS

2 tablespoons marzipan
Red food coloring gel
Brown food coloring gel
Green food coloring gel

### TOOLS

A toothpick

1. Color 1 tablespoon plus 2 teaspoons of marzipan with the red food coloring gel. Knead the paste to incorporate the color, adding more if necessary to achieve desired shade. Divide the remaining marzipan into three equal portions. Color one brown and another green in the same manner, and leave the remaining one natural.

2. Shape the red, green, and brown marzipan into a small globe, leaf, and stem, respectively. Make a small depression in the top of the apple. Attach the stem, then the leaf. Shape the natural marzipan into a worm. Using a toothpick, puncture the apple. Slide the worm in and close up the hole around it.

## SHOP IT

Fresh Golden Delicious, Granny Smith, Macintosh, Rome, or any bright red apples, overflowing from old-school ½-bushel baskets

Sour Patch apples, overflowing from old-school ¼-bushel baskets

Red, yellow, green, and tan malt balls, brimming in various-size apple crates and wood berry baskets

Caramel-filled foil-covered apples, brimming in an apple crate

## DISPLAY IT

Apple crates and handled baskets

DIY Wooden Cake Stands

Apple Print Tablecloth

"APPLE OF MY EYE" banner

Bamboo platters

Red ceramic mini-quiche pans

Wood berry baskets

## SWITCH IT

**GROW IT UP:** Serve with your favorite recipe for Appletinis or Apple Cart cocktails, a combination of 1 ounce apple brandy, ¾ ounce Cointreau, and ½ ounce lemon juice.

**GROW IT DOWN:** Serve with apple cider in mini apple barrel jars, each drink garnished with a cinnamon stick and a mini apple cider donut.

**COLOR IT:** Use an autumnal leaves palette: gold, orange, and brown.

# Perfectly Preppy

Apart from my favorite store in all of Manhattan, New York Cake and Baking (I mean it; more than Barneys, Bergdorf's, and Saks), my husband's closet is *the* best place to find inspiration for styling up sweets. The ginghams! The argyles! The stripes! The colors! There happens to be a ton of pink in his wardrobe—shirts but mainly ties—and I love it. He's not *that* into fashion, but he does show signs of budding fashionista-itis on the tie rack. There's nothing like a shot of fuchsia, bubble gum, petal, or raspberry pink to give corporate navy an adrenaline rush. Perhaps that's why men have no fear of wearing these colors to the office. But preppies have known this all along. Translating the pink and blue color combination to a sweets table is obvious to me.

10

# For this one, I started with a navy blue tablecloth. I added a handful

of ties interspersed with lengths of that preppy staple, grosgrain ribbon, cut into the shape of skinny and fat ties. The ties and ribbon make a cool and unexpected runner in any palette. It just goes to show you how endless the options are for jazzing up your table. (Best to use out-of-rotation ties, just in case a little strawberry mousse or frosting finds its way onto one.) Because the runner was my jumping-off point, I focused on the rest of the display before creating the menu. The key was to pile on pattern, just like any self-respecting preppy. With simple cotton fabric, ribbon, and buttons, I designed an eye-popping backdrop of huge diamonds that pick up where the ties leave off. Simple and sculptural white serving vessels lined with assorted candies provide a graphic look and allow the food to shine. You'll notice that the sweets here are predominantly pink, a conscious decision since navy blue isn't exactly an appetizing color and getting the hue of the right blue in desserts is tricky (unless, of course, we're talking about blueberries). However, I used blue M&M's to line a tray of icy white crispy rice diamonds. The stark contrast turns out to be a really clever way to create an argyle pattern. Sprinkles, sanding sugar, mousse, and marshmallows in varying shades of pink, combined with accents of royal, navy, and cobalt paper and ribbon, add up to a totally irresistible spread. A three-tiered cake, set on a footed cake plate and cake pedestal, spotlights the preppy tone—wide pinstripes, argyle, polka dots, and a bow. A pair of generous compotes flank it, "filled" (read on for my styling secret) to overflowing with truffles. You'll notice that I've arranged the food symmetrically—a good de-cluttering strategy when there is a lot of pattern at play. Not that you want anything about a preppy table to be minimalist; the more exuberant the better.

---

**INSPIRATION:** Pattern, fashion
**PALETTE:** Hot pink and navy
**PERFECT FOR:** Father's Day, his and her wedding shower, anniversary, milestone birthday party for him or her, major job promotion, graduation celebration for him or her

# Stripes and Argyle Cake

I've long admired Elisa Strauss's cakes, always wanting to have an occasion to have one for one of my own parties. What I love is how precise and clean her work is. She has a way that brings a feminine touch to everything she does; stripes and argyles could read pretty masculine, but with the simple addition of a bow, she gave it just the right amount of unisex appeal. Elisa graciously shared her decorating technique with me for my vanilla and strawberry cake, and I adapted it for those of you who don't work out of a professional kitchen. Thank you, Elisa!

**Makes one 9- × 4-inch tier.**

**Note:** You can replace the rolled fondant for the diamonds and stripes with gum paste, if you like. Gum paste is more durable and dries faster than fondant.

FOR THE CAKE:

1½ cups (3 sticks) unsalted butter, softened

3 cups granulated sugar

6 large eggs

2 tablespoons vanilla

6 cups all-purpose flour

2 tablespoons baking powder

1½ teaspoons salt

2 cups whole milk

FOR THE STRAWBERRY BUTTERCREAM:

Quick Vanilla Buttercream, page 14

¾ cup seedless strawberry jam

Pink food coloring gel

FOR THE FONDANT COVER AND DECORATIONS:

6½ pounds rolled fondant (1½ pounds for 6-inch dummy; 2 pounds for 9-inch edible cake; 3 pounds for 12-inch dummy)

2 pounds rolled fondant (for the diamonds and stripes)

Hot pink, pale pink, and navy blue food coloring gel

Royal Icing, page 15

FOR THE FAKE TIERS:

1 6-inch-square × 4-inch-high cake dummy

1 12-inch-square × 4-inch-high cake dummy

TOOLS AND MATERIALS FOR THE DECORATIONS:

4-inch diamond cutter

3-inch diamond cutter

Pastry brush

Stitching tool

Tape measure

Length navy blue grosgrain, ¼ inch wide

1. Spray two 9-inch-square baking pans with nonstick cooking spray and line the bottoms with parchment paper. Preheat oven to 350°F. To make the batter, follow the method for Vanilla Butter Cake, page 11, but using the measurements on page 236.

2. Divide batter equally between the pans and bake until golden and set, 35 to 40 minutes.

3. To make the buttercream, mix in the strawberry preserves in the last step of making the Quick Vanilla Buttercream, page 14, and then add drops of pink food coloring until desired shade of pink is achieved.

4. Once the cakes are completely cooled, see Decorating a Cake with Fondant, page 18, for assembling and covering with fondant. Cover the dummies with fondant as well. Stack the cakes on a 14-inch-square cake stand if you are making the tiered cake.

5. For the diamonds, tint 5 ounces of the fondant hot pink and 5 ounces pale pink. Roll each out onto a plastic mat or Omnigrid.

6. To decorate the middle tier, use a 4-inch diamond cutter to cut out 12 hot pink diamonds. Use a 3-inch diamond cutter to cut out 12 pale pink diamonds. Brush the back of the pale pink diamonds with a little water and center them on the hot pink diamonds. Brush the back of the double diamonds with water and affix to the sides of the cake, three across, with the points touching.

7. If desired, use the stitching tool to emboss the diamonds with an argyle pattern through their centers.

*Style It*

Ignore what your mother told you: Stripes and argyles *do* go together. And dots, too. The key is to limit the palette and vary the scale of both.

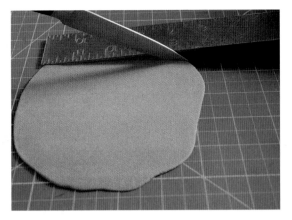

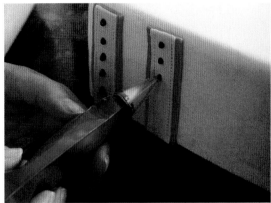

8. To decorate the striped tiers, tint 10 ounces more of fondant hot pink and 10 ounces pale pink. Roll each out onto a plastic mat or Omnigrid. For the top tier, cut ¼-inch-wide × 4-inch-high hot pink strips and ½-inch-wide × 4-inch-high pale pink strips. You will need 16 of each color for the top tier. Brush the backs of the hot pink strips with a little water and center them on the pale pink strips. Set aside. For the bottom tier, cut 1½-inch-wide × 4-inch-high hot pink strips and 1-inch-wide × 4-inch-high pale pink strips. You will need 20 of each color for the bottom tier. Repeat as you did with the top tier to create double strips, this time with the pale pink strips centered on the hot pink strips. Brush the backs of the double strips with water and affix to the cake dummies, placing the narrow strips on the top tier and the wider strips on the bottom tier, spacing them evenly apart. If desired, use the stitching tool to emboss the stripes, as shown in the photo.

9. Tint ½ cup of Royal Icing navy blue. Spoon it into a pastry bag or resealable plastic bag fitted with a Wilton Round Tip #2 and pipe dots in a straight line down the center of the strips.

10. Using the tape measure, measure the circumference of each tier. Cut a length of the ribbon plus 1 inch for the top and bottom tier and 10 inches to make the bow for the middle tier. Trim the bottom edge of each tier with the ribbon, securing the top and bottom ribbons in the back with a little Royal Icing. Tie the longer ribbon around the middle tier and fasten with a bow in the right-hand corner. Place the cake on a pedestal on the table.

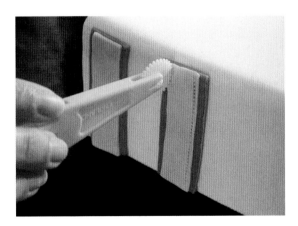

# Chipper Chocolate Cupcakes

These pretty little peaked cupcakes couldn't be easier to make and decorate; they're sweet and understated, just like a perfectly dressed prep.

**Makes 12.**

1 ounce semisweet chocolate, finely chopped

½ cup hot coffee

1 cup all-purpose flour

½ cup cocoa powder

⅔ teaspoon baking soda

¼ teaspoon baking powder

½ teaspoon salt

1 cup granulated sugar

1 large egg

¼ cup vegetable oil

½ cup buttermilk

½ teaspoon vanilla

½ recipe (2 cups) Quick Vanilla Buttercream, page 14

Pink sanding sugar, for garnish

1. Adjust the oven rack to the middle position and preheat oven to 350°F. Line a standard cupcake pan with cupcake liners. In a small bowl, whisk together the chocolate and coffee until the chocolate is melted. Set aside.

2. Sift together the flour, cocoa, baking soda, baking powder, and salt into a medium bowl. In a large bowl, whisk together the sugar, egg, vegetable oil, buttermilk, and vanilla until combined. Whisk in the chocolate-coffee mixture until combined. Whisk in the dry mixture until combined.

3. Divide batter equally among the cupcake cups and bake until just set and a toothpick inserted in the center comes out clean, 17 to 20 minutes. Let cool in pan for 5 minutes, then transfer to a wire rack to cool completely.

4. Using an offset spatula, cover each cupcake with a generous layer of frosting, using swirling motions to apply it. Sprinkle with the sanding sugar. Arrange on a tray lined with the rock candy crystals and set on the table.

# Simple Strawberry Mousse

This mousse is special on its own but a length of patterned grosgrain ribbon wrapped around the glass to secure a spoon is pretty and practical—and transforms it into a special treat. Use only high-quality white chocolate like Ghirardelli, Valrhona, or Callebaut.

**Makes about 12 3-ounce servings.**

- 12 ounces white chocolate, finely chopped
- 2 cups heavy cream
- 2 pints fresh strawberries, washed, hulled, and roughly chopped
- 3 tablespoons granulated sugar, divided
- 3 tablespoons fresh lemon juice
- 1 tablespoon gelatin

1. Prepare 12 3-ounce glasses with ribbon and a spoon (see photo, opposite page) and set aside.

2. In a medium microwave-safe bowl, combine the white chocolate and cream and melt on low power, stirring every 30 seconds until chocolate is melted and mixture is smooth. Cover with plastic wrap and refrigerate until thoroughly chilled, about 2 hours.

3. Meanwhile, combine the strawberries and 1 tablespoon of the sugar in the bowl of a food processor and puree until smooth. Press through a fine mesh strainer to remove seeds. Transfer the strawberry puree to a large bowl and whisk in remaining sugar and lemon juice.

4. Place 1 cup of the strawberry puree in a bowl and sprinkle gelatin over it. Set aside remaining puree. Stir until combined, then let sit to soften, at least 10 minutes. Pour the gelatin mixture into a saucepan set over medium heat. Cook, stirring constantly, until gelatin is dissolved. Whisk gelatin mixture into the reserved strawberry puree until combined. Cover with plastic wrap and refrigerate until it begins to thicken to a jelly-like consistency, about an hour and a half.

5. Meanwhile, in the bowl of a standing mixer fitted with the whisk attachment, whip the white chocolate–cream mixture on medium-high speed until it forms soft peaks, about 1 to 2 minutes. Whisk 2 tablespoons of the white chocolate–cream mixture into the remaining strawberry puree. Fold that mixture into the remaining white chocolate–cream mixture until it becomes light pink. Divide evenly among the glasses and chill until set, about 3 hours. Arrange the glasses on a tray lined with hot pink rock candy crystals and set on table.

*easy does it* *Pressed for time? Replace the mousse with strawberry Jell-O pudding. If you wish, swirl the cooked pudding with a dot of pink food coloring using a chopstick, to give it a colorful streak.*

ATTENTION: CHOCOLATE LOVERS!

# Spiced Chocolate Mousse

**Makes about 6 cups.**

*Note:* This mousse is made with uncooked eggs. It is at its creamiest when served immediately after making, but can be made ahead, chilled, and returned to room temperature before serving.

12 ounces bittersweet chocolate, finely chopped

4 tablespoons unsalted butter

6 eggs, separated, at room temperature

½ teaspoon ground cinnamon

¼ to ⅓ teaspoon cayenne pepper

1½ teaspoons granulated sugar

12 ounces heavy cream, chilled

1. In a large bowl set over a pan of simmering water, melt the chocolate and butter. While the chocolate is still warm, whisk in the egg yolks, cinnamon, and cayenne. Don't let the chocolate mixture cool too long before moving to the next step.

2. In the bowl of a standing mixer fitted with the whisk attachment, beat the egg whites and sugar to medium peaks. Fold ⅓ of the whites into the chocolate mixture to lighten, then fold in remaining whites until combined.

3. Whip the cream to soft peaks in the bowl of a standing mixer fitted with the whisk attachment. Gently fold into chocolate mixture until combined. Spoon into glasses and chill until set, about 1 hour. Arrange as for Simple Strawberry Mousse, page 243.

# Raspberry Truffles

It doesn't get much better than a bite-size ball of chocolate—except when it's rolled in blindingly pink sprinkles. These tend to disappear very fast, which is why I put two big bowls of them on the table (read Style It to learn one of the oldest tricks in the book for creating bounty!). Set them out just before guests arrive.

**Makes 2 dozen 1¼-inch balls.**

- 12 ounces semisweet chocolate, finely chopped
- ½ cup heavy cream
- 2 tablespoons unsalted butter, cut into ¼-inch pieces
- 6 tablespoons raspberry liqueur
- Hot pink sprinkles

1. Place chocolate, cream, butter, and liqueur in a microwave-safe bowl. Heat on full power, stirring every 30 seconds, until chocolate is melted and the mixture is smooth. Cover with plastic wrap and chill until firm, about 1 hour.

2. Line a baking sheet with parchment paper. Scoop tablespoon-size portions of the truffle mixture and, using your hands, roll each portion into a ball. (If the chocolate is too soft to roll into balls, chill until firm enough to work with.) Place on the baking sheet and chill again until firm.

3. Put the sprinkles on a dinner plate. Roll each truffle in the sprinkles to cover and return to the baking sheet. Chill until completely firm, about 1 hour. Keep chilled until ready to serve. Pile the truffles in a pyramid shape in a pair of footed compotes.

## Style It

Although it may not look like it, filling just one of these compotes would require more than 100 truffles! Instead, pump up the volume by filling them with crumpled parchment or waxed paper. Stay away from foil (too garish for a preppy gal!) or any other paper that might stick to the truffles.

# Sugar Cookie Pocket Squares

Mixing stripes and argyles is a preppy signature, but it's wise to keep the two patterns in the same color palette, especially if turning them loose on sweets. Add a selection of dotted cookies, though, if you really want to pile on the pattern. Christine Mehling from Better Bit of Cookies kindly shared the decorating technique for my cute little sugar cookie squares.

**Makes 20 2-inch square cookies.**

Sugar Cookies, page 12
Royal Icing, page 15, ½ recipe
Royal blue and pink food coloring gel
1 pound rolled fondant
Confectioners' sugar for dusting

SPECIAL TOOLS:

1 2-inch square cookie cutter
Fondant rolling pin
Palette knife
1 1-inch diamond-shaped cutter
Small paintbrush, for pastry only

1. Using the 2-inch square cookie cutter, stamp out cookies from dough and bake as directed.

2. Meanwhile, divide the Royal Icing equally between three bowls. Color one with the royal blue food coloring gel, one with the pink food coloring gel, and leave the last bowl white. Stir, adding more gel until the desired color is achieved for the pink and blue Royal Icing. Cover with plastic wrap and set aside.

3. Dust a work surface with confectioners' sugar. Roll out 8 ounces of fondant to ⅛-inch thickness and cut out 20 squares using the square cutter. Working with one cookie at a time, use a teaspoon of the white Royal Icing to drizzle a thin stream on top of each. Place a square of fondant over the icing, aligning the edges. Using a fondant rolling pin, flatten the fondant to make the surface as even as possible. Using a palette knife, straighten the four edges of the cookie.

4. To 4 ounces of white fondant, add royal blue food coloring gel to achieve the desired color. Repeat with the same amount of fondant and the pink food coloring gel. Roll out and cut 10 diamonds from each batch of fondant.

5. Brush the back side of 5 royal blue and 5 pink diamonds and affix one to the center of each cookie. Working one at a time with the remaining diamonds, cut them into quarters from point to point. Working with the color opposite the center diamond, brush the back side of each piece with water and affix one to each side of the square so that the longest edge is flush with the edge of the cookie.

6. To make the stripes going over the diamonds, cut strips of the pink and blue fondant about ⅟₁₆-inch-wide to fit the cookie. Affix with water.

7. To make the lined cookies, cut alternate strips of pink and blue fondant ⅛-inch-wide × 2 inches long and affix with water. Let dry in a cool dry place. Arrange the cookies on a platter lined with hot pink rock candy crystals and place on the table.

**easy does it** *Use purchased vanilla frosting in place of the Royal Icing and decorate with candy such as chocolate-covered Sunny Seed Drops or M&M's. Or color some of the frosting and pipe on the stripes and argyles.*

# Marquise-Cut Diamonds

Here's one way to turn a humble crispy rice cereal treat into a chic little dessert: Cut a pan of it into diamonds and cover each one in fondant, then sprinkle some sanding sugar on top.

**Makes 17.**

Basic Crispy Rice Cereal Treats, page 13
Confectioners' sugar, for dusting
1 pound rolled fondant
Hot pink sanding sugar

SPECIAL TOOLS:
4-inch round cutter
3-inch diamond cutter

1. Using a knife and a 3-inch diamond-shaped cutter as a guide, cut out 17 diamonds from the Crispy Rice Cereal Treats.

2. Dust a work surface with the confectioners' sugar. Roll the fondant to ⅛-inch thick. Using a 4-inch round cutter, and working one round at a time, stamp out rounds. Drape over the diamond rice crispy treat, gently pressing to adhere. Trim the edges with a sharp knife.

3. Sprinkle the diamonds with hot pink sanding sugar. Arrange in an argyle pattern on a tray lined with blue M&M's and place on the table.

## Style It

When the color palette is as saturated as this one, always go for white plates and platters—not only do they stand out, but they prevent the table from looking cluttered. Notice that for this table in particular, all of the tableware has clean edges, an intentional mimicking of the crisp lines of argyles and stripes. This is not a frilly moment! Show off those sharp edges!

# Buttoned-Up Argyle Screen

This "upholstered" (not to worry, there's no stitching involved, just a few different kinds of tape and a glue gun) backdrop is the epitome of preppy, but swap out the contrasting color palette for neutrals—creams and ivories—and it will showcase a wedding cake beautifully. My instructions include the screens that flank the tufted screen.

MATERIALS

- 7½ yards 48-inch-wide cotton batting, 2½ yards high each, cut into 3 equal pieces
- 3 1-yard × 2-yard × ½-inch-thick pieces foam core
- 7½ yards 54-inch-wide hot pink cotton/linen, divided 2½ yards high each
- 4½ yards 1½-inch-wide striped grosgrain ribbon
- 12 cover buttons (see Find It, page 358)
- ⅛ yard light pink taffeta

TOOLS

Tailor's chalk
Dressmaker pins

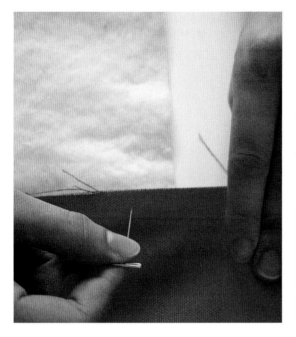

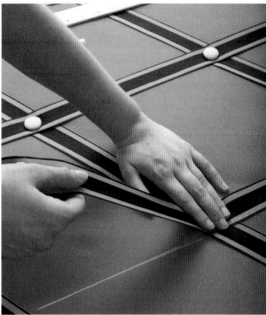

1. Lay one piece of the cotton batting on a work surface. Place one piece of foam core in the center of it. Fold the edges of the cotton batting onto the back of the foam core, working on one side then its opposite, pulling it taut. Secure with dressmaker pins. Repeat with the hot pink fabric. Repeat with the remaining two pieces of foam core.

2. To make the ribbon diamond on the middle panel, lay one of the covered foam core panels right side up on a work surface. Using the tailor's chalk, measure and mark a diamond design on the panel.

3. Using dressmaker pins, affix lengths of the ribbon along the chalk marks to form diamonds. Wrap any excess ribbon around the edge of the panel and onto the back. Secure with dressmaker pins.

4. Cover the cover buttons with the light pink taffeta as directed on the package. Hot glue a button at each intersection of ribbon.

5. Arrange the panels vertically on the table, leaning them against the wall, with the ribboned panel in the center.

# Preppy Pedestal

No matter the cake—single tier or tower—if you raise it up off the table just a few inches, you've made it a focal point. This cake could never be ignored—such a tailored design, with that perfectly preppy little ribbon and bow—but I'm all for making too much of a good thing.

**Makes 1 pedestal.**

MATERIALS

- 1  14- × 14-inch-square × 3-inch-high cake dummy or 2 shoe boxes taped together to create a square
- 1  14- × 14-inch square hot pink card stock Glue Dots
- 6  yards 1-inch-wide navy grosgrain ribbon, cut into 3 2-yard lengths
- 3  dressmaker pins

1. Affix the hot pink card stock to the top of the cake dummy with Glue Dots.

2. Wrap one ribbon around the sides of the pedestal so that the edge of the ribbon is flush with the bottom edge of the dummy. Secure with a dressmaker pin. Repeat with a second length of ribbon, overlapping the bottom ribbon slightly, beginning and ending at the same place, and securing with a dressmaker pin. Wrap the remaining ribbon in the same manner and secure it also with a dressmaker pin.

# Tie-Required Favor Box

The good news is that you really don't have to know how to tie a tie to make these pint-size versions. Of course, if you're throwing a boy/girl party, switch the teensy tie on top to a classic bow on half of the favor boxes. Fill with navy and pink M&M's, jelly beans, or foil-wrapped chocolates.

**Makes 1.**

### MATERIALS

3½-inch-square gift box

1  12-inch-square pink or navy waxed paper

Pink and navy M&M's, jelly beans, or foiled chocolates

⅔  yard ½-inch-wide royal blue satin ribbon

Double stick tape

### TOOLS

Hot glue gun

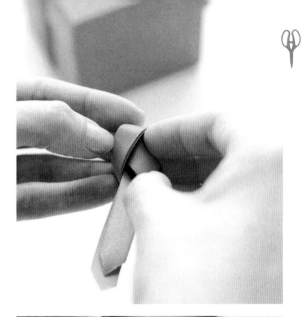

Place the waxed paper inside the box so that it overhangs the edges. Fill to ¾-full with the candy. Fold the excess waxed paper over the candy and replace the lid. Cut a 15-inch length of ribbon and wrap it around the box. Secure with double stick tape. Snip both ends of the remaining length of ribbon on the diagonal so that they come to a point. Fold the ribbon in half. Tie it in a knot at the folded end. Hot glue the "tie" to the box.

# Tied Together Candy Cup

Visual puns are my thing, and I'll take every opportunity I can get to put them into words. This favor goes perfectly with this table (I created a similar one for friends of mine who had just become engaged—ahem). See the Template Index, page 341, and download the "Tied Together" candy cup template at http://blog .amyatlas.com. You can make it in no time.

**Makes 1.**

MATERIALS

Basic Candy Cup, page 28

1 14-inch-square sheet royal blue waxed paper

Place the waxed paper in the cup, allowing the edges to shoot straight out of the container. Place the empty cups on the table and invite guests to fill them with their favorite treats to take home.

# Prepster Drink Flag and Candy Bag

In the fashion industry, designers have been incorporating flags into their lines for years (take Ralph Lauren, for example). I thought our preppy desserts should sport their own flags as well. Pair it with a candy bag for a head-to-toe Prepster look.

For the drink flag and the candy bags, see the Template Index, page 341, and download and print the templates at http://blog .amyatlas.com. Also see instructions on page 29. Fill the candy bags with hot pink M&M's.

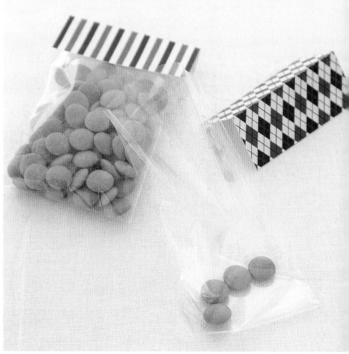

## SHOP IT

Petal pink marshmallows, arranged on their short side on a tray lined with argyle-patterned paper. See Template Index on page 341 and download and print at http://blog.amyatlas.com.

Pink lemonade

Pink and navy jelly beans, for filling gift boxes

Hot pink M&M's, for candy bags

Hot pink rock candy, for lining trays

Pink and navy barber poles, for lining trays over argyle-patterned paper. See Template Index on page 341 and download and print at http://blog.amyatlas.com.

## DISPLAY IT

Buttoned-Up Argyle Screen

Navy taffeta tablecloth

Preppy Pedestal

White platters, footed compotes, cake stands

Hot pink and navy patterned ties and grosgrain ribbons cut into tie shapes

## SWITCH IT

**GROW IT UP:** Serve with your favorite recipe for Pink Ladies.

**GROW IT DOWN:** Serve with pink lemonade.

**SWAP IT OUT:** Try kelly green and navy or bright yellow and navy.

# Movie Night

**W**hen I imagine movie night with my family or friends, I immediately think of an old-fashioned cinema that's decorated with get-your-glam-on colors like silver, gold, and red-carpet red. I picture hurrying to buy my popcorn and candy, walking up or down a set of stairs to find a seat, settling in, and waiting for the movie to start. I tried to capture all these moments and more in this table. My all-important vertical element is the red-carpeted steps positioned in the center of the table. (Not to worry, I'll tell you how to create them with items from your closet.) The candies are the stars, parading down the steps in old-fashioned glass jars filled to the brim.

## 11

# Gold foil-covered chocolate stars,

bright yellow M&M's and malt balls, red jelly beans and licorice—lots of saturated colors that look fabulous on that scarlet runner. I couldn't resist the idea of having Oscar awards on the table, so I mounted sugar cookies in the Oscar shape, set them on a circular base, and put them front and center. From there, I turned licorice wheels into movie reels and used amazing edible gold luster dust as a topcoat on star-shaped fudgy brownies. To give the table a slightly playful vibe while still retaining that vintage Hollywood feel, I mixed in old-school movie theater ephemera—strips of paper tickets and square pinstriped popcorn boxes. I needed a marquee moment, of course, which required a creative shout-out. I did it twice on the table—with a garland of cookies announcing its theme and also with the candy itself, arranged on a square tray to spell out the words that make every actor snap to attention, "Lights, camera, action!" I added a rectangular tray on top to turn the whole thing into a clapperboard. I did it a third time overhead—in paper—to mimic the marquee on a movie theater with a banner announcing "Movie Night." Set against an unapologetically glitzy fringed curtain in red, silver, and gold, the effect is unmistakably cinematic.

INSPIRATION: A passion

PALETTE: Red, gold, and black

PERFECT FOR: Oscar night, kids' slumber or birthday party, family movie night, movie premiere, new baby "a star is born" themed party

Red Velvet
Cupcakes

# Oscar Statuettes

Admittedly, these are a bit over-the-top. If you're feeling as ambitious as a Hollywood starlet, I say go for it. They're worth making if you're throwing a full-on, don-a-gown party to match the big Hollywood spectacle on television. See the Template Index on page 342 for the Oscar and download the Oscar cookie template at http://blog.amyatlas.com. Or see Find It, page 359, for a cutter. Getting the statuette to stand up straight is easy with isomalt, a sugar substitute that confectioners use to make decorations. The decorating technique comes from one of my favorite bakers, Patti Paige of Baked Ideas.

Makes 10 7-inch cookies.

Sugar Cookies, page 12
Royal Icing, page 15
Gold luster dust
Vodka or vanilla extract
Red and black food coloring gel
4 tablespoons Isomalt (see Find It, page 359)
2-inch circle cookie cutter

1. Using the Oscar template and a 2-inch circle cookie cutter, cut out 10 of each shape from the dough and bake at 350°F for about 18 minutes. Cool completely on wire rack.

2. To decorate, follow the instructions for Outlining and Flooding Cookies on page 17, dividing the icing among three bowls, with just ⅛ of it set aside for making red. Flood Oscar with the white, the base and the bottom of the statuette with the black, and reserve the red for writing.

3. Combine the luster dust with enough vodka or vanilla extract to create a loose paintlike consistency. If the luster paint becomes dry as you work, add more liquid. Paint the luster dust over the Oscars and let dry.

4. Fill a pastry bag or resealable plastic bag fitted with a Wilton Round Tip #1 with the red icing and pipe "BEST PICTURE," "BEST ACTRESS," "BEST SCREENPLAY," for example, on the bottom of each statuette. Let set and harden, about 3 hours.

5. Once both the rounds and the Oscars are dry, place the isomalt in a small pot over medium heat and cook just until the crystals have melted. Turn heat off, leaving pot on stove. Working with one circle and Oscar at a time, carefully dip the bottom of the Oscar into the isomalt and center on the top of the iced round. Hold in place for a few seconds until set. Arrange the statuettes on the red carpet just before guests arrive.

***easy does it*** For a children's party, skip the Oscar statuettes and serve Grauman's Handprint Cookies. Have your little guests roll out and press their hands into store-bought sugar cookie dough, just like my son, Josh, does here. Bake according to package directions.

# Golden Caramel Corn

This is a foolproof treat that will put your superb candy-making skills in the spotlight. Cooked sugar gets very hot, so take special care when working with it. Here I leave the caramel corn loose for filling up the cups, but you can also shape it into popcorn balls, which are an especially big hit with kids.

*Makes about 4 popcorn cups.*

- 3 tablespoons vegetable oil
- ½ cup popcorn kernels
- 1 stick (½ cup) unsalted butter
- 1½ cups packed light brown sugar
- ½ cup light corn syrup
- ¾ teaspoon salt
- 1 teaspoon vanilla extract
- ½ teaspoon baking soda

1. In a large saucepan combine oil and 4 popcorn kernels, cover, and cook over medium-high heat until 2 or 3 kernels pop. Add the remaining kernels and cook, shaking pan, until the kernels stop popping, about 4 minutes. Transfer popcorn to large bowl to cool.

2. Lightly spray 2 baking sheets with nonstick spray. Melt butter in a large saucepan over medium-high heat. Add brown sugar and corn syrup and heat, stirring to dissolve sugar. Bring to a boil and continue to cook, without stirring, until mixture registers 300°F on a candy thermometer, about 8 minutes.

3. Remove from heat and stir in salt, vanilla extract, and baking soda. Add popcorn and quickly stir to coat. Immediately spread onto baking sheets. When completely cool, separate popcorn into pieces.

4. Divide the popcorn equally among assembled cups (see Template Index on page 342, and download and print the template at http://blog.amyatlas.com), and see instructions, page 28. Arrange on the red carpet, along the steps.

*easy does it* *There are excellent gourmet caramel popcorns available, including my favorite, Hampton Popcorn. Popcorn Indiana also makes a yummy kettle corn. If you're pressed for time, buy a bag or two.*

# Red Velvet Cupcakes

Yes, old-school theater curtains inspired these. Crowned with an extravagant swirl of rich, fluffy cream cheese frosting and topped with a licorice-wheel movie reel, each cupcake is the picture of perfection.

Makes 12.

1¼ cups all-purpose flour

¼ cup cocoa powder

1 teaspoon baking soda

¼ teaspoon salt

⅔ cup granulated sugar

½ cup buttermilk

¼ cup sour cream

1 teaspoon vanilla

2–3 teaspoons red food coloring

½ cup vegetable oil

2 large eggs, beaten

Cream Cheese Frosting, page 14, doubled to pile on frosting high

12 licorice wheels

1. Adjust oven rack to middle position and preheat oven to 350°F. Line a standard cupcake tin with cupcake liners.

2. Sift flour, cocoa, baking soda, and salt into a medium bowl; add the sugar, mix, and set aside.

3. In a freestanding mixer, whisk together buttermilk, sour cream, vanilla, food coloring, oil, and eggs. Whisk in the flour mixture until well combined.

4. Divide the batter into cupcake cups and bake until just set or a toothpick inserted in the center comes out clean, about 20 minutes. Let cupcakes cool in pan for 5 minutes, then transfer to a wire rack to cool completely.

5. Fill a pastry bag or resealable plastic bag fitted with a Wilton Round Tip #1a with the frosting. Leaving a ¼-inch border around the top of the cupcake, pipe the frosting in gradually smaller circles, moving around the cupcake three times until you come to a peak. Top each with a licorice wheel. Line a platter with red M&M's, arrange the cupcakes over them, and place on the table.

Red Velvet
Cupcakes

# Walk of Fame Brownies

These moist, fudgy stars are dense enough to give clean edges when cut into stars with a very sharp knife. See the Template Index, page 342, and download and print the template at http://blog.amyatlas.com, or use a 3-inch star cookie cutter to guide you. (See Find It, page 359.) For the best results, let them sit overnight before stamping out. After cutting out the stars, let them chill in the refrigerator for 1 hour before dipping into the melted chocolate.

Makes 12.

Fudge-y Brownies, page 13

12 ounces good-quality semisweet chocolate, melted (see How to Melt Chocolate, page 16)

Gold luster dust

Vanilla extract

Small paintbrush

***easy does it*** *If you insist on baking your own brownies (Your guests will love you for it, trust me!) but can't take the time to cut them into stars, squares covered in chocolate and gold luster dust will be just as appealing. There's always boxed brownie mix, too!*

1. When brownies are ready to cut, use a sharp knife (with the template) or star cookie cutter dipped into hot water and wiped off. If you are using a cutter, after lifting out the brownie with it, gently stretch the cutter open to help release the star. Set stars on a wire rack.

2. Working with one brownie at a time, dip the top of each star into the melted chocolate, letting excess drip off. Set them on the wire rack and chill in the refrigerator, about 30 minutes.

3. Place ½ teaspoon of gold luster dust in a small bowl or cup. Stir in a few drops of the vanilla extract to create a paintlike consistency. With a small, clean paintbrush, brush a layer of gold luster onto the top of each brownie. Let dry. Line a square tray with licorice wheels, arrange the glittering stars on top, and set on the table.

# Clapperboard Ice Cream Sandwiches

Cookies and ice cream without the spoon! The chocolate wafers here are more cookie than cake-like—so good that they can stand on their own. I usually make a bunch of ice cream sandwiches using different flavors, wrap them in plastic, and store them in my freezer for a fun treat any day of the week. You can cut the cookies in half before baking if you want to make 3-bite versions, then handle the ice cream accordingly.

Makes 20 to 24 cookies or 10 to 12 sandwiches.

2⅔ cups all-purpose flour

⅔ cup plus ¼ cup extra dark or Dutch processed cocoa

1¼ cups (2½ sticks) unsalted butter, softened

1 cup granulated sugar

1 teaspoon salt

2 large egg yolks

1 tablespoon vanilla extract

½ gallon high-quality chocolate chip ice cream (or your favorite flavor), slightly softened

1. Adjust the oven rack to the middle position and preheat the oven to 350°F. Line two baking sheets with parchment.

2. Sift the flour and cocoa over a medium bowl and set aside. In the bowl of a standing mixer fitted with a paddle attachment, cream the butter, sugar, and salt on medium speed until light and fluffy, about 2 minutes. Add the yolks and vanilla and mix until thoroughly combined, using a rubber spatula to scrape down the sides of the bowl once or twice. Reduce the speed to medium-low and add the flour mixture in batches until combined.

3. Transfer the dough to a lightly floured work surface. Divide into 2 equal pieces. If the dough is too soft to handle, wrap and chill until firm enough to roll out. Working with one batch at a time, roll out into a ¼-inch-thick rectangle, about 10 × 8 inches. Using a ruler and knife or a cookie cutter, cut out 20 to 24 2- × 4-inch rectangles.

***easy does it*** *Use purchased chocolate wafer cookies in place of home-baked ones or, if you're really pressed for time, head to the freezer section and buy premade ice cream sandwiches and follow my styling suggestions.*

I'm always thinking about how to arrange sweets to fit a table's theme, but I love to go beyond that to the platters themselves. Note how the rectangular tray of ice cream sandwiches serves as the clapper of the "Lights! Camera! Action!" square clapperboard.

4. Transfer the rectangles to the prepared baking sheet, leaving a 1-inch space between them. Use the tip of a thermometer to poke 14 holes into each of the cookies.

5. Bake until the cookies stay firm when tapped in the center, 16 to 18 minutes. Let cool for 10 minutes, then transfer to a wire rack to cool completely. Repeat with remaining dough, incorporating any scraps into it.

6. Meanwhile, line the bottom of a 9- × 13-inch pan with parchment paper, allowing paper to overhang on two sides. It will act like a sling for the ice cream. Spread the softened ice cream into the pan, smooth the top, and freeze until firm, about one hour.

7. Run a knife along the exposed sides of the pan to loosen the ice cream. Holding onto the parchment paper, lift ice cream out of the pan and onto a work surface. Using the cookie cutter or one of the cookies as a template, cut into 10 to 12 2- × 4-inch bars. Peel off each ice cream piece and sandwich it between two cookies. Trim away excess ice cream with a sharp knife. Wrap each ice cream sandwich in plastic wrap and freeze until just before serving. To serve, arrange in a single layer on a tray lined with candy.

# CRAFT IT

## Glitzy Curtain

Three layers are better than one if you're doing anything Hollywood-style. Using three different-color Mylar curtains, one on top of another, gives an illusion of fullness. The glittery stars are easy to make.

Makes one 8- × 8-yard curtain.

MATERIALS

3  3-yard red Mylar curtains

3  3-yard silver Mylar curtains

3  3-yard gold Mylar curtains

Thumbtacks

12  5-inch cardboard stars

gold glitter

glitter glue

TOOLS

Stapler

⅛-inch hole punch

Fishing wire, enough to hang stars from the top of the Mylar curtains

### Style It

To determine how much of a certain kind of candy will fit into your jars, see Candy Math, page 39.

1. Lay one silver Mylar curtain on a clean work surface. Place one red curtain on top of it, aligning the top edges. Staple the curtains together. Staple one gold curtain over the red curtain. Repeat with remaining Mylar curtains. You will have three multi-colored panels at this point.

2. Attach the three curtains to each other horizontally by overlapping the top edges by about 3 inches and stapling.

3. To hang, thumbtack the curtains to the wall, about 5 feet above the table and each about 2½ feet apart. Alternatively, if you are hanging the curtain over a span of windows, affix it to the window casings using thumbtacks.

4. Glitter the stars. Place the glitter in a rimmed tray wider than the star. Apply a thin coat of glue all over one side of the star. Press it, glue-side down, into the glitter. Shake off excess. In areas where the cardboard still shows through, apply a bit more glue and spoon the glitter onto them. Shake off excess. Let dry completely.

5. To attach glittered stars to the glitzy curtain, cut the fishing wire at varying lengths, and set aside. Punch a hole at the top point of each star with the hole punch. Take the fishing wire and string it through the holes in the stars. Tie a knot at the top of each star.

6. Attach the stars to the curtain by hanging the fishing wire over the top of the curtain and tying a knot.

# Red Carpet Runway

The intrepid among you might take to building a staircase to nowhere, but for the rest of you, it's time to put all of those old shoe and boot boxes you store in the closet to good use! The red "carpet" is a panel of velour towel fabric, available at any fabric store.

MATERIALS

A selection of white shoe and boot boxes of the same height

1  3-yard × 9-yard piece crimson (or other red) velour fabric

Double stick tape

1. If your boxes aren't sturdy, fill them with books or magazines to strengthen them. Arrange shoe and boot boxes at the center of the table in such a way that they span 4 feet across and 2 feet deep. Stack more boxes on top of these boxes, set back about 12 inches. Do not allow the top "step" to overhang the back of the table—you need support underneath to hold the candy jars.

2. Drape the fabric along the steps as you would a runner, letting it fall down the front of the table to the floor. Secure to the steps with double stick tape.

# Classic Popcorn Boxes    Movie Night Marquee

It's a design that will trigger a memory of the aroma of fresh-popped popcorn—the tall red and white striped container, customized here with a graphic design and old-school movie tickets. See the Template Index, page 342, and download the template from http://blog.amyatlas.com.

Makes 1 box.

MATERIALS

1   Candy Cup (see Template Index, page 342; also see instructions, p. 28)

Strip of 4 movie tickets (see Find It, page 359)

Fill the cup with Golden Caramel Corn, page 263, until slightly overflowing. Tuck the strip of tickets into it and set on the red carpet. Make as many boxes as there are guests at the party.

I love the dots inside the letters on this banner—they remind me of the classic old movie theater signs that used to glow in yellow or white lights. See the Template Index on page 342 for the banner, and go to http://blog.amyatlas.com to download the template.

MATERIALS

10  sheets 11- × 14-inch white card stock

Sharp scissors

12  feet gold cord

Glue Dots or glue gun

Thumbtacks

1. Print template onto the card stock. Cut with sharp scissors. Lay the gold cord on a work surface. Beginning 12 inches from the left end, attach the letters "M-O-V-I-E" to the cord about 1½ inches from the top of the circle, using Glue Dots or glue gun. Leave about 1½ inches between the letters. Affix the letters "N-I-G-H-T" in the same manner, leaving about 12 inches between the two words.

2. To hang, thumbtack the loose ends of the cord to the Mylar curtain or apply Glue Dots to stick the banner to the window casing.

# Candy Clapperboard

Writing with sweets really gets the message across and guests are always charmed by it. For this table, it seemed only natural to fit a director's directive in, and after a few false starts, I finally figured out how to create the suggestion of a clapperboard without doing the obvious—which is piping one on a cake.

*Makes 1 platter.*

MATERIALS
Scrapbook paper
Yellow sugar candy beads
Black sanding sugar

TOOLS
Hot glue gun
Small paintbrush

1. Trim the paper to fit the platter you will be using. Using a pencil, write the words "Lights Camera Action!" onto the paper. Hot glue the yellow sugar candy beads to the letters on the paper.

2. Fill in around the candy beads with the black sanding sugar. Using the paintbrush, dust off any black sugar that has covered the yellow letters. Place the platter on the table and arrange the platter of ice cream sandwiches above it at a 45-degree angle.

# A Star Is Born Table Garland

...and aren't we all? Whether or not you're a fan of the Streisand hit (or the Judy Garland version), the sentiment is an uplifting one. Use the Template Index on pages 344–345 and download at http://blog.amyatlas.com, or use cookie cutters for the letters. Note that the cookies are hot glued to the garland, making them inedible—watch for little mouths that might be tempted to take a bite!

*Makes 1 garland.*

MATERIALS

Sugar Cookies, page 12

Royal Icing, page 15

Gold luster dust

Vanilla extract

TOOLS

2 yards gold cord

Small pastry brush

Hot glue gun

Masking tape

1. Cut the cookies from the dough using the templates or cutters and bake as directed. Decorate with the Royal Icing according to instructions for Outlining and Flooding Cookies with Royal Icing, page 17.

2. In a small bowl, combine the luster dust and enough vanilla extract to create a loose paintlike consistency. Using a small pastry brush, apply the luster dust to the cookies and let dry.

3. Lay the gold cord on a work surface. Arrange the letters along the cord to spell "A STAR IS BORN," beginning about 12 inches from the left loose end and leaving 12 inches loose at the right end also. Hot glue them to the cord at their very top and let dry thoroughly.

4. Hang the garland on the front of the table, affixing the loose ends to the underside of a platter with masking tape.

# Glamorous Glasses

On a night when style rules, leave no opportunity to dress up the table untapped. Deck out a plain drinking glass with a shimmering cuff and look-at-me red drink flag. Fill it with champagne or your favorite bubbly drink. See the Template Index on page 343 and download the drink flag template at http://blog.amyatlas.com.

*Makes 1 glass.*

MATERIALS

Gold glitter scrapbook paper

Glue Dots

White card stock, for drink flag

1  5-inch lollipop stick or straw

Strips of red paper movie tickets, for lining the serving tray (see Find It, page 359)

1. Cut a band of glitter scrapbook paper with the following dimensions: the circumference of the bottom of the glass + ½ inch × ¼ the height of the glass.

2. Wrap the cuff around the glass so that the bottom edge is flush with the bottom of the glass. Secure with a Glue Dot.

3. Download and print the template for the drink flag. Wrap the short, straight end around the lollipop stick (see page 29) and secure with a Glue Dot.

4. Fill the glass with champagne or your favorite bubbly drink, slide the flag in, and arrange all the glasses in single file on a rectangular tray lined with movie ticket strips.

# Star Tags

Stars are everywhere... To make these candy tags, go to http://blog.amyatlas.com to download the star template from page 342. There are two sizes—a larger version for the candy jars and a smaller one for the platters. You will find instructions for creating the correct size on my blog.

*Makes 1 tag.*

MATERIALS

    White card stock

    Black card stock, cut to fit the top of a candy jar lid

    Glue Dot

    Double stick tape

    Strips of red paper movie tickets, for lining
       the serving tray (see Find It, page 359)

Print the star template onto the white card stock and cut. Center it on the black cardstock lid cover with a Glue Dot. Attach to the jar lid with double-stick tape. For the stars on the dessert trays, simply print them onto white card stock, cut them, and tuck them into or lean them against each tray.

*Style It*

Use old-fashioned candy jars for this type of table. This is not a moment for dainty vessels.

# Movie Candy Favor Bags

What kind of movie experience is it without a bag, or box, of your favorite theater candy? You have to have something sweet and usually forbidden while you're sitting in the dark, watching the action on the big screen.

*Makes 1 bag.*

MATERIALS

    Decorative Candy Bags, page 29

    Patterned yellow card stock

    Red and yellow chocolate candy

    Strips of paper movie tickets (see Find It, page 359)

1. Fill the favor bags with a mix of red and yellow candy. Follow instructions for Decorative Candy Bags to complete.

2. Arrange the bags on a platter lined with strips of paper movie tickets and set on the table.

SHOP IT

## SHOP IT

Red jelly beans, to fill a candy jar

Yellow malt balls, to fill a candy jar

Foil-covered chocolate stars, to fill a candy jar

Red licorice nibs, to fill a candy jar

Yellow M&M's, to fill a candy jar

Red M&M's, to line a cupcake tray

Red and Yellow milkies, to fill favor bags

Yellow sugar candy beads, to line the ice cream
sandwich tray

Licorice wheels, to line the brownie tray and
embellish cupcakes

Black sanding sugar, to line the "Lights, Camera,
Action!" tray

## DISPLAY IT

Glitzy Curtain

Movie Night Marquee

Glittered Stars

Red Carpet Runway

A Star Is Born Garland

White tablecloth

Candy jars with lids

White platters, 10-inch-square and rectangular,
with small lip

## SWITCH IT

**GROW IT UP:** Serve with champagne or Casablan-
cas (a cocktail made with white rum, coconut
rum, pineapple juice, and grenadine syrup).

**GROW IT DOWN:** Offer sparkling cider.

# Vineyard Afternoon

There's nothing like a little taste of a vineyard to put guests into a relaxed mood. The very thought of such fragrant countryside is immediately transporting, which is the whole point of this quietly elegant table. Much like a fine wine—and you should bring out your best for this occasion—the spread slowly reveals its beauty (and delicious flavors) as the party goes on. I had no trouble deciding on the color palette, which is a departure from the rustic neutrals one might expect to see on a table like this. I chose vibrant shades that relate to the theme but exude a distinct, vivid personality. A beautiful red wine berry and a green the shade of olives or grapes seemed just right. I am forever raiding my closet for props, a move that came in handy for this particular table when I pulled a lightweight fringed scarf from a drawer—and saw it instantly as a table runner. Between the

12

# eye-catching palette and the unforgettable (and

incredibly fragrant!) rosemary wreath at the center of the table, there's not much more you need to make a statement here.

The vineyard concept gave me wonderful flavors to work with, and it lent itself to a striking rusticity when it came to planning the menu. You'll notice that this table is one of the few that features very little candy, but it is no less sweet. In fact, it's the only table in this book to offer up a selection of indulgent gourmet cheeses. Desserts predominate, however, primarily because the flavors and ingredients that hail from wine country are easily incorporated into cakes, cookies, and pies. Rosemary, pine nuts, hazelnuts, and olive oil all find their way into dessert here. Olive Oil Cake, one of my tried-and-true favorites, is always, always the first treat to be gobbled up. Funny, because its rather plain appearance doesn't even begin to suggest its deeply satisfying flavor. In fact, flavor drove every one of my sweets choices here; there's nothing subtle about the combination of rosemary and pine nuts in a crisp cookie; dark chocolate and dried figs; hazelnuts and rich, eggy store-bought biscotti; and tart, juicy berries in a buttery pie crust fresh from the bakery. And that's really the idea—to let the sweet offerings do all of the talking.

> **INSPIRATION:** Destination, Passion
> **PALETTE:** Red wine berry and olive green
> **PERFECT FOR:** Almost any celebration—book club gathering, wedding rehearsal party, intimate vineyard or at-home wedding, office gathering, birthday brunch, or deconstructed to use favorite elements for a concert in the park with friends

# Olive Oil Cake

Drenched in a subtly flavored, wine-infused simple syrup, this is a dense cake that is perfect both for dessert and with coffee in the morning. I've made it as an after-school snack cake for my boys (the wine in the simple syrup cooks off), minus the grapes and powdered sugar. But seriously, the greatest reason to recommend this cake is that it's as foolproof as it is delicious. Concord grapes offer the best flavor and color, but red seedless grapes can be substituted.

**Makes one 9-inch cake.**

- 1⅔ cups all-purpose flour
- ⅓ cup yellow cornmeal
- 2½ teaspoons baking powder
- 1¼ teaspoons salt
- 3 eggs
- 1 cup granulated sugar
- 1 cup olive oil
- 1 teaspoon orange zest
- ¼ cup white wine
- ½ cup milk
- 1 cup halved and seeded Concord grapes or purple grapes
- 1 bunch of Concord grapes or purple grapes

Confectioners' sugar, for dusting

FOR THE RED WINE SIMPLE SYRUP:
- ½ cup red wine
- ½ cup granulated sugar
- 2 tablespoons Concord grape jelly

1. Adjust an oven rack to the middle position and preheat oven to 375°F. Spray a 9-inch springform pan with nonstick cooking spray.

2. In a medium bowl, combine the flour, cornmeal, baking powder, and salt and stir to combine; set aside. In the bowl of a standing mixer fitted with the whisk attachment, combine the eggs and sugar and beat on medium-high speed until light, about 2 minutes. Reduce speed to medium and slowly add in oil. Add the orange zest and beat to mix. Reduce the speed to medium-low, add the white wine and milk, and beat until combined. Add the flour mixture and beat until combined. Remove the bowl from the mixer and fold in the grapes with a rubber spatula.

3. Pour the batter into the prepared pan and bake until the cake is golden brown and a toothpick inserted into the center comes out clean, 30 to 35 minutes. Place on wire rack.

4. In a small saucepan, combine the red wine, sugar, and jelly over medium heat and bring to a boil; set aside. While the cake is still warm, brush it with red wine syrup, letting syrup sink into top and down sides. Let cake cool in pan.

5. When ready to serve, remove cake from pan and set on serving plate. Place the grape bunch on the top and tap confectioners' sugar through a sieve and onto the cake.

## Style It

Rusticity rules this table: It's the ideal moment to bring out the chopping blocks, rattan and wooden platters, and slate cheese boards for serving vessels.

# Rosemary Pine Nut Cookies

I try to bake these as close to party time as possible because the aroma is irresistible: butter, fragrant rosemary, and toasted pine nuts. A killer combination!

**Makes about 40 2-inch cookies.**

¾ cup (1½ sticks) unsalted butter, softened
½ cup confectioners' sugar
¾ teaspoon salt
1 tablespoon minced fresh rosemary
½ teaspoon lemon zest
1 large egg yolk
2 cups all-purpose flour
1 egg white, lightly beaten
⅔ cup pine nuts

1. In the bowl of a standing mixer fitted with the paddle attachment, combine the butter, sugar, and salt and beat on medium speed until creamy, about 1 minute. Add the rosemary, lemon zest, and yolk and beat until combined. Add the flour and mix until thoroughly combined.

2. Transfer the dough onto a sheet of plastic wrap and roll into a 2-inch-diameter × 10-inch-long log. Roll up tightly, twisting ends of the plastic wrap to compact the log. Chill the dough until firm and sliceable, about 1 hour.

3. Adjust an oven rack to the middle position and preheat oven to 350°F. Line two baking sheets with parchment paper. Remove the plastic wrap and cut the log into ¼-inch-thick round slices. Place the slices on the pans, spacing them 1 inch apart. Brush around the edge of each cookie top with the egg white and press pine nuts in a single layer around the brushed edge.

4. Bake, one pan at a time, until cookies are light golden, 15 to 20 minutes. Let cookies cool on pan for 5 minutes, then transfer to wire rack to cool completely. Arrange the cookies on a cutting board in overlapping rows and place on the table. Garnish with the rosemary.

# Sangria on a Stick

Place these thirst-quenching pops on the table just as guests arrive—and offer them one immediately! Chill the serving tray first, then arrange the frozen treats on it.

**Makes 10 pops.**

- 1 cup red wine
- 1 cup diced apple
- ½ orange, diced
- ½ cup sliced raspberries
- ¾ cup orange juice
- ½ cup pineapple juice
- 3 tablespoons sugar
- 10 popsicle sticks
- Popsicle mold

When I first attempted the Rosemary Pine Nut cookies (opposite page), I sought to roll out the dough and cut them with cutters to get perfectly round circles. But perfection is not the point on a table with a rustic theme. If you plan to vary the menu, choose desserts accordingly.

1. Combine the red wine, apple, orange, and raspberries in a medium bowl and stir to combine. Set aside for at least 10 minutes.

2. Combine the orange juice, pineapple juice, and sugar in a small saucepan over medium heat. Heat, stirring occasionally, until the sugar just dissolves. Remove from the heat and let come to room temperature.

3. Meanwhile, set a strainer over a bowl and strain the fruit from the wine. Divide the strained fruit evenly among ten Popsicle molds. Add the wine to the cooled orange juice mixture. Pour the wine-juice mixture into each mold, filling to within ¼ inch of the rim at the top. Use a chopstick to dislodge any air bubbles. Freeze for 1 hour, then insert Popsicle sticks and freeze until completely firm, about 8 hours. As guests begin to arrive, set the popsicles out on a chilled tray and offer them one immediately.

CRAFT IT

# Provençal Wreath

Style It

The vertical element on a table doesn't always have to be edible! When a table needs the kind of height food just can't provide, focus on the backdrop, like I did with an oversize wreath.

I used half as many rosemary branches as I did olive branches here, and then tucked a lavender sprig in here and there. Use whatever combination of greenery you like; the trick is to use enough to create a lush wreath with no discernible gaps.

MATERIALS

Floral wire

Oval double wire frame, 4-foot-high × 3-foot-wide

Olive branches

Rosemary branches

Lavender

Command hook

TOOLS

Wire cutters

1. Leaving the floral wire on the paddle, attach the loose end to the crossbar on the wire frame.

2. Gather a small bundle of mixed greenery in your hand, lay it on the wire at the top of the oval (if you are making a round wreath, it doesn't matter where you begin) and wrap the wire securely around it, about three or four times. Do not cut the wire. Add another bundle, arranging it so that it overlaps the previous bundle, and wrap wire securely around it. Continue gathering, overlapping, and securing until you reach the point where you started.

3. Bring the wire to the back of the frame, wrap it around the wire frame a few times, and secure with a knot. Cut the wire, leaving about a 6-inch tail. Tie the end of the tail onto the wire frame to make a loop for hanging the wreath. Mount a Command hook on the wall, positioning it so that the wreath hangs in the center of the table and the bottom sits only slightly above the top of the table.

# Claret Favor Boxes

I love the shape and color of these take-aways, embellished with a grapevine handle and a rosebud. In vineyards, rosebushes are planted at the end of the rows of grapevines not necessarily for aesthetic reasons—though they are beautiful—but because they tip off the vintner if there are certain pests in the vineyard that might harm the grapes. Who knew?!! See the Template Index, page 343, for the leaves. Download and print them at http://blog.amyatlas .com.

**Makes 1.**

MATERIALS

    1 berry-colored trapezoid box, 4-inch-high ×
       2½-inch-wide × 1½-inch-wide at bottom

    Green twine

    10 inches floral wire

    Green floral tape

    Green construction paper, for the paper leaves

    Crepe paper rose (see Find It, page 360)

TOOLS

    Hole punch, ¼-inch

    Hot glue gun

1. Assemble box. Wrap the green twine on a diagonal around the floral wire and secure the ends with the floral tape to make the handle. Use the leaf template to trace the leaves onto the green construction paper. Cut out and set aside.

2. Flip open the larger of the 2 lids and punch two holes in the center, each ½ inch from the edge and parallel to the other. Bend the floral wire into a U-shape and tuck the ends into the holes. Bend back the ends on the underside of the lid to secure. Hot glue the leaves close to one side of the handle, then hot glue the flower at the base of the leaves.

# Sugar Dusted Fruit

A little superfine sugar and egg whites can turn a ho-hum bowl of fruit into an arrangement straight out of an Old Master painting. Gooorgeous! I've used supermarket grapes, apples, and pears here because they suit the theme, but this technique also works beautifully on citrus—lemons, limes, kumquats—for a holiday arrangement. Use as many egg whites as necessary to coat every piece of fruit you use. For these arrangements, about 6 whites should be enough. Remember, since there are raw egg whites, the dusted fruit is for decoration only.

MATERIALS

Superfine sugar
2 small bunches each green and purple grapes
12 small apples
12 D'Anjou or Seckel pears
Egg whites, beaten

TOOLS

All-paints paintbrush or small pastry brush
Green construction paper

1. Prepare two sheet pans with parchment and set aside.

2. Pour the sugar onto a dinner plate in a thin layer. Brush the fruit with a thin layer of egg white and roll in the sugar. Shake off excess. Transfer to the parchment and let dry.

The dusted fruit can be stored at room temperature in dry air up to 24 hours. Arrange the fruit in a tiered pie stand or compote, starting with the grapes and tucking the apples and pears in and among them.

3. To make the sugared fruits look more real, give them a leaf. See the Template Index, page 343, and download and print the template from http://blog.amyatlas.com.

# Cork Dessert Tag Holders

I love nothing more than an ingenious yet practical display solution, and this cork holder pretty much exemplifies that. Red wine should be opened in advance so that it can aerate, which means that if you're serving it, you can use the corks to make these. Keep in mind that not all wine is corked with real cork these days; you may need to stockpile these over the course of time. See the Template Index, page 343, and download and print the leaf template from http://blog.amyatlas.com.

**Makes 1 holder.**

MATERIALS

Green construction paper
1 cork wine cork

TOOLS

Utility knife

Using the leaf template on page 343, cut the green construction paper to make a leaf dessert tag. Using the utility knife, shave one side of the cork to make a flat edge. On the opposite side, make a ¼-inch horizontal slit down the length of the cork. Place the leaf dessert tag in the slit and set on table.

Blackberry or three-berry
pies with latticework
tops, set in pie stands
Pistachio nougat, ar-
ranged in overlapping
layers on a tray
Hazelnut and
chocolate-dipped
hazelnut biscotti,
arranged on a tray

Sugared jelly fruits,
arranged on a platter
Chocolate-dipped dried
figs
Selection of cheeses:
Goat, Bleu, Brie, Gouda,
Manchego, arranged on a
waxed paper–lined platter
Red wine

## DISPLAY IT

Chartreuse linen tablecloth
Berry wine–colored fringed scarf as table runner
Provençal Wreath
Slate platters for Sangria on a Stick and cheeses
Wrought-iron pie stands
Wooden cutting boards
Ceramic cheese markers

## SWITCH IT

**GROW IT UP:** In addition to a favorite wine, serve
an Italian Sunset (2 parts amaretto to 3 parts
each orange juice and club soda and a splash
of grenadine).

**GROW IT DOWN:** Serve sparkling grape juice.

**COLOR IT:** Try a monochromatic taupe palette
or orange and taupe.

# Spooktacular Halloween

probably don't need to mention that Halloween is one of
my favorite holidays of the year.
As a child, the whole idea behind this
candy-centric day seemed like a dream
come true. I could hardly believe that it was
completely acceptable to have all the candy
and chocolate I could eat—and that grown-
ups everywhere would happily push sweets
into my hands each time I shouted "trick or
treat!" (A note to my childhood neighbors:
If you were giving away Reese's Peanut
Butter Cups, I may have rung your door-
bell twice.)

This ultimate Halloween treat feast is
for fully costumed sweets: ghosts, witches,
pumpkins, jack-o'-lanterns, cobwebs—what
could be better than having all of that ico-
nography to inspire a spooktacular table?
The color palette, of course, is obvious.
Though the holiday is geared heavily
toward children, I wanted this table to

13

**appeal to all ages.** In other words, I was going for a festive yet elegant look. I started with a big visual punch, the centerpiece. It sets the tone. Spindly black-painted tree branches sprout from a neo-classical cast iron urn to create a spooky-chic focal point. The hanging licorice wheels give the goose bump–inducing impression that a spider might have just lowered itself down among the treats. Heighten this effect by sprinkling a handful of plastic creepy crawlies across the table and anywhere else where they might surprise an unsuspecting guest.

I took orange crepe fans, piled one atop another, and hung them so they creep across the wall in an undulating pattern. This brings a bit of energy to the setting. Allowing one color—orange—to predominate also gives the table a more sophisticated vibe; a few strong hits of black are all you really need to set it off. There's no shortage of playfulness, though. Who wouldn't love an oversize candy corn—that's actually a frosted brownie? Or a friendly witch, in a sugar cone hat with licorice hair and a candy corn nose, peering from atop cupcakes? There are ghosts, too, of course, cut from a pan of brownies, frosted in luminous white icing, and resting on their sides to appear as if they're floating across the room. Some of the offerings are more subtle—but all immediately bring to mind a symbol of the season. Simple orange paper bags filled with candy transform into pumpkins with just a wrap of floral tape; a cobweb of chocolate ensnares caramel apples; truffles coated in gold and orange sprinkles mimic a pile of gourds; and orange-tinted chocolate bark is cracked into foreboding shards. As for those colorful candy-coated chocolate-dipped pretzels? Call them witches' broomsticks! When you allow yourself to think even slightly out of the box, the sweets possibilities are endless. And isn't that what keeps every kid in us knocking on neighborhood doors on the most frightful night of the year?

**INSPIRED BY:** Holiday: a candy lover's favorite night of the year
**PALETTE:** Orange, black, and yellow
**PERFECT FOR:** Halloween party

# Bewitching Bark

The beautiful thing about this bark is that it can go from Halloween to the upcoming winter holidays with a switch of the food coloring. To get just the right shade of orange, mix the coloring gel in gradually. Of utmost importance, though, is the quality of the chocolate you use. A good-quality brand is essential—the chocolate will seize, or stiffen, if you use an inferior product.

**Makes 16 to 20 3-inch pieces.**

12 ounces good-quality white chocolate, such as Ghirardelli or Callebaut, finely chopped and melted (see How to Melt Chocolate, page 16)

Orange food coloring gel, to desired shade

4 ounces good-quality bittersweet chocolate, such as Ghirardelli or Callebaut, finely chopped and melted (see How to Melt Chocolate, page 16)

1. Line a baking sheet with foil and set aside.

2. Put a few dabs of the orange food coloring into the white chocolate, and stir, adding more color if necessary to achieve desired shade.

3. Spoon the orange chocolate into the prepared pan. Using a small offset spatula, spread to ⅛-inch-thick. Distribute the bittersweet chocolate over the orange chocolate by the tablespoonful in a random

ATTENTION: CHOCOLATE LOVERS!

# Chocolate Almond Bark with Sea Salt and Orange Peel

Rind of 1 navel orange, pith removed, chopped
    into ¼-inch pieces

½ cup granulated sugar

12 ounces bittersweet chocolate, finely chopped
    and melted (see How to Melt Chocolate,
    page 16)

⅔ cup chopped almonds

¾ teaspoon coarse or flaked sea salt

1. In a small saucepan, bring 2 cups of water to a boil. Add orange peel and simmer for 1 minute. Drain, rinse with water, and then repeat process with 2 more cups of fresh water.

2. Combine the sugar and ⅓ cup water in a small saucepan and heat over medium heat, bringing to a boil and stirring. Add the orange peel. Reduce heat to medium-low and simmer until the pieces are tender and become translucent, 20 to 25 minutes. With a slotted spoon, transfer peels to a baking sheet and let dry, about 1 hour.

3. Line a baking sheet with parchment. With an offset spatula, spread the chocolate onto parchment to ¼-inch-thick. Sprinkle the orange peel, almonds, and salt over the top. Chill until set, about 1 hour. Break into pieces and serve.

fashion. Drag a chopstick or butter knife through the chocolate in a swirled pattern, keeping the thickness of chocolate to ⅛-inch. Jiggle or tap the pan on the counter to settle the chocolate and smooth the top.

4. Cover with plastic wrap, making sure the plastic doesn't touch the chocolate, and chill until set, about 1 hour. Remove the bark from the pan and break into 3-inch pieces. Arrange on a footed cake stand and serve immediately or chill until ready to serve. Tie a 2-inch-wide ribbon into a bow around the stem of the cake stand.

# Wicked Pumpkin Cupcakes

Chocolate sugar cones for hats and shoelace licorice for hair—what could be more fun to share with a band of trick-or-treaters? These are ideal for making with grade-schoolers, who can't resist sneaking a few candy corns while turning them into noses!

**Makes 12.**

1¼ cups all-purpose flour
2 teaspoons baking powder
1 teaspoon baking soda
1½ teaspoons ground cinnamon
1 teaspoon ground ginger
½ teaspoon ground nutmeg
¼ teaspoon ground cloves
½ teaspoon salt
6 tablespoons unsalted butter, softened
½ cup packed light brown sugar
¼ cup granulated sugar
2 tablespoons vegetable oil
1 large egg
¼ cup sour cream
1 teaspoon vanilla
1 cup pumpkin puree
Quick Vanilla Buttercream, page 14
Orange food coloring gel
12 chocolate sugar cones
Black shoelace licorice, cut into 3-inch lengths and
    ½-inch lengths
24 chocolate M&M's, for the eyes
12 candy corns, for the noses

1. Adjust oven rack to middle position and preheat oven to 375°F. Line a cupcake tin with yellow cupcake liners.

2. Sift the flour, baking powder, baking soda, cinnamon, ginger, nutmeg, cloves, and salt into a medium bowl and set aside.

3. In the bowl of a standing mixer fitted with the paddle attachment, combine the butter, brown sugar, and granulated sugar and beat on medium-high speed until light and fluffy, about 3 minutes. Add the vegetable oil and beat until combined. Add the egg and beat until combined, scraping down the sides of the bowl once or twice.

4. Reduce the speed to medium and add the sour cream, vanilla, and pumpkin puree and beat until combined.

5. Reduce the speed to medium-low and add the flour mixture until just combined. Give the batter a good stir with a rubber spatula to insure that it's thoroughly combined.

6. Divide batter evenly among the cupcake liners, filling them to the brim to get a domed-top shape for the witches heads. Bake until just set, about 20 minutes. The cupcakes should spring back when tapped in the center. Let cool in the pan for 5 minutes, then remove and let cool completely on a wire rack.

7. Add a few dabs of the orange food coloring gel to the buttercream and stir to combine thoroughly. Add more coloring as necessary to achieve a light orange tint. Spoon about two tablespoons of buttercream onto each cupcake and, using an offset spatula, spread until smooth all over.

8. Place an ice cream cone "hat" onto each buttercream "head," tilting it slightly to leave room for the "face." Tuck the longer strands of licorice into the buttercream around the sides and back of the rim of the hat. Place the shorter strands in the front, for the bangs. Create eyes and a nose with the chocolate M&M's and candy corn.

9. Fill two deep-rimmed trays with orange, yellow, and black M&M's. Arrange the cupcakes on top and place on the table.

Style It

Angle the hats slightly to the back on the cupcakes to bring the witches to life!

***easy does it*** *Jell-O Instant Pudding and Pie Filling makes a delicious pumpkin spice pudding for an easy swap-out for homemade whoopie pies. Chill it in votive glasses and arrange on the pedestal.*

# Pumpkin Whoopie Pies

As a pumpkin-lover, I get full-on excited by this seasonal take on the classic chocolate and vanilla combination. Cinnamon, ginger, and clove-spiked (don't be alarmed by the amount of spices used here; you need every speck of them!) cake-like cookies are spread with unctuous cream; they are the perfect handheld goodie on Halloween and every other day of autumn.

**Makes 12 3-inch pies.**

2¼ cups all-purpose flour
1 tablespoon ground cinnamon
1 tablespoon ground ginger
¾ teaspoon ground cloves
¾ teaspoon salt
¾ teaspoon baking powder
¾ teaspoon baking soda
1 large egg
1 large egg yolk
1½ cups packed light brown sugar
2 teaspoons vanilla
1¼ cups pumpkin puree
¾ cup plus 1 tablespoon vegetable oil
Cream Cheese Frosting, page 14

1. Adjust oven rack to the middle position and preheat oven to 350°F. Line 2 baking sheets with parchment paper.

2. Sift flour, cinnamon, ginger, cloves, salt, baking powder, and baking soda into a medium bowl; set aside. In a large bowl, whisk together the egg, egg yolk, and sugar until combined. Whisk in the vanilla until combined. Add the pumpkin puree and oil and whisk until the mixture is smooth. Add the flour mixture in batches and whisk until smooth after each addition.

3. Fill a pastry bag fitted with a plain tip (Wilton Round Tip #2a) with the batter. Pipe 2¼-inch round mounds onto prepared baking sheets, spacing them 2 inches apart. Bake, one pan at a time, until just firm, 15 to 17 minutes. Let cool in pan for 5 minutes and then transfer to a wire rack to cool.

4. Meanwhile, make the frosting. Spoon it onto the flat side of half the pumpkin cookies. Top each with another cookie, flat side down. Arrange directly on the pedestal, in a pyramid, and set on the table. The whoopie pies can be made one day in advance and kept, tightly covered and refrigerated.

# Candy Corn Brownies

What could be cuter than a brownie shaped and decorated like the season's iconic sweet, candy corn? Use a knife and the candy corn template (see page 343 and download the template at http://blog.amyatlas.com) or a candy corn–shaped cookie cutter (see Find It, page 361) to cut these out.

**Makes 8.**

Fudge-y Brownies, page 13
Royal Icing, page 15
Orange food coloring gel
Yellow food coloring gel
Orange sanding sugar

1. Turn the cooled brownies out onto a work surface in a single piece. Cut out using a knife and the template as your guide. Alternatively, dip a candy corn cutter into hot water, wipe down, and cut out the brownies.

2. To decorate, follow the instructions for Outlining and Flooding Cookies with Royal Icing, page 17, dividing the icing among three bowls for orange, yellow, and white. Use the orange icing to outline the bottom section of the candy corn, the yellow to outline the middle section and the white to outline the top section. Allow to dry for around an hour. Then flood each section, spreading out the icing with a toothpick. Immediately sprinkle the bottom section with orange sanding sugar and leave to dry.

3. With the remaining orange icing, pipe squiggly lines across the candy corn at the places where the colors meet. Let dry for at least 4 hours. Arrange the candy corns on their sides directly on pedestals.

# Hauntingly Good Hazelnut Truffles

Hazelnut and chocolate melted together, chilled, formed into Ping-Pong-size balls, and rolled in sprinkles: scarily good. These tend to disappear quickly, so it's not a bad idea to stick a stash in the refrigerator to replenish the supply.
I find that sometimes the truffle mixture can become quite sticky on your palms and refuse to roll properly. Simply wash your hands and continue rolling!

**Makes 2 dozen.**

   1 cup good-quality bittersweet chocolate chips, such as Ghirardelli, melted (see How to Melt Chocolate, page 16)
  12 tablespoons hazelnut spread
   6 tablespoons unsalted butter, very soft
   ½ cup chopped hazelnuts
   ¾ cup yellow and orange sprinkles

1. In a large bowl, add the hazelnut spread and butter to the melted chocolate and stir with a wooden spoon until thoroughly combined. Stir in the hazelnuts. Chill until firm enough to scoop, 45 minutes to 1 hour.

2. Dump the sprinkles onto a rimmed plate. Scoop a flat tablespoon of the chocolate mixture into the palm of your hand and roll into a ball, then roll in the sprinkles and place on a sheet pan.

3. Chill again until firm, at least 30 minutes. Arrange the truffles in footed compotes and place on the table.

*easy does it* Replace the truffles with Entenmann's seasonal Pop'Ems or Dunkin' Donuts chocolate Munchkins.

# Ghost Brownies

Royal Icing makes the perfect ghost costume—so luminous and ethereal that it can appear spooky. Use a knife and the ghost template (see page 343 and download the template at http://blog.amyatlas.com) or a ghost-shaped cookie cutter (see Find It, page 361) to cut these out.

Makes 8.

Fudge-y Brownies, page 13

Royal Icing, page 15

White luster dust

Vodka or vanilla extract

Black candy for eyes, like small chocolate M&M's

1. Turn the cooled brownies out onto a work surface in a single piece. Cut out using a knife and the template as your guide. Alternatively, dip the ghost cutter into hot water, wipe down, and cut out the brownies.

2. To decorate, follow the instructions for Outlining and Flooding Cookies with Royal Icing, page 17. Pipe an outline around each ghost and leave to dry for around 1 hour. Then flood the brownie, using a toothpick to spread out the icing. Let it dry for at least 1 hour.

3. Combine the luster dust with enough vodka or vanilla extract to create a loose paintlike consistency. If the luster paint becomes dry as you work, add more liquid. Paint the luster dust over the Royal Icing. Add two candies to each ghost for eyes. Let dry.

4. Arrange the ghosts on their sides directly on the pedestal.

## Style It

Arrange the ghosts on their sides so that they look as though they're flying off the table.

# Witches' Broomsticks

Salty, sweet, and colorful—is there anything more one could want from a pretzel? These rods are dipped in chocolate and rolled in sprinkles, chocolate chips, and Reese's Pieces, and will fly off the table faster than a witch's broomstick.

**Makes 20.**

- 1 cup Reese's Pieces
- 1 cup mini semisweet chocolate chips
- 3 cups orange, yellow, and brown sprinkles
- 12 ounces good-quality dark chocolate, such as Callebaut or Ghirardelli, finely chopped and melted (see How to Melt Chocolate, page 16)
- 20 8-inch pretzel logs

1. Line a baking sheet with parchment paper and set aside.

2. Place the Reese's Pieces, chocolate chips, and sprinkles on 3 separate pieces of parchment paper.

3. Hold a pretzel by one end over the bowl of melted chocolate and spoon the chocolate over it, turning the pretzel until all but 1 inch is coated. Use the back of the spoon to scrape excess back into the bowl.

4. Holding the rod over the parchment sheets, first sprinkle the sprinkles over the pretzel and then sprinkle the chocolate chips over it, turning the rod as you go. Let the excess candy fall back onto the parchment sheets. Lay the rod on parchment paper and then press the Reese's Pieces over the rod. Repeat with remaining pretzel rods. Chill until completely set, at least 30 minutes.

5. Arrange the rods directly on a pedestal on the table, stacking them in a pyramid shape.

# Broomsicles

There's no double, double, toil and trouble here, no fire burning, no cauldron bubbling. Instead, I went for the chill. A frothy float made with sparkling orange soda and vanilla ice cream spiked with vanilla vodka seemed better suited to this table, and it gave me the opportunity to use the perfect stirrer, a tiny upended broom. Skip the alcohol and serve it to tiny monsters, too! Instead of placing it on the table, serve the drink to guests as they arrive.

**Makes 1 6-ounce drink.**

- 5 ounces orange soda
- 1 ounce vanilla vodka
- 2 small scoops vanilla ice cream, enough to fill an 8-ounce glass half-full

1. Combine the orange soda and vanilla vodka in a large measuring cup.

2. Put two small scoops of ice cream into an 8-ounce glass. Pour the vodka-soda mix over it, tilting the glass slightly while pouring, to minimize foam. Slide a broomstick stirrer into the glass and serve (see page 308).

# Haunted Forest Tree

Branches always make an excellent centerpiece, whether they are stripped of their leaves for a macabre vibe or are bursting with blossoms and foliage for a more cheerful occasion. They never fail to deliver the vertical element every table needs—and in this case, the perfect hooks for party favors.

**Makes 1 centerpiece.**

MATERIALS

Floral foam, cut to fit within 1 inch of urn rim

Urn or fluted vase, 18 inches high

Armload of slender tree branches, stripped
    of foliage

Orange pumpkin malt balls, enough to cover
    the floral foam

3  orange 12-foot streamers

2  black 12-foot streamers

"Boo" spider or your desired stamps (see Find It,
    page 361)

Black ink pad

Orange ink pads

24  3-inch-wide × 4-inch-tall glassine envelopes

Seasonal licorice pastels, for filling bags

Orange embroidery thread, cut into 8-inch lengths

Glue Dots or double stick tape

Licorice wheels

1. Put the floral foam into the vase and insert the branches, one at a time, to mimic the shape of a tree. Fill the vase with the pumpkin malt balls.

2. Hang the streamers from the branches, allowing them to drape in extended U shapes.

3. Stamp the glassine envelopes. Fill one envelope with the licorice pastels and fold the top over on itself by 1 inch. Slide a length of embroidery thread along the crease of the fold, then secure the fold with Glue Dots or double stick tape. Tie the ends of the thread together and hang from a branch on the tree. Slide a length of embroidery thread through the hole in a licorice wheel, tie off, and hang from a branch.

4. Repeat with remaining bags and wheels, distributing them evenly among the branches.

# Pumpkin Orange Pedestals

Apart from the urn filled with branches in the center of the table, there was little in the way of height on this table, so I created it myself with these fabric-wrapped boxes.

**Makes 4.**

MATERIALS

- 2 12- × 12-inch × 3-inch-high pieces of Styrofoam, cake dummy, or floral foam
- 2 6- × 6-inch × 3-inch-high pieces of Styrofoam, cake dummy, or floral foam
- 3 yards orange silk shantung
- 5 yards ¼-inch orange satin ribbon
- Dressmaker pins

See Pretty Pedestal, page 25, to wrap the forms. Trim the top edge with the ribbon, securing every few inches with a dressmaker pin.

## Style It

When choosing store-bought candies, give your inner sugar-loving child free rein and candy up with the good stuff! Use a heavy hand and go for all the seasonal favorites like candy corn, licorice, and M&M's. It just isn't Halloween without them.

# Pumpkin Goodie Bag

A take-away treats bag is an absolute must—whether your invitees are candy-crazed children or just kids at heart. This one could not be easier, but it has a huge visual impact. Orange bag plus candy plus brown floral tape equals a sweet, sweet pumpkin.

**Makes 1.**

MATERIALS

- 1 orange mini craft bag (6¼-inch-high × 3½-inch-wide × 2-inch-deep)
- Black, orange, and gold licorice pastels
- Brown floral tape
- Orange embroidery thread

Fill the bag to ¾-full with the licorice pastels. Twist the bag closed to form a stem. Stretch the floral tape slightly, then wrap it around the stem, beginning at the bottom of the stem and working your way to the top. Wrap the tape around the top several times. Tie a length of thread around the stem and double knot it, leaving 5-inch tails. Make 1 for each guest and arrange them on either side of the table.

# Patch of Pumpkins Garland

Here's a good example of the power of many. On its own, a crepe foldout fan is pretty, but hang two dozen of them in an overlapping amorphous pattern and they become something else altogether.

**Makes one 8-foot wall hanging.**

MATERIALS

24 orange foldout honeycomb fans (see Find It, page 361)

Glue Dots

Orange embroidery thread, cut into varying lengths depending on the height of your wall

Thumbtacks

1. Open up the fans and secure with Glue Dots if the fans do not have a hook to secure them. For the lowest lying fans, tie lengths of thread to the existing string on the fans, so you can hang them very low. Vary the lengths so that the layer flows with the height of the branches. Affix the thread to the wall with thumbtacks.

2. Add a third layer of fans in a random pattern along the length of the backdrop. Affix with thumbtacks. Repeat with a fourth, fifth, and sixth layer, positioning the fans to create dimension.

# Chocolate Favor Boxes

A refined way to package Halloween treats for the adults at the gathering.

Makes 1.

MATERIALS

1 small black linen box (3¼-inch-wide × 2¾-inch-high × 2¼-inch-deep)

Orange malt balls, for filling

28 inches ⅛-inch satin ribbon

Fill the box to ¾-full with the malt balls and close. Wrap the ribbon around the middle of the box two times, making an X pattern on the front. Tie off in a bow in the back.

## Style It

If you love cobwebs, I say go for it and craft a simple DIY table runner using faux spiderwebs. You can buy the basic white cotton fluff everywhere. Make it much spookier by spray-painting it black and then drape it loosely across the table. The overall effect is striking. Swap out the black serving pieces for your everyday white ones. They'll absolutely pop against all the black "webs."

# Broomsicle Stirrer

Makes 1.

MATERIALS

Length of raffia

Wooden skewer

Glue Dots

1. Cut 10 pieces of raffia, 5 inches long each. Fold each piece in half. Cut another piece of raffia, also 5 inches long.

2. Gather the 10 pieces together into a bunch to make a "broom." The cut sides should be up. Wrap the single 5-inch piece around the bunch, ¼ inch from the bottom.

3. Slide the skewer into the raffia broom, so that the broom is at the top of your skewer. If necessary, secure with a Glue Dot or use a hot glue gun.

## SHOP IT

Orange, yellow, and black licorice pastels in a
   lidded candy jar and for lining vessels
Licorice allsorts, orange, black, and white only,
   piled onto a small tray
Candy corn, piled on a small tray
Orange- and candy corn–flavored saltwater
   taffy, piled onto a small tray
Ghost and jack-o'-lantern brownies on a stick
Cobweb caramel apples

## DISPLAY IT

Patch of Pumpkins Wall Hanging
Haunted Forest Tree
Urn filled with pumpkin malt balls
Orange silk shantung tablecloth
Black-rimmed trays, compotes, cake stand, and
   small dishes
Fabric-covered pedestals
Tiny plastic ants
Pumpkin Goodie Bags

## SWAP IT OUT

Nothing says fall quite like a caramel
apple. Swap out the purchased cobweb
caramel apple for the Caramel Lady Apples
on page 220.

## SWITCH IT

**GROW IT UP**: Serve with Broomsicles (page 303) or
   classic Zombies.
**GROW IT DOWN**: Serve Virgin Broomsicles (page 303).

# New Year's Eve Buffet

**H**appy New Year! Yes, I know fountains of champagne glasses are what you would normally expect at a New Year's party, but I'm not much of a drinker. I'll take a fountain of pretty, delicious candy to ring in the New Year any day. And that's where the inspiration for this table began. Champagne from a fountain is the kind of thing that mesmerizes even the teetotalers at a party. What's better than a sky-high stack of anything indulgent? So, as you might have guessed, I created not one, but three fountains of sweet tidings for the New Year. This is not necessary, but you must admit that they certainly scream,

**14**

# "There's no other day of the year like this one."

Short of getting the candy to flow from one dish to another (as champagne would if I actually included one of those fountains), I figured out how to create the illusion of movement with this table and at the same time allow it to exude a beautiful stillness. It's a yin-and-yang sensibility that I often like to achieve, and it's especially relevant for ringing in the New Year. Who doesn't resolve to bring balance into their lives?

But back to those fountains. Because they provide the striking vertical element for this table, I next considered the horizontals. Bring on the parade of paper lanterns, hung in two rows from table end to table end. Strung with ethereal snowflake garlands, they make the whole table seem as if it's floating. A perforated white table runner picks up where the lanterns leave off. With all of that height and weightlessness, all I needed to round out this winter wonderland was a menu of memorable treats—season-inspired gingerbread cupcakes, not-too-sweet crispy rice cereal bars grown up with flaky coconut; buttery, nutty shortbread snowballs; and elegant ice-blue petits fours topped with silver nonpareils. And then there are the homemade snowy marshmallows, perhaps the most potent symbol here: They're all sweetness and light. And isn't that just how the coming year should be?

INSPIRED BY: Holiday
PALETTE: Ice blue, silver, and white
PERFECT FOR: New Year's Eve buffet, wedding (minus the snowflakes, if desired), baby shower

# Coconut Crispy Rice Cereal Bars

If you've flipped through this book, you may have noticed that I owe a debt to puffed rice cereal. There aren't many other desserts that can handle a variety of add-ins and -ons and can be cut into almost any shape. In keeping with the ethereal look of this table, I added shredded coconut straight from the package to mimic the idea of fresh fallen snow. You can also toast the coconut for a nuttier flavor (see directions below). Use a stockpot to melt the marshmallows in; anything smaller and the mixture tends to overflow when mixing in the crispy rice cereal.

**Makes 45 2½- × 1-inch rectangles.**

  5 cups coconut, divided
  8 tablespoons (1 stick) unsalted butter
  ⅜ teaspoon salt
20 ounces marshmallows
  ½ teaspoon coconut extract
9½ cups crispy rice cereal
  1 cup confectioners' sugar

1. Spray a 9- × 13-inch pan with nonstick cooking spray and set aside. Adjust oven rack to middle position and preheat oven to 350°F. Spread 4 cups of the coconut onto a large, rimmed baking sheet and bake until just golden, about 10 minutes, stirring once or twice so coconut bakes evenly. Let coconut cool completely.

2. In a large stockpot combine the butter and salt and melt over medium heat. Add the marshmallows and melt, stirring constantly. Remove from heat and stir in the coconut extract. Add the toasted coconut and crispy rice cereal and stir to combine. Using a clean spatula that has been sprayed with nonstick spray, immediately spread mixture into prepared pan. Let set at room temperature, about 1 hour.

3. In a medium bowl, stir together confectioners' sugar and 1 to 3 tablespoons water until smooth. Spread over rice crispy mixture and top with remaining coconut. Let topping set, about 1 hour. Cut into 2½ × 1-inch rectangles and arrange on a tray lined with paper, spacing the treats about ½ inch apart.

*easy does it* Sometimes a little embellishment on a packaged sweet is all you need. Buy prepared crispy rice cereal treats and frost and top with coconut as above.

# Pound Cake Ice Cubes

Tinted ever so slightly with food coloring gel, the luminescent glaze on these buttery little bites hardens to create a surface as slick as an ice cube. A single pearlized nonpareil, applied with a tweezer for ease, dots the center.

**Makes 24 1-inch pound cake cubes.**

Simple Glaze, page 15, doubled
Light blue food coloring gel
2 loaves store-bought pound cake
White pearlized nonpareils

1. Prepare a baking sheet with parchment and set a rack over it. Set aside. In a bowl, add a few dabs of the food coloring gel to the glaze and stir until thoroughly incorporated. Add more gel to achieve desired color if necessary. Cover with plastic wrap and set aside.

2. Using a serrated knife, trim the crust from the pound cakes on all sides. Slice the pound cakes into 1- × 1-inch cubes, using an exaggerated sawing motion to get a smooth cut. Transfer to the rack.

3. Using a teaspoon, drizzle the glaze over each pound cake cube, then patch the exposed parts on the sides with more. Using an offset tweezer, place a single pearlized nonpareil in the center of each cube. Let set in a cool, dry place for at least 1 hour. Arrange in a single layer on a platter lined with the pearlized nonpareils and set on the table. The pound cake cubes will keep, stored in an airtight container, up to 2 days.

*easy does it* Swap out the pound cake for white chocolate–covered Oreos. Dress them up with a nonpareil pressed into their centers.

# Snowcapped Gingerbread Cupcakes

Winter holidays beg for warm spices, so I anointed these cupcakes my signature New Year's confection. Spread with ridiculously delicious white chocolate buttercream (just *try* not to eat a spoonful or two!) and dotted with nonpareils, they're a wonderful wintry sweet.

Makes 12.

- 1⅛ cups all-purpose flour
- 2 teaspoons ground ginger
- ½ teaspoon ground cinnamon
- ¼ teaspoon baking soda
- ¼ teaspoon salt
- ⅛ teaspoon ground cloves
- ⅛ teaspoon ground nutmeg
- ½ cup granulated sugar
- 1 egg
- ⅓ cup molasses
- 4 tablespoons (½ stick) unsalted butter, melted
- 1 tablespoon vegetable oil
- ½ cup buttermilk

FOR THE WHITE CHOCOLATE BUTTERCREAM:

- ¼ cup granulated sugar
- 1 large egg white
- Pinch salt
- 7 tablespoons unsalted butter, cut into pieces and softened
- ½ teaspoon vanilla extract
- 4 ounces good-quality white chocolate, such as Ghirardelli or Callebaut, melted and slightly cooled (see How to Melt Chocolate, page 16)
- Light blue nonpareils

1. Adjust an oven rack to the middle position and preheat oven to 350°F. Line a standard cupcake tin with cupcake liners. In a medium bowl, whisk together the flour, ginger, cinnamon, baking soda, salt, cloves, and nutmeg; set aside. In a large bowl, whisk sugar, egg, molasses, butter, oil, and buttermilk. Add the flour mixture to the wet mixture and whisk until just combined.

2. Divide the batter among the cupcake cups and bake until cupcakes are just set and a toothpick inserted in the center comes out clean, about 17 minutes. Let cupcakes cool in pan for 5 minutes, then transfer the cupcakes to a wire rack to cool completely.

3. Meanwhile, make the buttercream. In the bowl of a standing mixer fitted with the whisk attachment, combine the sugar, egg white, and salt and whisk on medium speed until combined. Place the bowl over a pan of simmering water and whisk with a hand whisk until temperature reaches 150°F on a kitchen thermometer. Return the bowl to the mixer and whisk on medium-high speed until the mixture is thick and glossy, about 1 minute. Reduce the speed to medium and add the butter, one piece at a time, until combined. Reduce the speed to medium-low and add vanilla and white chocolate and beat until smooth.

4. Using an offset spatula, frost the cupcakes, using a swirling motion to give the tops a billowy look. Sprinkle the nonpareils on top. Arrange on a tray lined with paper, spacing the cupcakes an inch apart.

# Classic Marshmallows

If you've never had a homemade marshmallow, pop one of these in your mouth; you will resolve never to eat the supermarket version again. They are so easy to make and so tasty (and less loaded with ingredients you can't pronounce). Of course, the artisanal variety work as well as homemade if you're time-pressed, so go right ahead and Shop It at your favorite bakeshop or sweetery.

**Makes 16 2-inch cubes.**

- 2 cups confectioners' sugar, divided
- 2 tablespoons plus 2½ teaspoons unflavored gelatin
- 2 cups plus 2 tablespoons granulated sugar, divided
- ½ cup light corn syrup
- 2 large egg whites
- 1 tablespoon vanilla

1. Prepare an 8- × 8-inch baking pan with vegetable oil, rubbing it on the bottom and sides. Place ⅓ cup of the confectioners' sugar in the pan and tilt and tap to coat.

2. Place ½ cup of water in a small bowl and sprinkle the gelatin over it. (If there is any dry gelatin on the top, sprinkle a bit of water over the top and gently stir so all of the gelatin will soften.) Let mixture sit until gelatin has softened, about 10 minutes.

3. In a medium saucepan, combine ½ cup water with 2 cups of the granulated sugar and the ½ cup corn syrup. Stir over medium-high heat until sugar has dissolved. Using a pastry brush, brush sides of pan to return any sugar crystals to the mixture. Cook, without stirring, until syrup registers 240°F on a candy thermometer.

4. Remove from the heat and gently whisk in the softened gelatin until dissolved.

In the bowl of a standing mixer fitted with the whisk attachment, whip egg whites on medium-high speed until frothy. Add the remaining 2 tablespoons of granulated sugar and continue to whip until egg whites form stiff but not dry peaks; transfer to a small bowl. Immediately rinse and dry mixer bowl and whisk attachment and return these to the mixer.

5. Pour the syrup mixture into a very clean mixing bowl and whisk on high speed until thick, white, glossy, and the consistency of shaving cream, about 5 minutes. Reduce the speed to medium and mix in vanilla.

6. Using a rubber spatula, gently fold in whipped egg whites until completely combined. Immediately spread the mixture into the prepared pan and lightly smooth top. Sift ⅓ cup of the confectioners' sugar over the top. Let marshmallows set at room temperature, at least 3 hours.

7. Place the remaining confectioners' sugar in a medium bowl. Using a greased knife, cut marshmallows into 16 2-inch squares. Toss marshmallows in sugar, one at a time, to coat. Arrange the marshmallows in a pyramid on a footed cake stand and set on the table.

**easy does it** *Only artisanal substitutes will do! I have my sources, which you can find on page 362.*

# Shortbread Snowballs

Also known as Mexican Wedding Cookies, these buttery, nutty little numbers melt in your mouth like a snowball and are terrifyingly addictive. The pretty little pyramids of them tend to come down fast, so I always make extra to build them back up. If you share your New Year's celebrations with children, it's wise to set out a small bowl of snowballs for little hands—reaching for them at the tippity top of the tower of compotes can cause the towers to tumble!

**Makes 36 to 40.**

1 cup unsalted butter, softened

½ cup plus 1 tablespoon confectioners' sugar, plus more for coating cookies

¾ teaspoon salt

1 teaspoon vanilla extract

1¼ cup walnuts, finely chopped in the food processor

2¼ cups all-purpose flour

1. In the bowl of a standing mixer fitted with the paddle attachment, combine the butter, sugar, and salt, and cream them on medium speed until combined. Reduce the speed to medium-low, add the vanilla, and mix until combined. Add the walnuts and flour and mix until completely combined. Chill until firm enough to handle, about 1 hour.

2. Line 2 baking sheets with parchment paper. Roll the dough into 1-inch balls. Place balls on prepared pan, spacing 1 inch apart. Chill dough balls on pan until very firm, about 1 more hour.

3. Adjust oven rack to the middle position and preheat oven to 400°F. Bake one sheet of cookies at a time until they are set, about 10 minutes. Let cool on pan.

4. Meanwhile, dump confectioners' sugar onto a dinner plate. Roll the warm cookies in the sugar. Let cool completely and roll again. Arrange the cookies in pyramids in a pair of footed compotes and set on table.

***easy does it*** *Replace the cookies with Dunkin' Donuts powdered sugar Munchkins or Entenmann's Pop'Ems.*

## Style It

Candy comes in handy when you need to give your sweets a lift. Whether filling up a footed vase or a deep, rimmed tray, rock candy crystals, M&M's, nonpareils, lemon sours, jelly beans, Life Savers—I could go on—make enticing fillers. See page 36–37 for the possibilities.

# White Birch Pretzel Rods

It might sound corny, but my little boys really do inspire me—these salty, chocolatey rods being a case in point. They're among Zach and Josh's favorite things to make (and eat) with me since we love the combination of sweet and salty. We usually set out ramekins filled with toppings and the boys create little masterpieces by sprinkling the rods with all types of candy (see pages 36–37). Here is my decidedly adult version—dipped and decorated for the occasion.

*Makes 16 to 20.*

Silver dragées

12 ounces good-quality white chocolate, such as
    Ghirardelli or Callebaut, melted (see How to
    Melt Chocolate, page 16)

20 8-inch pretzel rods

1. Line a baking sheet with parchment paper and set aside. Place the bottom of an egg carton wrong side up on a work surface and poke rod-size holes in each egg holder. Set aside. Alternatively, line a sheet pan with a piece of parchment. Pour the dragées on a dinner plate and set aside.

2. Hold 1 pretzel rod at a time by one end over the bowl and spoon chocolate over it, turning the pretzel until it is entirely coated beyond your fingers. Use the back of the spoon to scrape off excess back into the bowl.

3. Holding each rod over the plate of dragées, sprinkle them all over it, turning the rod as you go. Let the excess sprinkles fall back onto the plate. Place the uncoated end of the rod into a hole in the egg carton or lay the rod on the parchment. Repeat with all the pretzel rods. Chill until completely set, about 30 minutes. Repeat coating and sprinkling on the exposed end of the pretzels and return, wet side up, to the egg carton or lay the rods on the parchment. Chill until set. Fill a footed vase with a few inches of white rock candy crystals. Fan the pretzel rods in the compote and place on the table.

# Spiked White Hot Chocolate

Frosty, complete with magic black hat (Oreo Cakester) and scarf (yarn),
warms up this frothy rum-flavored chill chaser.

**Makes 6 8-ounce drinks.**

- 5 cups whole milk
- 1 teaspoon cinnamon
- 2 cardamom pods
- 1 vanilla bean, halved and seeds scraped and reserved, or 2 teaspoons vanilla extract
- 6 ounces good-quality white chocolate, such as Ghirardelli or Callebaut, roughly chopped
- ¼ cup rum
- Whipped cream, for garnishing

FOR THE SNOWMAN STIRRER:

- 12 marshmallows
- Orange, black, and red edible markers
- 6 5-inch lollipop sticks
- 6 Mini Oreo Cakesters
- 24 6-inch strands winter blue merino yarn

1. In a medium saucepan, combine milk, cinnamon, cardamom, and vanilla seeds. Bring the milk to a boil, then remove from the heat and set aside for 15 minutes, allowing the spices to steep in the milk as it cools.

2. Strain the milk to remove the spices, then return it to the pot. Add the white chocolate and rum. Heat the milk until the white chocolate has melted, stirring with a wooden spoon. When ready to serve, ladle into mugs and top each with a dollop of whipped cream. Tuck a Snowman Stirrer in each and serve.

3. To make a Snowman Stirrer, make a face on 1 marshmallow using edible markers. Slide it and 1 more marshmallow onto the top of a lollipop stick, pushing the stick through so that it comes out the other side. Slide a Cakester onto the stick just far enough to catch it. Tie the yarn around the seam where the two marshmallows meet.

# Snowflake Garland

I love the way these snowflakes look as if they are constantly falling; the way they flutter when guests walk past the table. Fishing line helps to create the illusion, and I, for one, can't live without it. It disappears and lets the delicate flakes twinkle in the air. In addition to the garland, you may want to attach a single snowflake from a length of fishing line and hang it vertically from the wire on the bottom of each lantern.

**Makes 1 16-foot-long garland.**

MATERIALS

    3  each of 8-, 10-, 12-, and 16-inch white paper lanterns

    Command hooks or thumbtacks

    Opalescent lavender scrapbook paper

    Opalescent baby blue scrapbook paper

    6  yards fishing line

TOOLS

    Arctic snowflake punch, 2-inch (see Find It, page 362)

    Hot glue gun

1. Hang the lanterns in two rows from Command hooks or thumbtacks in the ceiling.

2. Punch out eight each of the lavender and baby blue snowflakes. Hot glue the fishing line to each snowflake, beginning 6 inches from one end of the fishing line and alternating the lavender and baby blue snowflakes. This will be your garland.

Paper punches are just one of my secret weapons—they come in tons of designs and can turn a simple piece of paper or paper container into a handmade decoration, just like that. They're especially handy when you want to add a little dash to a purchased sweet.

3. To hang the garland, secure one end to the bottom wire of the lantern that hangs the farthest left. Thread it through the bottoms of three or four paper lanterns, allowing excess to hang from each one. Secure the remaining loose end to the bottom wire of the lantern that hangs the farthest right.

4. Make a second garland and hang as above from remaining paper lanterns.

# Candy Fountain

My dream—an endless waterfall of candy! In order to steady these, it's essential to hot glue them together, a move you may not want to make with fine crystal, so save the fancy dishes for another gathering. The glue can be removed, of course, with Goo Gone or other adhesive removers.

**MATERIALS**

3 different-size footed compotes

**TOOLS**

Hot glue gun

Run a bead of hot glue around the bottom rim of the middle footed compote. Set it into the center of the bottom compote and let dry thoroughly. Repeat with the top compote, but set it into the middle compote. Set the tower on the table, then fill with candy.

## Style It

Stacked compotes make a fabulous table display, but they're best used for grown-up gatherings. Skip them for the bar or bat mitzvah or the tenth birthday party. There's beauty in practicality; for the younger set, create vertical elements that can stand up to their energy.

# Silver Sweets Box

These little fortune boxes are meant to bring just that for the New Year. There's almost nothing to putting these together—you can enlist the help of little hands to punch the snowflakes out of lightweight lavender paper, a color that complements beautifully the limited palette. Invite guests to fill their box with a mix of sweets from the table.

*Makes 1.*

MATERIALS

1 silver mini takeout box, 2¾-inch-wide ×
2½-inch-high × 2-inch-deep
1 small sheet lavender card stock

TOOLS

Arctic snowflake punch, 1-inch
(see Find It, page 362)
Hot glue gun

Assemble the box and raise the handle. Punch a single snowflake from the card stock and affix it to the handle with a tiny dot of hot glue. Repeat to make as many boxes as there are guests at the party. Arrange in a cluster on the table.

### GETTING THE BLUES

There are hundreds of hues of blue and some are better suited for a table of sweets than others. When ordering candy online, be careful to study the shade of blue you are choosing—sometimes an aquamarine reads much lighter than it actually is, for example. For this table, stay in the cool/icy blue range. Shimmery, glittery candies work best.

# Chill-Out Chocolate Bar

I love the way a single snowflake gives a flat candy bar a little dimension;
tied on with a length of soft, feathery, mohair yarn, a simple bar of chocolate
becomes a special gift.

**Makes 1.**

MATERIALS

Baby blue card stock, 12 inches × 12 inches

Length of ivory mohair yarn

Baby blue mulberry wrapping paper, 12 inches ×
12 inches

TOOLS

Arctic snowflake punch, 2-inch
(see Find It, page 362)

Hot glue gun or Glue Dot

Follow the instructions for Custom Candy
Bar Wrappers, page 27, using the card
stock. Wrap the yarn four times lengthwise
around the candy bar, beginning and
ending on the back. Tie in a double knot
to secure. Punch a snowflake from the
scrapbook paper. Hot glue or affix it with
a Glue Dot to the center of the candy bar.
Make one for each guest. Arrange the
chocolate bars on a tray lined with rock
candy crystals.

Teal, white, and gray barber poles, arranged in a glass footed vase

White dusted truffles, in a medium glass footed compote

Light blue Sunny Seed Drops, in a medium glass footed compote

Silver dusted toffee almond truffles, in a small glass footed compote

Glittery, opalescent truffles, in a small compote

Periwinkle chocolate dragées, in a large glass footed compote

White mint lentils, in a medium glass footed compote

Sky blue truffles, in a small footed compote

Pearl opalescent Sixlets, in a medium footed compote

Silver M&M's, in a medium footed compote

Vanilla ribbon candy, stacked in a pyramid on a footed cake stand

White rock candy crystals for displaying

Pastel blue pearlized sprinkles or sugar pearls for displaying

Wedgwood blue linen taffeta tablecloth

Perforated white linen table runner

Snowflake Garland

Double-face satin ribbon for bows on footed compotes

Mulberry wrapping paper

Candy-lined white trays

Footed glass compotes and cake stands

## SWITCH IT

**GROW IT UP:** In addition to your favorite bubbly, serve with Spiked White Hot Chocolate, page 326.

**GROW IT DOWN:** Serve with seltzer and a swizzle stick.

**COLOR IT:** Try yellow and white for a baby shower; sea foam green and white for Mother's Day.

# *Template Index*

On the following pages, I've provided snapshots of the templates you read about throughout the book. Use this index as a visual reference. To access the actual templates, go to http://blog.amy atlas.com. Download the template you want and print it on the specified paper. Then follow the instructions for the project. It's as easy as that!

Some of the templates incorporate text. If you want to change the text, print the template, scan it into your computer, and use a program such as Illustrator to swap in your own creative touch.

## Picnic in the Park

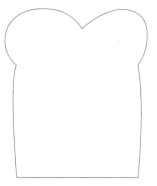

Bread slice: 74

## Take Me Away

Square vessel liner: 95, 99

Rectangular vessel liner: 94, 97

Take Me Away Take-aways: 103

Ready-to-Wear Candy Bag: 104

Ready-to-Wear Drink Flags: 104

## Mad for Zig Zag

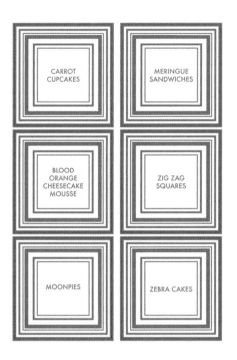

CARROT CUPCAKES

MERINGUE SANDWICHES

BLOOD ORANGE CHEESECAKE MOUSSE

ZIG ZAG SQUARES

MOONPIES

ZEBRA CAKES

Private Label Dessert Tags: 122

## Pastel Pretty

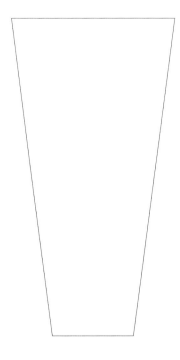

Colorful Cotton Candy Sticks wrap: 143

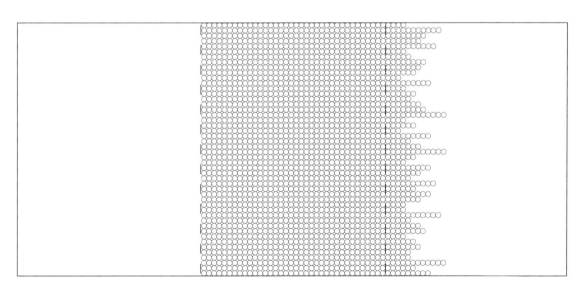

Necco Wafer Runner: 140

## Darling Dots

Never-Melt Crispy Rice Ice Cream Cones: 155

## Honey, I Love You

peanut butter
malt balls

bee
macarons

chocolate beehive
cupcakes

honey
panna cotta

honey beehive
cake

Beeswax Dessert Tag: 185

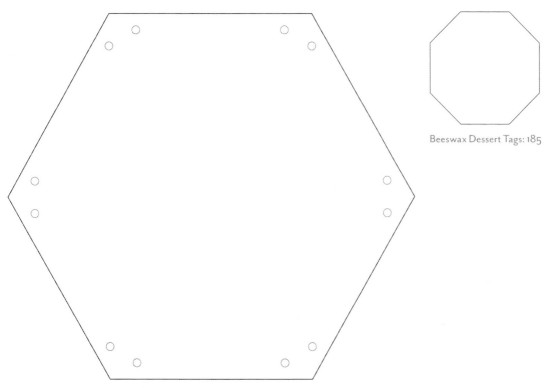

Beeswax Dessert Tags: 185

Haute Honeycomb backdrop: 178

*Game Night!*

| 9 | 14 | 4 | 28 | 67 |
| 73 | 80 | 1 | 37 | 20 |
| 11 | 2 | ★ | 33 | 64 |
| 38 | 1 | 59 | 3 | 77 |
| 10 | 27 | 39 | 63 | 22 |

Bingo! card: 189, 196

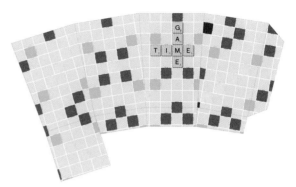

Game Time Candy Cups: 203

Poker Chip Dessert Tags: 206

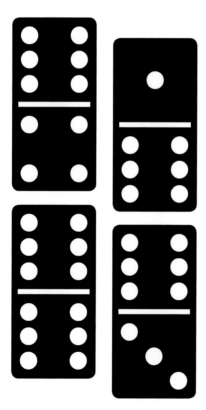

Domino Streamer: 203

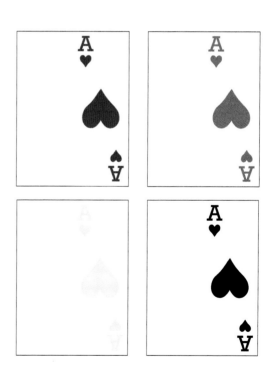

Ace Candy Bags: 206

# Apple of My Eye

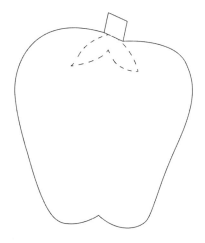

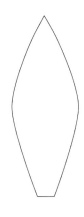

Brownie Apples: 223

Apple leaf: 220, 229

"Apple of My Eye" Banner: 224

# Perfectly Preppy

Tied Together Candy Cup: 254

Prepster Drink Flag: 254

Prepster Candy Bag: 254

Square vessel liner: 255

# *Movie Night*

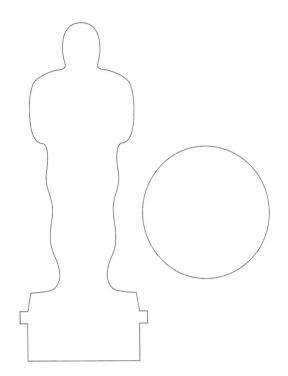

Oscar Statuettes: 260

Classic Popcorn Boxes: 272

Walk of Fame Brownies and Star Tags: 266, 276

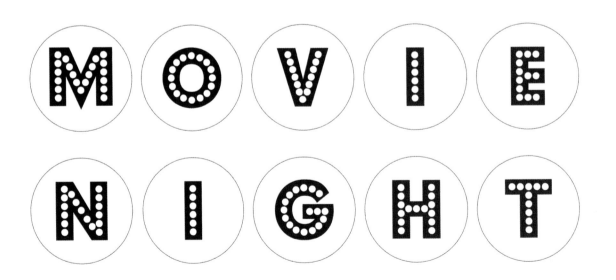

Movie Night Marquee: 272

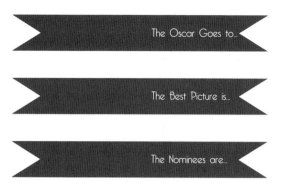

Glamorous Glasses flags: 275

## Spooktacular Halloween

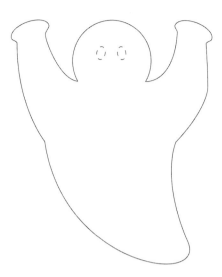

Ghost Brownies: 302

## Vineyard Afternoon

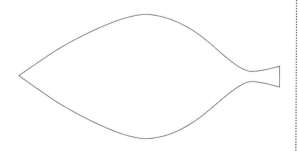

Leaf for Claret Favor Boxes, Sugar Dusted Fruit, and
Cork Dessert Tag Holders: 287, 288

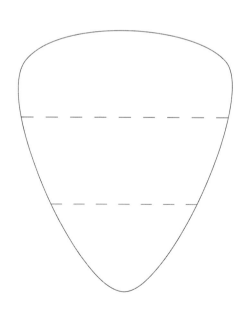

Candy Corn Brownies: 300

# Alphabet Template

152, 169, 225, 274

# R S T U
# V W X
# Y Z

# Essentials

# Find It
## Sourcing Everything in Sweet Designs

### Basics

**Food Coloring Gel:** Wilton, www.wilton.com or
  AmeriColor, www.americolorcorp.com

**Fondant:** N.Y. Cake & Baking Distributor,
  www.nycake.com or Wilton, www.wilton.com

**Pastry Tips:** Wilton, www.wilton.com or Ateco,
  www.atecousa.com

**Cupcake wrappers:** Wilton, www.wilton.com

**Foil wrapped chocolate bars:** Candy Wrapper Store,
  www.candywrapperstore.com

**Styrofoam forms or Cake dummy:** N.Y. Cake &
  Baking Distributor, www.nycake.com

**Glue Dots:** Michaels, www.michaels.com

**Scrapbook paper:** Michaels, www.michaels.com

**Extra long card stock:** A.I. Friedman,
  www.aifriedman.com

**Card stock for printing templates:** Paper
  Presentation, www.paperpresentation.com

**Cellophane bags:** Uline, www.uline.com

### Forever Chanel

#### COUTURE VASE COVER

**Fabric to cover couture flower vases:** B&J Fabrics,
  www.bandjfabrics.com, and Lace Star,
  www.lacestar.com/fabrics.html

**Decorative ribbon for tying around vases:** Mokuba
  New York, www.mokubany.com

**Ranunculus and garden roses:** Associated Cut
  Flower, www.associatedcutflower.com

#### PRETTY PEDESTAL

**Cake dummy or Styrofoam:** N.Y. Cake & Baking
  Distributor, www.nycake.com

**Fabric to cover couture flower vases:** Lace Star,
  www.lacestar.com/fabrics.html

**Decorative ribbon:** Mokuba New York,
  www.mokubany.com

## BOATER BOX

**Hatboxes:** Michaels, www.michaels.com
**Yellow acrylic paint for boater boxes:** Michaels, www.michaels.com
**Paintbrushes:** Michaels, www.michaels.com
**Cord for boater boxes:** M&J Trimming, www.mjtrim.com
**Gold cord for tags:** M&J Trimming, www.mjtrim.com
**Camellias for boater boxes:** Tinsel Trading Company, www.tinseltrading.com
**Tissue paper for lining boater boxes:** Kate's Paperie, www.katespaperie.com

## DESSERT TAGS

**Tags:** Paper Presentation, www.paperpresentation.com
**Gold Cord:** M&J Trimming, www.mjtrim.com

## LINEN

**Tweed Tablecloth:** Lace Star, www.lacestar.com/
**Yellow ribbon for tailored bow:** Masterstroke Canada, www.masterstrokecanada.com

## VESSELS AND GLASSWARE

**China:** PropHAUS: www.prophaus.com
**Small bell jar:** Dean & Deluca, www.deandeluca.com
**Glass pitcher:** Crate & Barrel, www.crateandbarrel.com
**Glasses:** CB2, www.cb2.com

## CANDY AND SHOP IT DESSERTS

**Calissons:** Crossings, www.crossingsfrenchfood.com
**Malt balls:** Koppers Chocolate, www.kopperschocolate.com
**Rose mints:** Hilliards House of Candy, www.hilliardscandy.com
**Pound cake:** Entenmann's, www.entenmanns.com
**Dragées for petits fours:** India Tree, www.indiatree.com

# Picnic in the Park

## FESTIVE BUNTING

**Red and white scrapbook paper for bunting:** Michaels, www.michaels.com
**Ribbon:** M&J Trimming, www.mjtrim.com

## DIY LUNCH BOX

**Medium handled kraft gable boxes:** Nashville Wraps, www.nashvillewraps.com
**White labels on kraft boxes:** Paper Presentation, www.paperpresentation.com
**Gingham ribbon:** Mokuba New York, www.mokubany.com
**Ladybugs:** Tinsel Trading Company, www.tinseltrading.com

## PINWHEEL FAVOR BOXES

**Red favor boxes:** Paper Presentation, www.paperpresentation.com
**Gingham scrapbook paper:** Michaels, www.michaels.com
**Brads for pinwheels:** Paper Presentation, www.paperpresentation.com
**Lollipop sticks for pinwheels:** N.Y. Cake & Baking Distributor, www.nycake.com, or Wilton, www.wilton.com

## SCALLOPED CHERRY SACKS

**Kraft bag for cherries:** Michaels, www.michaels.com
**Scalloped scissors:** Michaels, www.michaels.com
**Baker's twine:** Paper Presentation, www.paperpresentation.com

## SWEET TAGS

**Dessert tags:** Paper Presentation,
www.paperpresentation.com
**Kraft sticks for tags:** Michaels, www.michaels.com

## GINGHAM SANDWICH WRAPPERS

**Gingham tissue paper:** Nashville Wraps,
www.nashvillewraps.com
**Red curling ribbon:** Nashville Wraps,
www.nashvillewraps.com

## LINEN

**Red and white French ticking striped tablecloth:**
Wolf Home, www.wolfhomeny.com

## VESSELS AND GLASSWARE

**Trifle dish for Strawberry Trifle:** Crate & Barrel,
www.crateandbarrel.com
**Scalloped red and white pie dishes for Sweet Cherry
Pies:** Fishs Eddy, www.fishseddy.com
**Red and white striped galvanized drink bucket:**
Macbeth Collection,
www.themacbethcollection.com
**12 × 4 inch white platter:** Crate & Barrel,
www.crateandbarrel.com
**White scalloped cake stand:** Rosanna,
www.rosannainc.com
**Picnic basket:** Pier 1, www.pier1.com
**Round metal tray:** PropHAUS, www.prophaus.com
**Barrel jars for red zinger tea:** Fishs Eddy,
www.fishseddy.com
**Mason jars with handles:** Pottery Barn,
www.potterybarn.com

## SPECIALTY BAKING SUPPLIES

**Slice of bread cookie cutter:** Copper Gifts,
www.coppergifts.com

## CANDY

**Gummi Twin Cherries:** Candy Warehouse,
www.candywarehouse.com

## *Take Me Away*

## CABANA CURTAINS

**Peacock fabric for curtains:** Trina Turk for
Schumacher and Decorators Best,
www.fschumacher.com and
www.decoratorsbest.com

## AQUAMARINE CAKE PEDESTAL

**Aqua fabric to cover pedestal:** B&J Fabrics,
www.bandjfabrics.com
**White cord ½ inch:** M&J Trimming,
www.mjtrim.com
**Cognac leather scraps for rope ends:** M&J Trimming,
www.mjtrim.com
**16 × 4 inch Styrofoam or cake dummy:** N.Y. Cake &
Baking Distributor, www.nycake.com

## CREPE-COVERED CYLINDERS

**Cylinder vases 4 inch diameter × 12 inch tall:**
Jamali Floral & Garden Supplies,
www.jamaligarden.com
**Navy crepe paper for wrapping around vase:**
Castle in the Air, www.castleintheair.com
**Young green hydrangea:** Dutch Flower Line,
www.dutchflowerline.com
**White rope ½ inch wide:** M&J Trimming,
www.mjtrim.com
**Cognac leather scraps for rope ends:** M&J Trimming,
www.mjtrim.com

## TAKE ME AWAY TAKEAWAYS

**Green favor bags:** Michaels, www.michaels.com
**Blue cord:** M&J Trimming, www.mjtrim.com
**Card stock for printing templates on labels:** Paper
Presentation, www.paperpresentation.com

### CRINKLE CANDY WRAPS

**Navy crepe paper for wrapping around taffy:**
Castle in the Air, www.castleintheair.com

**Green Sour Punch Straws to tie taffy:**
Candy Warehouse, www.candywarehouse.com

**Salt water taffy:** Candy Warehouse,
www.candywarehouse.com

### READY TO WEAR DRINK FLAGS
### AND CANDY BAGS

**Cello bags for candy:** Paper Presentation,
www.paperpresentation.com

**Card stock for printing templates on tags and flags:**
Paper Presentation, www.paperpresentation.com

### LINEN

**Aqua fabric:** B&J Fabrics, www.bandjfabrics.com

**Ikat runner fabric and Suzani print:** Quadrille
Fabrics, www.quadrillefabrics.com

### VESSELS, VESSEL LINERS, AND GLASSWARE

**6 × 14 inch white tray:** Crate & Barrel,
www.crateandbarrel.com

**5 × 10.5 inch white tray:** Crate & Barrel,
www.crateandbarrel.com

**12 inch square tray:** Crate & Barrel,
www.crateandbarrel.com

**Drink glasses:** CB2, www.cb2.com

**Grasshopper lucite tray:** Dabney Lee at Home,
www.dabneyleeathome.com

**Cake Stands:** Martha Stewart for Macy's,
www.macys.com

**Card stock for printing templates on vessel liners:**
Paper Presentation, www.paperpresentation.com

### SPECIALTY BAKING SUPPLIES

**Lollipop sticks for lime popsicles:** N.Y. Cake & Baking
Distributor, www.nycake.com

### CANDY

**Green ribbon candy:** Candy Warehouse,
www.candywarehouse.com

**Green fruit jelly slices:** Candy Warehouse,
www.candywarehouse.com

**Green jelly beans:** Candy Warehouse,
www.candywarehouse.com

**Green Sunny Seed Drops:** Candy Warehouse,
www.candywarehouse.com

## *Mad for ZigZag*

### PLEATED PEDESTAL SKIRTS

**Scrapbook paper:** Michaels, www.michaels.com

**Orange fabric:** B&J Fabrics, www.bandjfabrics.com

**Styrofoam:** N.Y. Cake & Baking Distributor,
www.nycake.com

### PEAKS AND VALLEYS WALL DECORATION
### AND RUNNER

**White Canson paper for zigzag runner and orange card
stock for wall decoration:** A.I. Friedman,
www.aifriedman.com

### CHIC CANDY BAR WRAPS

**Orange card stock:** A.I. Friedman,
www.aifriedman.com

**Foil wrapped chocolate bars:** Candy Wrapper Store,
www.candywrapperstore.com

**White herringbone ribbon for chocolate bars:** Masterstroke Canada, www.masterstrokecanada.com

### PRIVATE LABEL DESSERT TAGS

**Card stock for printing template of labels:** Paper
Presentation, www.paperpresentation.com

### RICKRACKED RAMEKINS

**Orange ½ inch rickrack ribbon:** Masterstroke Canada,
www.masterstrokecanada.com

### ZIG AND ZAG FAVOR BOXES

**Orange favor boxes:** Paper Presentation,
www.paperpresentation.com

**White paper for orange favor boxes:** A.I. Friedman,
www.aifriedman.com

## LINEN

**Orange tablecloth:** B&J Fabrics,
    www.bandjfabrics.com

## VESSELS AND GLASSWARE

**Vases:** Jonathan Adler, www.jonathanadler.com,
    and Urban Batik, www.urbanbatik.com
**V shaped platters:** PropHAUS, www.prophaus.com
**12 inch × 6 inch white platters:** Crate & Barrel,
    www.crateandbarrel.com
**Candleholder for faux cake stand:** Crate & Barrel,
    www.crateandbarrel.com
**Plate on top of candleholder for faux cake stand:**
    Williams Sonoma, www.williams-sonoma.com
**12 inch × 12 inch platter:** Crate & Barrel,
    www.crateandbarrel.com
**Glasses:** CB2, www.cb2.com
**White ramekins for Cheesecake Mousse:**
    Dean & Deluca, www.deandeluca.com
**Orange and white chevron tray:** Macbeth Collection,
    www.themacbethcollection.com

## CANDY AND SHOP IT DESSERTS

**Orange slices:** Candy Warehouse,
    www.candywarehouse.com
**Zebra cakes:** Little Debbie, www.littledebbie.com
**Orange Moonpies:** MoonPie, www.moonpie.com
**M&M's:** Mars, Incorporated, www.mms.com
**Sanding sugar:** India Tree, www.indiatree.com
**Orange rock candy:** Candy Warehouse,
    www.candywarehouse.com
**Orange and white striped candy sticks:** Hammond's
    Candies, www.hammondscandies.com
**Square orange bark:** Sensational Sweets,
    www.sensationalsweets.com
**Orange and white pillow mints:** Stewart Candy
    Company, www.stewartcandy.com

## FLOWERS

**Gerber Daisies, Farmer's Market**

## Pastel Pretty

## NECCO WAFER RUNNER

**Necco Wafers:** Candy Warehouse,
    www.candywarehouse.com
**Netting for runner:** Michaels, www.michaels.com
**Straight edge (Omnigrid):** A.I. Friedman,
    www.aifriedman.com

## ETHEREAL YARN CURTAIN

**Mohair yarn for backdrop:** Purl Soho,
    www.purlsoho.com
**Glassine paper:** Kate's Paperie,
    www.katespaperie.com
**Scalloped Paper Shapers 3 inch punch:** Michaels,
    www.michaels.com

## COLORFUL COTTON CANDY STICKS

**Cotton candy sticks:** Web Restaurant Store,
    www.webstaurantstore.com
**Mulberry paper for covering cotton candy sticks:**
    Kate's Paperie, www.katespaperie.com
**Lucite trays holding cotton candy:** The Container
    Store, www.containerstore.com
**Nonpareils for filling Lucite trays:** India Tree,
    www.indiatree.com

## POLKA DOT PARTY BAGS

**Gusseted plastic bags:** N.Y. Cake & Baking
    Distributor, www.nycake.com
**Stamps for favor bags:** Michaels, www.michaels.com

## CONFETTI DECORATION

**Pastel confetti:** Pink Poodle Boutique,
    www.pink-poodle-boutique.com

## LINEN

**Sea Green Silk Taffeta tablecloth:** Wolf Home,
www.wolfhomeny.com

## VESSELS AND GLASSWARE

**Scalloped pastel ceramic dishes:** Magenta,
www.magenta-inc.com

**Rectangular pink platters:** Mudd for ABC,
www.abchome.com

**Small and large candy dishes:** PropHAUS,
www.prophaus.com

**Pastel translucent spoons:** Gelato Supply Company,
www.gelatosupply.com

**Peach tongs:** Sabre, www.gracioushome.com

**Long pink serving spoons:** Sabre,
www.gracioushome.com

## SPECIALTY BAKING SUPPLIES

**Rectangular treat cups for Pink Éclairs :** N.Y. Cake &
Baking Distributor, www.nycake.com

## CANDY AND SHOP IT DESSERTS

**Cotton candy floss sugar in lemon and lavender:**
Great Western, www.gwproducts.com

**White cotton candy:** 1890 Caramel Corn,
www.1890caramelcorn.com

**Purple and pink Sunny Seed Drops:** Candy Warehouse,
www.candywarehouse.com

**Pink and purple pastel dragée sprinkles:** India Tree,
www.indiatree.com

**Pastel marshmallows:** Butter Baked Goods,
www.butterbakedgoods.com

**Pastel pillow mints:** Candy Warehouse,
www.candywarehouse.com

**Pastel ribbon candy:** Hammond's Candies,
www.hammondscandies.com

**Pastel Dragées:** Crossings,
www.crossingsfrenchfood.com

**Pastel licorice pastels:** Candy Warehouse,
www.candywarehouse.com

**Strawberry Petites:** Little Debbie,
www.littledebbie.com

**Turquoise taffy:** Sweet Candy Company,
www.sweetcandy.com

**Small blue nonpareils:** India Tree, www.indiatree.com

## Darling Dots

## DOTTED SWISS CANDY BOARDS

**Foam board for favor boards:** A.I. Friedman,
www.aifriedman.com

**Dot fabric for favor boards:** Purl Soho,
www.purlsoho.com

**Fabric scraps for cello bags:** Purl Soho,
www.purlsoho.com

**Cello bags:** Paper Presentation,
www.paperpresentation.com

**Thick pink satin ribbon:** M&J Trimming,
www.mjtrim.com

## SWEET FAVOR BOXES

**Red favor boxes:** Paper Presentation,
www.paperpresentation.com

**Labels for favor boxes:** Paper Presentation,
www.paperpresentation.com

**Ribbon:** M&J Trimming: www.mjtrim.com

## MIX AND MATCH CHOCOLATE BARS

**Scrapbook paper:** Michaels, www.michaels.com

**Labels:** Paper Presentation,
www.paperpresentation.com

**Foiled Hershey bars:** Candy Wrapper Store,
www.candywrapperstore.com

## LINEN

**Pink cotton linen:** B&J Fabrics, www.bandjfabrics.com

## VESSELS, VESSEL LINERS, AND GLASSWARE

**Pink milk glass cake stands:** Fishs Eddy,
www.fishseddy.com
**Pink milk glass bowls:** Fishs Eddy, www.fishseddy.com
**White platters:** Crate & Barrel,
www.crateandbarrel.com
**Scrapbook paper for vessel liners:** Michaels,
www.michaels.com

## CANDY

**Long marshmallows for knotted marshmallows:**
Arnaud Soubeyran, www.nougatsoubeyran.com
**Pink and white square marshmallows:** Baked,
www.bakednyc.com
**Ribbon candy and pillow mints:** Hammond's Candies,
www.hammondscandies.com
**Malt balls, Milkies, and Valentine's Day licorice pastels:**
Koppers Chocolate, www.kopperschocolate.com
**Taffy, jelly beans, gummy hearts, pillow mints, and
pink wafers:** Candy Warehouse,
www.candywarehouse.com
**Red dragées:** Mariebelle, www.mariebelle.com

## *Honey, I Love You*

## HAUTE HONEYCOMB

**Vellum paper for backdrop:** Paper Presentation,
www.paperpresentation.com
**Copper circles for backdrop:** B&J Florist Supply Co.,
no website, (212) 564-6086
**Mini bees:** Tinsel Trading Company,
www.tinseltrading.com

## BEESWAX PEDESTAL

**Beeswax sheets:** Toadily Handmade,
www.toadilyhandmade.com
**Cake dummy or Styrofoam:** NY Cake & Bake,
www.nycake.com

## HONEY, TAKE ME HOME JARS

**Honey and honeycomb:** Savannah Bee Co.,
www.savannahbee.com
**Jars for honey:** Fishs Eddy, www.fishseddy.com,
and Dean & Deluca, www.deandeluca.com
**Wooden honey spinners:** Dean & Deluca,
www.deandeluca.com
**Paper for top of honey jars and to line plates:** A.I.
Friedman, www.aifriedman.com
**Honey sticks:** Chelsea Marketplace,
www.chelseamarket.com

## BEESWAX BELLY BANDS

**Card stock:** A.I. Friedman, www.aifriedman.com
**Beeswax sheets:** Toadily Handmade,
www.toadilyhandmade.com
**Foiled Hershey bars:** Candy Wrapper Store,
www.candywrapperstore.com

### GOLDEN GIFT BAG

**Yellow gusseted bags:** Michaels, www.michaels.com

**Black 1 inch ribbon:** M&J Trimming, www.mjtrim.com

**Pipe cleaners for bees:** Michaels, www.michaels.com

### BEESWAX DESSERT TAGS

**Beeswax sheets:** Toadily Handmade, www.toadilyhandmade.com

**Card stock for printing template of labels:** Paper Presentation, www.paperpresentation.com

### LINEN

**Honey Linen fabric:** New York Elegant Fabrics, www.nyelegantfabrics.com

### VESSELS, VESSEL LINERS, AND GLASSWARE

**Yellow cake stands:** Potluck Studios, www.potluckstudios.com

**12 inch × 12 inch white platters:** Crate and Barrel, www.crateandbarrel.com

**Bell jars:** Dean & Deluca, www.deandeluca.com

**Domed Cake stands:** Williams Sonoma, www.williams-sonoma.com

**Beehive drink dispenser:** Pier 1, www.pier1.com

**Glasses for Honey Panna Cotta:** Crate & Barrel, www.crateandbarrel.com

**Beehive glasses:** ABC Home, www.abchome.com

**Decorative paper for vessel liners:** Paper Presentation, www.paperpresentation.com, and A.I. Friedman, www.aifriedman.com

### SPECIALTY BAKING SUPPLIES

**Beehive baking cake tins:** Williams Sonoma, www.williams-sonoma.com

**Beehive cupcake wrappers:** NY Cake & Baking Distributor, www.nycake.com

**Marzipan for bees for honey beehive cake:** NY Cake & Baking Distributor, www.nycake.com

### RIBBON

**Ribbon around cake platters and Honey, I Love You cookies:** Mokuba New York: www.mokubany.com

**Twine:** M&J Trimming, www.mjtrim.com

### CANDY AND SHOP IT DESSERTS

**Macaroons used for bee macaroons:** La Maison du Chocolat, www.lamaisonduchocolat.com

**Graham cracker under cupcake:** Nabisco, www.nabiscoworld.com

**Jordan almonds:** Koppers Chocolate, www.kopperschocolate.com

**Butter waffle cookies:** Jules Destrooper, www.destrooper.com

**Peanut butter malt balls:** Koppers Chocolate, www.kopperschocolate.com

**Lemon Bark:** Sensational Sweets, www.sensationalsweets.com

**Bit-O-Honey candy:** Candy Warehouse, www.candywarehouse.com

## Game Night!

### GAME TIME CANDY CUPS

**Card stock for printing template:** Paper Presentation, www.paperpresentation.com

**Orange waxed paper for stuffing candy cups:** Kate's Paperie, www.katespaperie.com

### GAMING PURSE

**Orange bags:** Michaels, www.michaels.com

**Suit toothpicks:** Pick on Us, www.pickonus.com

**Card chocolates:** Candy Warehouse, www.candywarehouse.com

## DOMINO STREAMER

**Card stock for printing template:** Paper Presentation, www.paperpresentation.com

**Twine:** M&J Trimming, www.mjtrim.com

## COMING UP ACES CANDY BOARDS

**Foam core boards:** A.I. Friedman, www.aifriedman.com

**Orange Canson paper for foam core borders:** A.I. Friedman, www.aifriedman.com

**Fabric for wrapping around boards:** B&J Fabrics, www.bandjfabrics.com

## ACE CANDY BAGS

**Cello wrappers:** Michaels, www.michaels.com

**Card stock for printing template on candy bags:** Paper Presentation, www.paperpresentation.com

## POKER CHIP DESSERT TAGS

**Card stock for printing template:** Paper Presentation, www.paperpresentation.com

## LINEN

**Lemon yellow fabric for tablecloth:** B&J Fabrics, www.bandjfabrics.com

## VESSELS, VESSEL LINERS, AND GLASSWARE

**Crossword glasses:** Fishs Eddy, www.fishseddy.com

**Glass cake stands:** Fishs Eddy, www.fishseddy.com

**16-inch yellow tray for Cheery Checkerboard:** Crate & Barrel, www.crateandbarrel.com

**White platters:** Crate & Barrel, www.crateandbarrel.com

**Small and large lucite trays:** The Container Store, www.containerstore.com

**Card stock for printing Bingo vessel liners:** Paper Presentation, www.paperpresentation.com

## SPECIALTY BAKING SUPPLIES

**Lollipop sticks for Twister Inspired Cheesecake Pops:** N.Y. Cake & Baking Distributor, www.nycake.com

**Cupcake liners:** Wilton, www.wilton.com

**Diamond cookie cutter:** N.Y. Cake & Baking Distributor, www.nycake.com

## CANDY AND SHOP IT DESSERTS

**Dice lollipops:** Candy Warehouse, www.candywarehouse.com

**Foil wrapped Oreo cookies:** Williams & Bennett, www.williamsandbennett.com

**Green Jordan almonds:** Koppers Chocolate, www.koppershocolates.com

**Skittles:** Candy Warehouse, www.candywarehouse.com

**Yellow jelly beans:** Candy Warehouse, www.candywarehouse.com

**Jujubes:** Candy Warehouse, www.candywarehouse.com

**Strawberry and cream malt balls:** Koppers Chocolate, www.koppershocolates.com

**Poker chip chocolates:** Madelaine, www.madelainechocolate.com

**Aqua M&M's:** Mars, Incorporated, www.mms.com

**Yellow and blue sanding sugar:** N.Y. Cake & Baking Distributor, www.nycake.com

**Green Sixlets:** Candy Warehouse, www.candywarehouse.com

**Light Blue Sunny Seed Drops:** Candy Warehouse, www.candywarehouse.com

**White Sunny Seed Drops to make checkerboard:** Candy Warehouse, www.candywarehouse.com

**Yellow M&M's to make checkerboard:** Mars, Incorporated, www.mms.com

**If sourcing marshmallows:** Baked, www.bakednyc.com

## Apple of My Eye

### APPLE OF MY EYE BANNER

**Card stock for printing template:** Paper Presentation,
www.paperpresentation.com

### APPLE PRINT TABLECLOTH

**Acrylic paint and paintbrushes for apple stamping:**
Michaels, www.michaels.com
**White tablecloth:** B&J Fabrics,
www.bandjfabrics.com

### DIY CAKE STANDS

**Dowels and wooden circles:** Woodcrafter.com,
www.woodcrafter.com

### U-PICK GOODY BAG

**Red and yellow favor bags:** Michaels,
www.michaels.com
**Floral tape for apple bag:** Michaels,
www.michaels.com

### SEED BAG OF SWEETS

**Burlap bags:** Jamali Floral & Garden Supplies,
www.jamaligarden.com
**Apple scrapbook paper for apple tags:** Michaels,
www.michaels.com

### VESSELS, VESSEL LINERS, AND GLASSWARE

**Bamboo wooden platters:** Fishs Eddy,
www.fishseddy.com
**Wooden shelves:** Ikea, www.ikea.com
**Apple berry baskets:** Pottery Barn,
www.potterybarn.com, and Fishs Eddy,
www.fishseddy.com
**Red apple pie dishes for Mini Apple Pies:** Le Creuset,
www.lecreuset.com
**Small wood berry baskets:** Wasserstrom Co.,
www.wasserstrom.com
**Wooden apple crates:** Colonial Trading Company,
www.colonialtrading.com
**Decorative paper for vessel liners:** Michaels,
www.michaels.com

### SPECIALTY BAKING SUPPLIES

**4-inch apple cookie cutter:** Copper Gifts,
www.coppergifts.com
**Sticks for Caramel Lady Apples lollipop sticks:** N.Y.
Cake & Baking Distributor, www.nycake.com

### CANDY AND SHOP IT DESSERTS

**Red and yellow pretzel balls:** Koppers Chocolate,
www.kopperschocolates.com
**Green malt balls:** Koppers Chocolate,
www.kopperschocolates.com
**Peanut butter malt balls:** Candy Warehouse,
www.candywarehouse.com
**Green Sour Patch Kids:** Candy Warehouse,
www.candywarehouse.com
**Green Gummi for cupcake leaf on Delicious Apple
Cupcakes:** Candy Warehouse,
www.candywarehouse.com
**Foiled caramel apples:** Madelaine Chocolate,
www.madelainechocolate.com
**If sourcing candy apples:** Hammond's Candies,
www.hammondscandies.com

# *Perfectly Preppy*

## BUTTONED-UP ARGYLE SCREEN

**Pink fabric on backdrop:** B&J Fabrics,
www.bandjfabrics.com

**Blue and pink ribbon on backdrop:** M&J Trimming,
www.mjtrim.com

**Button kit:** Purl Soho, www.purlsoho.com

**Fabric for covering buttons:** Wolf Home,
www.wolfhomeny.com

## PREPPY PEDESTAL

**Pink paper under cake:** A.I. Friedman,
www.aifriedman.com

**Navy ribbon around cake dummy:** M&J Trimming,
www.mjtrim.com

**14 inch square × 3 cake dummy or Styrofoam:** N.Y.
Cake & Baking Distributor, www.nycake.com

## TIE-REQUIRED FAVOR BOX

**Pink favor boxes:** Paper Presentation,
www.paperpresentation.com

**Blue satin ribbon for tie knots on favor boxes:** Kate's
Paperie, www.katespaperie.com

## TIED TOGETHER CANDY CUP

**Blue glassine paper in favor boxes:** Kate's Paperie,
www.katespaperie.com

**Card stock for printing template:** Paper Presentation,
www.paperpresentation.com

## PREPSTER DRINK FLAG AND CANDY BAG

**Cello Bags:** Michaels, www.michaels.com

**Card stock for printing template on flags and candy
bag wrappers:** Paper Presentation,
www.paperpresentation.com

## LINEN

**Navy silk taffeta tablecloth:** Wolf Home,
www.wolfhomeny.com

**Ties:** Pink, www.thomaspink.com; Faconnable,
www.faconnable.com; Tommy Hilfiger,
www.tommy.com

## VESSELS, VESSEL LINERS, AND GLASSWARE AND SPECIALTY BAKING SUPPLIES

**Deep footed compote:** Martha Stewart for Macy's,
www.macys.com

**Cake stand:** Martha Stewart for Macy's,
www.macys.com

**Mousse glasses for Simple Strawberry Mousse:**
Crate & Barrel, www.crateandbarrel.com

**Mini spoons for Simple Strawberry Mousse:**
Fishs Eddy, www.fishseddy.com

**Pink and white ribbon around Simple Strawberry
Mousse glasses:** M&J Trimming,
www.mjtrim.com

**Card stock for printing template for vessel liners:**
Paper Presentation, www.paperpresentation.com

## SPECIALTY BAKING SUPPLIES

**Diamond cookie cutter:** N.Y. Cake & Baking
Distributor, www.nycake.com

## CANDY AND SHOP IT DESSERTS

**Pink and navy mint lentils in preppy candy bags:**
Koppers Chocolate, www.kopperschocolate.com

**Pink rock candy crystals:** Candy Warehouse,
www.candywarehouse.com

**Pink and blue striped candy sticks:** Papabubble,
www.papabubble.com

**Pink marshmallows:** Better Bit of Butter,
www.betterbitofbutter.com

# Movie Night

## GLITZY CURTAIN

**Mylar curtains:** Party City, www.partycity.com
**Cardboard stars:** Party Fair, www.partyfair.com
**Gold glitter for stars:** Michaels, www.michaels.com

## RED CARPET RUNWAY

**Red velvet curtains and runner:** Wolf Home, www.wolfhomeny.com

## CLASSIC POPCORN BOXES

**Card stock for printing template:** Paper Presentation, www.paperpresentation.com

## MOVIE NIGHT MARQUEE

**Card stock for printing template:** Paper Presentation, www.paperpresentation.com

## A STAR IS BORN TABLE GARLAND

**Gold cord for cookie sign:** M&J Trimming, www.mjtrim.com

## GLAMOROUS GLASSES

**Movie ticket roll:** Staples, www.staples.com
**Drink glasses:** Crate & Barrel, www.crateandbarrel.com
**Gold pebbled wrapping paper:** Kate's Paperie, www.katespaperie.com

## MOVIE CANDY FAVOR BAGS

**Cello Bags:** Michaels, www.michaels.com
**Card stock for printing template on candy bags:** Paper Presentation, www.paperpresentation.com

## LINEN

**White tablecloth:** B&J Fabrics, www.bandjfabrics.com
**Black and white film paper:** Paper Presentation, www.paperpresentation.com

## VESSELS AND GLASSWARE

**Candy jars:** Bed Bath & Beyond, www.bedbathandbeyond.com
**Metal scoops:** Bowery Kitchens, www.bowerykitchens.com
**Square 12 inch × 12 inch platters:** Crate & Barrel, www.crateandbarrel.com
**Rectangular platters for Clapperboard Ice Cream Sandwiches:** Crate & Barrel, www.crateandbarrel.com

## SPECIALTY BAKING SUPPLIES

**Gold cupcake liners for Red Velvet Cupcakes:** N.Y. Cake & Baking Distributor, www.nycake.com
**Isomalt Magic Pearls (to make Oscar Statuette cookie stand):** Chef Shop, www.chefshop.com
**Oscar cookie cutter for Oscar Statuette:** Cheap Cookie Cutters, www.cheapcookiecutters.com
**Gold luster dust:** N.Y. Cake & Baking Distributor, www.nycake.com
**Star cutter for Walk of Fame Brownies:** Cheap Cookie Cutters, www.cheapcookiecutters.com

## CANDY AND SHOP IT DESSERTS

**Yellow pretzel celebrations:** Koppers, www.kopperschocolates.com
**Yellow sugar candy beads:** Candy Warehouse, www.candywarehouse.com
**Black sanding sugar:** N.Y. Cake & Baking Distributor, www.nycake.com
**Gold foil-wrapped stars:** Candy Warehouse, www.candywarehouse.com
**Jordan almonds:** Koppers Chocolate, www.kopperschocolates.com
**Yellow lentils:** Koppers Chocolate, www.kopperschocolates.com
**Red lentils:** Koppers Chocolate, www.kopperschocolates.com
**Licorice Wheels:** Candy Warehouse, www.candywarehouse.com
**If sourcing popcorn:** Hampton Popcorn, www.hamptonpopcorn.com, or Popcorn Indiana, www.popcornindiana.com

# Vineyard Afternoon

## PROVENCAL WREATH

**Form for wreath:** Michaels, www.michaels.com
**Ribbon:** M&J Trimming, www.mjtrim.com
**Rosemary:** local farmer's market

## CLARET FAVOR BOXES

**Raspberry trapezoid favor boxes:** Paper Presentation,
www.paperpresentation.com
**Paper flowers:** The Green Vase,
www.thegreenvase.com
**Floral wire handles:** Michaels, www.michaels.com

## CORK DESSERT TAG HOLDERS

**Green card stock for leaves:** A.I. Friedman,
www.aifriedman.com
**Corks:** WidgetCo, www.widgetco.com

## LINEN

**Chartreuse tablecloth:** Wolf Home,
www.wolfhomeny.com
**Berry runner:** Matta NY, www.mattany.com

## VESSELS

**Slate boards:** Crate & Barrel,
www.crateandbarrel.com
**Tiered stands:** Crate & Barrel,
www.crateandbarrel.com
**Wooden cake stand:** Fishs Eddy,
www.fishseddy.com
**Wooden cheese boards:** Dean & Deluca,
www.deandeluca.com
**Cheese markers:** Magenta, www.magenta-inc.com
**Cheese knife:** Be Home, www.be-home.us

## SPECIALTY BAKING SUPPLIES

**Popsicle sticks for Sangria Pops:** Michaels,
www.michaels.com
**Popsicle mold for Sangria Pops:** Williams Sonoma,
www.williams-sonoma.com

## CANDY OR SHOP IT DESSERTS

**3 berry pies:** Little Pie Company,
www.littlepiecompany.com
**Pistachio nougat:** Crossings,
www.crossingsfrenchfood.com
**Chocolate covered figs:** Fran's Chocolates,
www.franschocolates.com
**Biscotti:** Dean & Deluca, www.deandeluca.com
**Jelly fruits:** Leonidas for Chelsea Marketplace,
www.chelseamarket.com

# Spooktacular Halloween

## HAUNTED FOREST TREE

**Orange and black streamers:** Luna Bazaar, www.lunabazaar.com

**Urn:** Jamali Floral & Garden Supplies, www.jamaligarden.com

**Branches:** B&J Florist Supply Co., no website, (212) 564-6086

**Glassine bags:** Paper Presentation, www.paperpresentation.com

**Halloween stamps for glassine bags:** EK Success, www.eksuccessbrands.com

**Orange yarn:** Purl Soho, www.purlsoho.com

## PUMPKIN ORANGE PEDESTAL

**Styrofoam or cake dummy:** N.Y. Cake & Baking Distributor, www.nycake.com

**Orange silk fabric:** Wolf Home, www.wolfhomeny.com

## PUMPKIN GOODIE BAG

**Orange bags:** Michaels, www.michaels.com

**Floral tape for stems for pumpkin favors:** Michaels, www.michaels.com

## PATCH OF PUMPKINS GARLAND

**Orange honeycomb paper fans:** Luna Bazaar, www.lunabazaar.com

## CHOCOLATE FAVOR BOXES

**Black favor boxes:** Paper Presentation, www.paperpresentation.com

## LINEN

**Orange Silk Linen:** Wolf Home, www.wolfhomeny.com

## RIBBON

**Orange ribbon:** M&J Trimming, www.mjtrim.com

**Raffia for Witches' Broomsticks:** Michaels, www.michaels.com

## VESSELS

**Black rectangular trays:** Jamali Floral & Garden Supplies, www.jamaligarden.com

**Black cake stands:** PropHAUS, www.prophaus.com

## SPECIALTY BAKING SUPPLIES

**Candy corn cookie cutter for Candy Corn Brownies:** Copper Gifts, www.coppergifts.com

**Ghost cookie cutter for Ghost Brownies:** Copper Gifts, www.coppergifts.com

## CANDY AND SHOP IT DESSERTS

**Ghost and pumpkin pops:** BrowniePops, www.berries.com

**Cobweb candy apples:** Mrs. Prindables, www.mrsprindables.com

**Candy corn taffy:** Sweet Candy Company, www.sweetcandy.com

**Halloween licorice pastels:** Koppers Chocolate, www.kopperschocolate.com

**Pumpkin malt balls:** Koppers Chocolate, www.kopperschocolate.com

**If sourcing candy corn and ghost brownies:** Simply Divine Brownies, www.simplydivinebrownies.com

**If sourcing whoopie pies:** One Girl Cookies, www.onegirlcookies.com, or Wannahavacookie, www.wannahavacookie.com

**Orange licorice, gummies, and candy corn:** Candy Warehouse, www.candywarehouse.com

**Licorice wheels:** Candy Warehouse, www.candywarehouse.com

# New Year's Eve Buffet

## SNOWFLAKE GARLAND

**White paper lanterns:** Luna Bazaar,
www.lunabazaar.com
**Snowflake punches:** EK Success for Michaels,
www.michaels.com

## CANDY FOUNTAIN

**Glass compotes:** Anthony Garden Boutique,
no website, (212) 737-3303

## SILVER SWEETS BOX

**Silver takeout containers:** Paper Presentation,
www.paperpresentation.com
**Lavender card stock for snowflake punches:**
Paper Presentation, www.paperpresentation.com

## CHILL-OUT CHOCOLATE BAR

**Mohair yarn for chocolate bars:** Purl Soho,
www.purlsoho.com
**Mulberry wrapping paper for Chocolate Bars:** Kate's
Paperie, www.katespaperie.com
**Foiled Hershey bars:** Candy Wrapper Store,
www.candywrapperstore.com

## SNOWMAN STIRRER FOR SPIKED
## WHITE HOT CHOCOLATE

**Merino yarn:** Purl Soho, www.purlsoho.com
**Lollipop sticks:** Wilton, www.wilton.com

## LINEN

**Wedgwood blue silk taffeta linen:** Wolf Home,
www.wolfhomeny.com
**Perforated runner:** New York Elegant Fabrics,
www.nyelegantfabrics.com

## RIBBON

**Silver satin ribbon:** Kate's Paperie,
www.katespaperie.com

## VESSELS, VESSEL LINERS, AND GLASSWARE

**Silver rimmed urns for White Birch Pretzel Rods:**
Jamali Floral & Garden Supplies,
www.jamaligarden.com
**12 inch square white platters:** Crate & Barrel,
www.crateandbarrel.com
**Irish coffee mugs for snowman drink:** Crate & Barrel,
www.crateandbarrel.com
**Gingerbread cupcake liners:** N.Y. Cake & Baking
Distributor, www.nycake.com
**Rice paper for vessel liners:** Kate's Paperie,
www.katespaperie.com

## CANDY AND SHOP IT DESSERTS

**Blue pearlized sprinkles:** India Tree,
www.indiatree.com
**Blue silver bon bons:** Bedazzle My Bon Bons,
www.bedazzlemybonbons.com
**Blue dusted truffles:** Anna Shea Chocolates,
www.annasheachocolates.com
**Silver M&M's:** Candy Warehouse,
www.candywarehouse.com
**Periwinkle dragées:** Mariebelle, www.mariebelle.com
**White chocolate lentils:** Economy Candy,
www.economycandy.com
**Chocolate powdered truffles:** Koppers Chocolate,
www.kopperschocolates.com
**Blue Sunny Seed Drops:** Candy Warehouse,
www.candywarehouse.com
**Teal and silver barberpoles:** Papabubble,
www.papabubble.com
**If sourcing Marshmallows:** Baked,
www.bakednyc.com
**Vanilla Thin Ribbon Candy:** Candy Warehouse,
www.candywarehouse.com

# Amy's A-list of Favorite Sources

**Kitchen Aid.** Their appliances are sturdy and timeless. I can bake basically anything with their mixer, food processor, and blender in my kitchen.

**Michaels.** The craft mecca. From paint to scrapbook paper to glitter, this place is my one-stop shop for crafting. They also now have a bakeware section. I live here!

**Crate&Barrel.** Their classic white serving platters and cake stands will show off any dessert and are staples on my tables.

**Williams-Sonoma.** Their specialty serveware (think ruffled and scalloped cake stands) and baking tins (honey beehive tins) bring special touches to my tables.

**Pottery Barn.** Their glass vases and seasonal serving pieces always find a way onto my tables.

**NY Cake & Baking Distributor.** The baking mecca. The store is filled with anything I can possibly need to bake. From colored sprinkles to fondant to baking tins, I can find it all here.

**West Elm.** I love West Elm's seasonal items, and whenever I'm looking for a serving tray, I can find it here.

**Target.** A fantastic place to find inexpensive but great party décor, including melamine plates.

**Sur La Table.** A great stop for specialty baking tins.

**Anthropologie.** I love shopping here for eclectic vessels.

**Bloomingdale's.** A great place to find pretty tabletop items and timeless china.

**Paper Presentation.** I shop here for craft punches, specialty/scrapbook paper, and stamp pads in every color of the rainbow.

**Fishs Eddy.** My go-to place to find novelty platters/glasses like the crossword puzzle glasses in Game Night.

**Kate's Paperie.** I shop here when I'm looking for beautiful specialty paper, like mulberry and rice paper.

**A.I. Friedman.** I come here to stock my tool kit with X-Acto knives, bone folders, straight edges, and my favorite extra large card stock paper (Canson).

**B&J Fabrics.** From burlap to cottons to patterned linens, I shop here to find the perfect fabrics for custom linens on my tables.

**Wolf Home.** When I am looking for fancy fabrics, like silk taffeta and velvet, this is my spot.

**M&J Trimming.** Filled with walls of ribbon in every color, texture, and pattern, M&J is my place to find the best trimmings for my tables.

**Candy Warehouse.** My go-to place for old-fashioned candy.

**Joanns.** A fantastic place for fabrics.

**Hobby Lobby.** A great place for more craft items.

**Duncan Hines.** I love to use their boxed mixes when time is an issue.

**Pillsbury.** Best store-bought cookie dough when in a crunch.

# Sweet Words of Thanks

I t takes a village. Those are four simple words that resonate more intensely now for me than ever before. Who knew that the seemingly rational suggestion to turn the work I'd been so passionately producing for the last several years into a book would require an equal amount of passion from a group dedicated to putting my vision into print? I was lucky enough to have a hamlet of top-notch talent, supportive family members, and patient friends.

Judy Linden, my agent nonpareil, is everything a girl with a growing business and busy family life could ask for. I'm not sure there's anyone else who could have made it to the finish line with this Type-A girl! What's more, she loves candy. It's true. Seriously, though, Judy believed in this book before I believed in it, and I'm so thankful for her vision and loyalty. She worked tirelessly with me on every step of the book, from the proposal stage to the very last stage. She is a trusted advisor and dear friend. Her colleagues at Stonesong Press, Ellen Scordato and Alison Fargis, were also very supportive. Ellen wins the award for most unflappable person and Zen approach on a photo shoot, which was desperately needed! Thank you also to Nola Soloman and Sarah Passick, who kept the book on track.

Everyone should be so lucky to have a Commander in Sweets, Managing Director, and right-hand person who seems to know what you're going to say, not to mention think, before you do. Lisa Hauptman is that person for me. She keeps Amy Atlas Events running as smoothly as poured fondant. Thank you for also reminding me to smell the roses, for the many laughs, and for enriching our company on a daily basis. We are truly living the sweet life.

The talented Natalie Blake spent hours and hours with me, crafting all of the beautiful and cool decorations on each table, and took on the unenviable task of recording the nitty gritty details included in these pages. While she was in the craft room with a glue gun, Jo Keohane took over my kitchen, testing and retesting (and retesting again) every single recipe with grace and perseverance. Jo was as meticulous with recipe testing as I am with styling, and she worked with me until we nailed each and every recipe.

A very big, sweet thank-you to photographer Johnny Miller, whose professionalism is as attractive as his gorgeous photography. A big thanks to Livia Cetti, who ran all over town with me looking for the perfect props, worked with me to vet out my concepts, and helped with styling. Thank you to my sweet friend Valerie Velez for hair and makeup.

Thank you to Kathleen Hackett for her wonderful editorial contribution. I spent many a late night trading emails with Kathleen searching for the perfect term to describe each treat, and her creative phrases brought life to all of my styling, crafting, and baking tips.

Thank you to the rest of my fabulous team who contributed to this book:

Yvonne Ruperti, Joyce Sangiarardi, Lisa Homa, Loren Simons, Adina Greenhaus, Erica Miller, Katie Rosenhouse, Kelly Phillips, Justin Conly, Keri Levitt, Marc Jacobson, and Arisara Srisethnil. Thank you also to Wendy Kromer, Elisa Strauss, Jill Adams, Patti Paige, Christine Mehling, and Andy of Empire Set Shop for your contributions.

A big shout-out to the many vendors (see page 348–363) who have kept me in sweets all these years. I consider you all my friends.

My fondest regards to the team at Hyperion, not least my editor, Leslie Wells, Editor-in-Chief Elisabeth Dyssegaard, and Publisher Ellen Archer, Swanna MacNair, Kristina Miller, Karen Minster, Kerri Kolen, Beth Tondreau of BTDNYC and her associates Maura Spellman and Noom Kittayarak. Thank you for believing in my book.

There would be no book, no business, if it were not for a few very important people in my life . . . I love you all.

My beloved dad and cheerleader, whom I dedicate this book to, for teaching me to never give up and letting me know I was special enough to achieve all of my dreams. I got my moxie from you and know you are reading this proudly somewhere while snacking on Halvah.

My mom, for believing in me, flying in to give me TLC, your undying support, and unconditional love. I love you more than any words can say, Mom. Thank you.

Savta, thank you for your support, business advice, love, and for helping with the kids through all of the stages with the book.

Jonathan, for teaching me to appreciate life, during busy and quiet times, and to appreciate the journey. For being a mentor and for all of our late night talks. Your love is a gift. I'm so lucky to have such a wonderful brother.

Rick, you are my rock, my sounding board, my love, and my best friend. Thank you for being so supportive of my dreams and for keeping me grounded. You make me a better person. I love you. As promised, your monument is being built.

Zachary and Joshua, life with you is as sweet as it gets. You both complete me. I hope this book will inspire you to follow your dreams (whatever they are) as Grandpa Al always told me. Thank you for being patient during the many late nights Mommy had to work and for sampling lots of sweets. PS, you can now have your mommy back!

Thank you to the rest of my family and friends who have been supportive over the years.

Finally, thank you, readers. Without you, there would be no book. Your enthusiasm keeps this little village alive. I don't take that for granted for one minute, and I am so thankful for your loyalty and support.

# Index